PORTRAIT OF A PUTNEY PUD

Portrait of a Putney Pud
An Unpredictable Career in Teaching

by

PATRICK TOBIN

The Memoir Club

First published in 2004 by
The Memoir Club
Whitworth Hall
Spennymoor
County Durham

British Library Cataloguing in
Publication Data.
A catalogue record for this book
is available from the
British Library.

ISBN: 1 84104 089 4

Typeset by George Wishart & Associates, Whitley Bay.
Printed by CPI Bath.

To Margery I dedicate this story, with love and huge gratitude. It is a hymn of thanks to her, to Matthew, Emma, Lucy and Sophie, and to many others who have shaped my life, endured its excesses and advised on its telling.

Contents

Illustrations

Foreword

PATRICK TOBIN, retiring to the Isle of Wight, has written an autobiography which encompasses a lifetime's experience of education.

The opening chapters offer a nostalgic and intricate picture of the post-war world of South West London, a world of steam engines, trolley buses and tug boats, and of rambles over heaths, commons and transport networks then unthreatening to the exploring child.

The Tobin family home held diverse political and societal traditions within an energetic intellectual and temperamental resolution. No influence was stronger than that of the Roman Catholic Church. It accounted for the long journey to a school many miles away, and it resonates in the tensions – educational, moral, spiritual and practical – which dominate Patrick's accounts of secondary education in Ealing and of his fruitful but cloistered undergraduate years at Christ Church Oxford.

There were clearly many professions and vocations which would have welcomed the young History graduate, but teaching it was to be. Diversity abounds in the three posts which follow. These include a return to St Benedict's Ealing (on the one hand an unambitious move, but leading on the other to a predictably feisty Common Room performance); an idyll of kinds amidst the hills and Rugby tournaments of Brecon; and a final spell at Tonbridge, in a Common Room competitive and relaxed simultaneously, and allowing the opportunity for experiencing a completely different way of doing things with an exchange placement at The King's School Parramatta.

Though the career progression appears at times arbitrary for someone later to become the HMC expert on professional development, that arbitrariness necessarily acquires a steely contrariness and courage as Patrick takes on his first Headship at Prior Park, becoming the first lay Head of an all-but-closed Catholic boarding school, soon to be steered towards co-education. Many were the wiles required, and much, we are engagingly told, the serendipity experienced.

All change. The next move is to Daniel Stewart's and Melville College and the Mary Erskine School, an Edinburgh conglomerate of no mean proportion, with many resources, and many sites, and all of them with many corners, most of them vigorously fought over. But the Headmaster's operational principles and practice remain broadly the same. The mind of Dr Johnson, a friend remarked, should be compared to an elephant's trunk: strong to buffet even the tiger; pliant to pick up even the pin. Something of that Lexicographer's mental versatility (as also quizzical approach to Scots custom) characterizes Patrick's account of these Edinburgh years.

The autobiography reaches a climax with the chairmanship of HMC in testing times. The Jersey conference of 1998 was a personal tour de force whose importance this book in some ways underplays. The arrival of Estelle Morris, the first Labour minister to address the Conference, was a landmark. But the acumen and skills required of the Chairman were not only political. They were also those of the diplomat, the civil servant, and the administrator. The chosen theme, Educating Into Goodness, contextualized all these skills within a characteristic philosophical, religious and educational framework. What was on offer was not just a vision of education but, in a masterfully chaired AGM, a grammar of its implementation and administration, rounded off by a splendid service with wonderful singing by Patrick's school choir, of which one of his own daughters was a member. Patrick's family, it should be added, prove a charming and ironic source of intellectual counterpoint as the narrative unfolds.

Patrick's year of office brought HMC not only a new divisional structure but also, as indubitably and even more importantly, a new organizational feel, a new stability. The Chairman drew the best out of the *genus loci*. Jersey, in educational terms, provided new off shore trust for lasting mainland benefit. HMC developed professionally.

WH Auden once dubbed Tennyson the most instinctive rebel in the society in which he was the most perfect conformist. This is the fascinating biography of a less brooding Isle of Wight author, a teacher, Headmaster and Chairman who, time and again, proves himself the most instinctive conformist in the vocation and religious tradition in which he has been the most logical and complete reformer.

Timothy Hands
Headmaster of The Portsmouth Grammar School

CHAPTER 1

Putney

THREE OF MY children live in Putney now. Lucy and Sophie are in Lower Park. Matthew and his wife Sarah have a flat on West Hill. A few hundred yards away are St Thomas of Canterbury's, where my parents Denis and Una were married, and the small flat on Upper Richmond Road in which they and Una's sister Kathleen launched their ménage à trois.

The 'old block' of Lower Park is one of the last of the grand villas that once dotted the slopes of Putney and Roehampton. Half way up Putney Hill, with Doric portico and classical proportions, it looks splendid from Lytton Grove, until you see the windows blocked off to minimize the Window Tax. At the end of the 1930s, in a more radical concession to economy, Putney's oldest house was converted into flats. Into the largest of these, just before my birth in 1941, moved my father and mother and aunt.

The extraordinary thing is that, throughout my childhood, I looked on our set-up as, if not normal, then at least as utterly desirable. After Margery and I married in 1970, after a courtship so whirlwind that she had rarely visited Lower Park, she accused me of deliberately concealing from her the family she had taken on. The truth is that it was only when I saw my own upbringing through a matrimonial filter that I realized how odd it had been. I guess that this is a not uncommon sensation.

Denis and Una had met on the golf course. They had nothing in common except golf, Catholicism and Irish extraction. He was the rootless child of Empire, born in Madras, sent to boarding school at the age of four, then packed off to England and the Polytechnic at nineteen. She was the literate and artistic ex-head girl of a convent school and one of the very small number of female graduates of King's College, London. Denis had left behind him the parents whom he scarcely knew – the father who died in 1942 and the mother who only re-entered England and his life in 1944. Una never moved more than a mile from the Upper Richmond Road and wherever she lived she took with her Kathleen and the imprint of her driving Irish father.

James Flanagan had been born in 1875 in Tullamore, County Offaly. He was the eldest of many children and he was probably the most ambitious. Family legend was that he came under the influence of a mad and ultra-nationalistic teacher. In coming to London, therefore, he was doing more than seeking his fortune. He was also entering the capital of the enemy.

James Flanagan put down roots in London. He worked in the telephone exchange in Acton Vale, he married Nellie Daly – herself half Irish, half English – and he became the proud and aspiring father of three children. Kathleen was born in 1903, Pat in 1906 and Una in 1908. By then the family was established in the genteel surroundings of East Sheen. Forty years later, my mother would walk us through Richmond Park to that leafy, suburban home – and remind herself, no doubt, of paradise lost.

By 1916 the London Irish were confronted by tensions at least as sharp as those experienced today by Moslem immigrants. Divided by religion from the English Establishment, in the middle of a war to the death between Britain and Germany, Catholic Irish like the Flanagans could only see the Dublin Easter Rising of 1916 as a sharp test of loyalty. My grandfather had no doubt where his attachment lay. Pat was sent to Hammersmith to pick up copies of republican papers. On Empire Day, in a road lined with Union Jacks, James Flanagan put out the Sinn Fein flag.

For many the Peace was as harsh as the War. The 'flu of 1918 decimated Europe. Nellie Flanagan died of mastoid, shrieking frightful things, Kathleen recalled, in her final delirium. Kathleen became the effective mother of the family, qualifying as a dispenser but never imagining for herself a life beyond her home. Una grew up knowing that where she was, Kathleen would be with her.

I don't know when the Flanagans moved to Southfields from Sheen, but it would have been before the roundabout replaced the crossroads at Tibbet's Corner, because this, or so my father told me, was deemed necessary when a car knocked James Flanagan off his bike and nearly killed him. Elsenham Street, round the corner from Southfields Station, is a street of Edwardian terraced houses. Now they are sought after by young City lawyers as their first family homes. In 1930 they would have seemed dreary and artisan. As boys we were often taken to see Una's old neighbours, with their aprons and extraordinary cockney accents, but at the time, when young men escorted her home, she took care to detach herself from them before they reached Elsenham Street and her shamingly humble neighbourhood.

For Una saw herself as better than the ordinary. Her father drove her hard, training her with such ferocity to win her sprint races that she spat blood. The Sacred Heart nuns of Wandsworth also fostered her self-belief. Mother Burnett made her head girl – 'If the whole of Ireland cannot rule my lord of Kildare, then let my lord of Kildare rule all Ireland.' One day she was taken to the convent in Roehampton and was mildly horrified to realize that Mother Burnett saw her as a potential novice. The nuns paid for her degree at King's College, London, where she studied Geography so that she could return to West Hill as a teacher. This was probably a mistake, insofar as Una's tastes were literary rather than scientific. Every day she walked an hour each way to catch the tram and in the end she got a Third. She was employed as a teacher nonetheless and I have no doubt that she was very good.

Vivacious and effervescent, Una wanted marriage but was wary of entanglement. So, when she met the tall, dark and handsome young man on the golf course in Priory Lane, Roehampton, she enjoyed his company but held out for someone more sophisticated. After all, Denis Tobin was younger than she by over three years. Beyond sport, what did he have to offer? It was hardly surprising that she and Kathleen came across him one day in company with another woman. Perhaps the callow young man and the apparently accomplished but actually hesitant young woman would never have got married had Mother Burnett not intervened. She told Una that it was time to make up her mind and the rest followed.

Denis was the second of the three children of George and Teresa ('Budgie') Tobin. George was a civil engineer, an overseer in the Madras office of The Eastern Extension Australasia and China Telegraph Company, his father having gone out from Ireland with the army. Budgie Enright's father had also been born in Ireland and he was another engineer – for the Rajah of Venkatigiri. The rajah had been looking for someone to build bridges and maintain his roads and Thomas Enright had been recommended to him. Budgie's mother liked a drink and achieved distinction when, following a drink or a stroke, she fell down and her hair allegedly changed colour overnight – from white to red. The Enrights were very religious, going every evening to church to say the Rosary.

When Denis was born in 1912 his family were living in Madras. The Tobins soon moved from Vepery to 'Leith Castle', a former residence of the Portuguese governors in Mylapore. Then they acquired 5 East Parade, a desirable property on the maidan in Madras. George Tobin's sister Amy and her husband, Captain Morris, had another house on the square. They were wealthy but childless, as was another sister, Topsy Brookes. Budgie Tobin had two sisters, Minnie Clements and Eileen Mahony. Minnie, tall and slim, had married the superintendent of the local gaol. They had four children, three of whom entered the Navy. Noel was very good looking. Brian would go down with the *Hood*. Georgie was a close friend of Denis.

So Denis grew up in an Irish world within an imperial world, but it was an Irishness that sought expression through, not away from, the British Empire. I never detected in the Tobins a whiff of Irish nationalism, let alone of anti-English sentiment. On the contrary, Denis took from his Indian upbringing an enduring faith in the civilizing order conferred by the Raj.

In old age, my father's mind returned endlessly to the scenes of his childhood. Yet Denis never returned to the land he had left at nineteen. He preferred to live with the memories – the time when, about to open a door, he saw that a rattle-snake had wrapped itself around the handle, so he grabbed a hockey stick and killed it, or, much earlier, at Leith Castle when, flying a kite, he backed into a cactus bush and his mother applied castor oil from head to toe to pull out the spikes, John and Sheila, his brother and sister, taunted him by calling him 'Salome' and their mother got very cross.

Denis and John were packed off to boarding school when Denis was not yet five. They were not, of course, of the class or caste or religion that belonged to the great public schools in England. Rather they went to Montfort High School, Yercaud, in the Cheverroy Hills. 5,000 feet above sea level, Yercaud was a summer retreat for the English, the 'Poor Man's Ooty', and Montfort is one of the many enduring echoes of the Raj. *'This school is for the elite…The student who comes out of this school is an all-rounder.'* John and Denis travelled overnight by train and were then carried some miles to the school by native bearers, with Denis imitating their song. The Brothers were French and Denis thought highly of them. One Brother whom he particularly liked would tweak his nipple hard when he misbehaved and strike him across the shoulder with a cane. Denis and his friends would give away parts of their clothing to Indian boys in return for the local beetles which they would wire to kites and turn into flying beetles.

At eleven Denis transferred with John to the Jesuits and St Joseph's College, North Point, Darjeeling. It took several days to travel from Madras to the Himalayas and the boys returned home only once a year. As the 'toy train' climbed the final miles towards Darjeeling, John and Denis would jump out and race up three or four loops before clambering aboard. There are magnificent views of Kanghenjunga from Darjeeling but Everest is almost always in cloud.

Denis loved St Joseph's. He was a brilliant sportsman – the first boy in his school to score a century, a dynamic hockey winger whose team reached the all-India final, where they lost to a team of bare-footed Indians. He was clearly a bright and attractive pupil. On 15 August one year the Headmaster, Father de Gheldere, gave him a special medal for his recitation of Prevot's *Vision*. Once, on the loose during another feast day, he decided to leap across a gap between two rocks. But he was wearing leather soled shoes and he slid helplessly towards the precipice until he landed on a Huntley and Palmer's biscuit tin embedded in the soil. Years later, a younger boy from East Parade, the son of an Australian jockey who had once won the Sydney Cup, asked Denis whether he was the Tobin of 'Tobin's Rock'. John alas fared less well at St Joseph's and it was decided, much to Denis' disappointment, that the two boys should return to Yercaud.

In 1931 John and Denis took the ship to England, John into accountancy, Denis into the family tradition as an engineer. He trained at Chiswick Polytechnic, where he enjoyed the sport and did well enough to be apprenticed with Armstrong Siddeley. For a while he and John were billeted in Barnes and I imagine that this led to his encounter with Una Flanagan on the golf course in Roehampton. As war loomed the government needed specialists in aeronautical engineering. Denis was seconded to the Air Ministry as a Technical Officer and the wedding certificate records him as living in Farnborough.

When you marry, you acquire another family. That was true for Denis rather than Una. With his siblings he had arrived from India with little or no baggage. His father and majestic mother were a world away. There was a real sense in which theirs had been the privileged background, with servants and the sense of being one of the heaven-born, while the Flanagans were but one step from the bog. Denis' experiences had been far richer and more exotic than Una's. But he was younger than Una and over eight years junior to Kathleen and he was new to the centre of Empire. He seems to have accepted, as the raw colonial boy, that he must learn and assimilate. Not until war and widowhood decanted another and more stately Mrs Tobin into their lives would there be a challenge to the Flanagan world picture.

For the London Flanagans were thriving and confident. James' sister, Mary Goodwin, had acquired through her husband, George, five children and bourgeois prosperity in Coulsdon. Tough, witty and caustic, she exercised so fierce and domineering a matriarchy that she and George were no longer on speaking terms. Winnie Coombes, the only daughter of Nellie Flanagan's half-sister Albertina, was by now an up-and-coming civil servant. As for the Flanagans, they had become accustomed to driving holidays in France, Italy and Switzerland. Denis trailed along with the family. At times the cultural veneer cracked. As they processed reverentially through the Catacombs in Rome, James Flanagan had only one thought. Finally, he could bear it no longer and the silence was broken by his anguished whisper, 'Who won the Fight?' Needless to say, the Irish priest knew whether Dempsey had beaten Tunney.

Una and Denis were married by Father Donovan in St Thomas of Canterbury's on September 3 1938. The wedding breakfast was in Zeeta's, on the corner of Putney Hill and the Upper Richmond Road, and they then set off on their honeymoon. They may have had a night or two on their own but that was all. Soon they were joined by Kathleen and Pat and they all drove in Pat's car through France to the Alps. In Brecon forty years later, briefly away from Putney, Denis would tell Margery that he 'should have been stronger' about Kathleen. He wasn't and the die was cast.

Una had given up teaching, de rigeur, as soon as she married but the months of relatively carefree marriage were to be few. The first child was soon conceived, Una developed high blood pressure and kidney problems, Mary was born prematurely and died within hours.

War broke out on my parents' first anniversary. At first it made little impact. Denis was in a reserved occupation and was therefore spared enlistment. Una became secretary to a Wing Commander in Whitehall. 1940 was a different matter – rout in France, the Blitz, fear of invasion. Nothing daunted, my parents conceived me. They moved into Lower Park in the summer of 1941, as Hitler struck at Russia. Una left her job in Whitehall – the last employment she would ever have – and the Wing Commander beckoned me poetically into the world:

May 1942, at 7 months – with my parents in the garden at Lower Park.

> Yet still shall shine the brisk September sun
> On berry-jewelled hedge and dew pearled grass.
> Ridiculous, the bob-tailed rabbits run
> And man-made wars and woes shall fade and pass.
> Surely my fate-fraught life I will not shun
> And having you for mother might be fun.

I was born on 4 October – in a nursing home, it hardly needs to be said, on the Upper Richmond Road. Soon afterwards I was taken for baptism by Father Donovan at St Thomas of Canterbury's Church and was given the names of Patrick (after Una's brother), Francis (as I was born on his feast) and John (after Denis' brother).

It is a matter of regret that I can speak with no authority on the world war into which I was born. If I suffered from those nights spent in the cellar of Lower Park, as the aircraft droned and the bombs and anti-aircraft shells thudded and the windows were blown out by nearby blast, I have no memory of it. I can recall walks with my mother to inspect the latest damage – peering at a house whose walls had been blown away to reveal, like a dolls-house, the bathroom within. My Putney landscape became dotted with such ruin and destruction. Watching the trains from Barnes coal yard my mother observed that one of them was full of German prisoners of war. Down Priory Lane, where there is now the Bank of England sports ground, we went to inspect the pigs.

I remember instead the stories told to me – of Father Tanner climbing on to the roof of St Simon's church to knock a blazing fire bomb off the roof; of my mother leaving Thames House one day and hearing the engine of the flying bomb cut out, so that her legs turned to jelly; of our mini-evacuation from the flying bombs to my aunt Sheila's home in Broughton and of the immediate explosion there of a wayward 'V1'; of my solemnly dropping four of their kittens into a pond, chanting *'Ding Dong Bell, Pussy's in the Well'* – they all survived.

And I remember little bits about the end of the war – the fly-past that reduced Tiggy Roller to tears as we assembled in the Lower Park garden to watch, the unveiled destination panels of the buses previously covered with black-out paint, a sudden encounter, as we walked across Barnes Railway Bridge, with a very strange locomotive called *'Liberation'*.

Little did I realize then the central part my father had played in one of the great developments of that time, Frank Whittle's prototype of the jet-engined aircraft. In effect, Denis was the Ministry's representative and on 15 May 1941, as Resident Technical Officer with Power Jets, he was one of the famous few to witness at Cranwell the first flight of the E.28. Later, as fifteen references in *Jet* confirm, Whittle saw Denis as the person who was primarily responsible for the transfer of the work from Rover to Rolls Royce. During my first years, therefore, my father would have been an intermittent figure in my life. In addition to his work at Farnborough, he had to make many train journeys to Derby, blacked out amid the air-raids. I was brought up, in effect, by two anxious women. When my father re-entered regular family life after the war he was for me a mercurial, unpredictable and somewhat threatening intruder.

For my first five years I shared a bedroom with Kathleen, or 'Koo' as she will henceforth be known. Michael was in my parents' room. Michael Lawrence was born on 10 August 1943, the feast day of St Lawrence, two names sufficing as both uncles had been used on me. I had been light. He (at 4¾ pounds) was lighter. Sean, born dead in 1946, terminated my mother's unhappy experience of child-bearing. She had had enough. Sex was a beastly business. The only way for her to stop babies from risking her life was to sleep apart from Denis. So she moved in with Koo and I entered the male dormitory. I look back over the decades and feel for my father. Small wonder that he was moody and unpredictable. My mother never hinted at regret.

The miracle is that Denis and Una and Koo made everything feel so normal for Michael and me at the time. It was, of course, much easier for children than for their parents to accept the world of 'austerity'. *We* could have no sense of the 1930s prosperity that had been lost. Ration cards were just another feature of shopping. Our father and mother did not drive, but then few did. The only heating in the flat until the 1980s consisted of some two-barred electric fires, with the second lit only in severe frost. There was a hot bath once a week but we normally washed hands and faces in cold water. In winter that water was very cold indeed, never more so than in worst weeks of the winter of 1946-47.

When Michael and I would complain Denis would hold up to us, as a model of stoic fortitude, 'old man Flanagan'. We were assured that Grandad took a cold bath every morning and he certainly seemed to be vigour and energy personified. Grandad was never ill. It was the more shocking when my mother and father suddenly dashed off to Tankerton one Sunday in September 1948 and returned to tell us that he was dead. In retirement he had remarried and become Secretary of the golf club in Whitstable. The local constabulary formed a guard of honour at the funeral of this pillar of the English establishment.

Visitors to Lower Park had to adjust to its limitations. In summer months the 'Blue Room' might be open for hospitality. This was very large but faced north down Putney Hill. Two bars of the electric fire would not normally suffice to do more than take the edge off the chill. Michael and I used it mainly for our train sets. So for meals and all other purposes we would squeeze instead into the one room that faced west. The many hours of sunshine served, alas, to illuminate a peculiarly Catholic catastrophe. My father was a devoted member of the Society of St Vincent de Paul. He would bring alms and succour to the unfortunate, having stood and smiled winningly at the church door, collection plate in hand. Father O'Kelly commended to him as a very deserving object of family patronage one Machin, a 'skilled paper-layer'. So it was that we awaited with eager anticipation the hanging of the new wallpaper on the dining room wall. Charity forbids a description of the outcome. It was typical of my parents that, confronted daily with this disaster, they did nothing whatever to secure restitution, repair or replacement.

Lower Park may have been only a flat but we rarely visited a house and, in any case, it offered everything that we could wish. There were two long corridors, up and down which Michael and I would pretend to be buses. The big garden in which we played together and with the other children offered a further facility, the back wall of the garages. Michael and I hammered tennis balls at it for hours, so that there must have been universal relief when the pre-war tennis court was restored and we could hit balls at each other. Three bus routes ran on Putney Hill and we were familiar with every aspect of them – numbers, makes and advertisements. They shook the old building as they raced

On Putney Heath.

down the hill. On snowy winter days we would watch expectantly as they reached the bus-stop opposite, hoping that they would slither and slide.

At the top of the hill lie the green expanses of Putney Heath and Wimbledon Common. Just after the war, *The Times* evoked a John Major-like image of rustic peace and tranquillity with a photograph of cricket on Putney Heath – with Koo, incredibly, watching from a push chair. With my father we would walk or run across Wimbledon Common, all the way there and all the way back, stand on the slim pedestrian bridge over the railway line, spot the tell-tale smoke above the roofs of Earlsfield, listen for the 'doom-doom' of the approaching monster and gaze in adoration as a Merchant Navy or West Country or Battle of Britain or King Arthur or Lord Nelson thundered underneath.

My father taught us both to cycle. It was nearly fatal to Michael. One Sunday afternoon we had all ridden up the slope by the Anglican church in Roehampton and come over the brow. Michael began furiously to pedal down the slope towards the main road and then shouted that he did not know how to stop. Koo's frantic efforts to keep up with him were to no avail. A bus appeared, then another bus, Michael hurtled between them and smashed into a fence on the far side.

As war receded the Tobins made a regular Christmas pilgrimage to the West End. The magic of our first pantomimes, *Peter Pan* and *Rainbow's End*, lingers still, although my fondest memory is of *Jack and the Beanstalk* in Wimbledon Theatre, where from the front row of the stalls Michael took on Frankie Howerd in a memorable duel of wit and repartee.

And there was an ever-expanding world of fantasy that Michael and I came to share. Lower Park was a zoo and we were, variously, monkeys or bears. I was Monkey Toolow F (Ferdinand) and he was Monkey Toolow E (Edward). Or I was Ponzo and he was Bunto (bears). There were football and cricket teams – and two bus companies, 'Monkeys Transport' and 'Zoo Corporation', with designated routes and parking spaces within the flat grounds. I devised elaborate timetables for them. On one birthday my parents, fatally, gave me as a present 'Balyna', a roll of cloth which opened to form a cricket pitch, on which there were wickets and fielders. The bowler delivered down a shoot and the batsman operated a 'bat' that swung off a metallic arm and was operated by a string. I learned to dispense with Michael and bowled with my left hand while batting with my right. Hours and days were spent on cricket series, each meticulously recorded and each contributing to a veritable *Wisden* of batting and bowling averages for my legions of imaginary players.

My parents bought us model boats, a yacht for Michael and a steam ship for me. The *Azalea* was magnificent when it worked. It ran on methylated spirits and would chug most elegantly across ponds. The Round Pond at Kensington was an expanse too far. *Azalea* expired half way across. My father plunged in, and cut his foot so badly on some glass that we all rushed off to St Mary Abbot's Hospital.

Gradually our world expanded. On a bus trip to Epsom my father pointed out the hospital in North Cheam where George Bernard Shaw had just died after falling into his fire. We would take the train to Godalming to see Una's cousin, Winnie Coombes, in her cottage in Hascombe. She always thought that Michael and I got away with murder and believed in getting us to 'do something'. So Michael was given a fork to dig her flower bed. He plunged it through his Wellington boot and was whisked off for his first tetanus injection. We stayed with our cousin Peter, Uncle Pat and Auntie Dorothy in Wallasey, seeing the docks of Liverpool in their grim majesty, fighting mock battles in the dunes above the Dee and learning how lucky we were to live in the South. Pat was one of those uncles who was marvellous as a short-term guest – witty, sardonic and interesting – but who was less fun as the full-time dad to an only son. I saw him as a kindred spirit, the more so when my mother gave me for a

Balyna scorebook a handsomely bound exercise book half-filled with Southern Railway timetables meticulously copied by Pat around 1920.

By today's standards, ours was an amazingly small world, as ordered as it was circumscribed. Tea time meant 'Children's Hour'. After supper we would sit around the table and attend to the reading, first of David Copperfield and then of The Fellowship of the Ring, with all of us except Koo taking turns to read. Sunday lunch was not complete without The Critics, to which we all listened in melancholy and, I suspected, uncomprehending silence.

Led by Denis, by now an MBE for his contribution to the jet, we were equally devout in our formal monarchism. The royal Christmas broadcast was obligatory, with Denis standing for the National Anthem, and we were all bystanders in February 1952 as the funeral cortege took King George VI to his rest. We were present in a different sense at Queen Elizabeth's coronation. Mrs Roe had invited us into No. 6 to watch the great event on television. I was not at all sure that it was proper that we should participate, even via television, in such a palpably Church of England service, but the experience convinced my mother and aunt that we too must have a television. From then on all the easy chairs in the dining room were angled towards the little box.

As Michael and I grew, the whole flat seemed to take on new dimensions. My mother embarked on a systematic programme of aggrandisement via auction. She would see the advertisement of a country house sale and we would all troop off to Kent or Surrey. Then my father would be instructed to bid for huge wardrobes or ornate bookcases or the immense Tudor table which ran the length of our living-and-dining room – and which supplied the perfect surface for Balyna.

Before I leave the age of happiness, let me drool for a moment on its most lovely feature, our English family holidays. We had the first of these in 1947, at Combenteignhead in Devon, and it was idyllic – the archaic little bus in Newton Abbot, the steep lanes down which we hurtled on the back of our parents' bikes, the red sands of Teignmouth, the GWR expresses racing past the beach at Dawlish.

Next Easter we took a week on the Isle of Wight in a house at Seaview owned by one of the Putney parishioners. Balcombe was – and is – a Victorian semi-detached house a few hundred yards from the beach. It was probably not an especially big house, but compared to our flat it seemed cavernous. At the top of its own little flight of stairs, tucked under the eaves, was my own bedroom. The door had a latch. In the breakfast room downstairs was an illustrated map of the island. Everywhere, it seemed, it was threaded with railway lines, along which tank engines puffed. And that was the way it really was in those pre-Beeching days. On the days we weren't paddling or building sand castles or playing cricket, we would be wheeling our bikes along the sea wall to Ryde and watching expectantly as train after train would steam across the pier before us to

With the family on holiday in Seaview.

meet the ferries at the pier head. Then our train would rumble in along the pier and draw up, its individually named tank engine loudly hissing and clanking. We would load our bikes in the guard's van and then we would be off – to Ventnor, or Freshwater, or Cowes – standing at the window of our Victorian carriage.

By no stretch of the imagination were they luxury holidays. An ice cream was a treat, while tea in the '*Black Cat*' at Shanklin was a once-a-holiday ritual. But the happiness of childhood ended with our Balcombe holidays and not only for me. To the end of her life, if she could not get to sleep, my mother would imagine walking along the sea wall to Ryde. She never reached the end.

CHAPTER 2

'A Minimis Incipe'

'Begin from the Smallest'
Motto of St Benedict's School, Ealing

IT WAS UNUSUAL then for boys to attend their mother's old school but such a consideration would not have checked Una. In September 1946 I was delivered at the Sacred Heart Convent, West Hill. I remember little of the next three years. There were nuns and statues and a few boys amid the mass of girls. I realized rapidly enough that boys were potentially nasty and threatening. This may account for the fact that, when my class was being rehearsed for prizegiving and all the girls came up in turn to curtsey and I was then told to show what a boy should do, I too curtseyed, to general mirth.

Una walked me down to school and escorted me home, usually by bus. Michael came too, first as companion, then as fellow-pupil. The walk took a short cut across the District Line railway and by a small hut, used, I think, by the Territorial Army. On one occasion, Michael made his own way from school and was pulled into the hut by a man and abused. The three of us trooped into Wandsworth Police Station to register the incident and that was that.

I seem to recall academic promotion. This enabled my mother, when she registered me for St Benedict's Ealing, to argue that I should join the year group in advance of my age. This made sense, in that I had an October birthday and was evidently intelligent, but its consequence was to consign me to a school career in which I was for ever less mature, physically and emotionally, than my peers. In the end my own age group caught up!

The choice was between St Benedict's and Wimbledon College. Wimbledon, miles nearer home, was run by the Jesuits, who were reputed to be somewhat fierce. The Benedictines of Ealing had a reputation that was more kindly, urbane, religiously moderate and, above all, *English*.

St Benedict's celebrated its centenary last year. I have known it for more than half of its existence and I find that strange, for it seemed middle-aged then, in 1949, this red-brick cluster of houses on Eaton Rise and Montpelier Avenue. The headmaster who awarded me my place is as august, aquiline, tall and unbowed now as he was then. Dom Bernard Orchard recalls instantly the small scholarship he later gave me – to tilt my parents away finally from Wimbledon College – and remarks that at the time he had had to fight to ensure that the school itself would remain open.

How different my life might otherwise have been. A Jesuit toughness perhaps instead of my spiritual mediocrity? School friends in Putney and Wimbledon. No marriage to Margery and none of my children. Probably no career as a teacher – and certainly not one launched at Ealing. That first visit to Ealing in 1949 and that little scholarship of £50 changed my life irrevocably.

So, instead of the short bus ride to Wimbledon, I was given an immensely complicated, over-river, expedition to Ealing. This evidently caused last-minute misgivings. My mother found out from the school that another boy, Michael Bundy, made approximately the same journey. So on Day 1 we met Bundy and he showed me the ropes – bus to Putney Bridge (penny), trolley-bus to Hammersmith (penny ha'penny), train to Ealing (thruppence ha'penny), bus to school (penny). I did not detect enthusiasm in Bundy for his new role. It also struck me that his choice of route was open to criticism. The Piccadilly line from Acton Town to South Ealing seemed inferior to me to the District option to Ealing Broadway, closer to the school and offering two bus routes rather than one. So next day I made my own way. I was still only seven years old.

By today's standards such parental neglect must seem shocking. To me the daily journey was an experience to savour and relish. It was, for a start, a series of tactical challenges. The easy bus stop on Putney Bridge brought with it the risk that the trolleybus (626, 628, 630 or 655) might have filled up at the previous stop, accessible only if you jumped off the bus at the lights and crossed the High Street. At Hammersmith, did you catch the bird in the hand, the slow Ealing Broadway District, or wait for the bird in the bush, the fast Piccadilly that might catch up an earlier District train? I became expert in reading meaning into signals. My greatest coup, seeing my Piccadilly held at red in Hammersmith, was to jump on the Piccadilly that came into the *District* platform and then gaze smugly as my train passed a whole series of stationary Piccadillies. I think that Koo became nervous about my independence. I was briefly persuaded to accompany her to Earls Court on her journey to work, a less stressful but more boring itinerary.

Every journey to school was potentially educational. There were media studies (Michael and I appraised every new advertisement – assiduously memorizing, for instance, the latest version of the doggerel that faithfully ended, '*Remember then the golden rule, There is no substitute for Wool*'), urban studies (washing lines and dereliction from Ravenscourt Park to Turnham Green), gender psychology (why did girls endlessly chatter and giggle?), health education (those mysterious advertisements relating to venereal disease), current affairs (how many MIGS had been shot down by Sabres over the Straits of Quemoy?), social anthropology (the reading tastes conveyed by the back page of other passengers' papers), cinema (especially Brigitte Bardot) and, above all, a doctorate in the efficiency and slow technological development of London Transport.

It was in 1949 the end of a transport era. The 93s from Epsom into Putney were stately, slow and booming 'D's (Daimlers). For a few weeks the 65s up to school were 'LT's – the distinctive, petrol-engined *smell* of the bus that lumbered up to South Ealing Station on my first day lingers with me still – while the 97s were short, stumpy and lumbering 'B's (Bristols). On Saturday mornings – we had Saturday morning school for several years – there were handle-door trains on the District Line. And the trolley-buses, silently gliding, ghostly emerging from the fog, seemed to take with them a working-class world of their own. Returning home at lunchtime on winter Saturday mornings, I would sit upstairs amid the cloth caps and cigarette fug as the hordes assembled for Chelsea or Fulham. The trolley-buses were an unrivalled excuse for lateness. When one was late, all were late – especially if, as often happened, its arms left the wires, wildly thrashing around, and the driver would have to pull from under the vehicle a long bamboo pole, hook the errant arms and get them back on to their wires.

The trolleybuses were to endure throughout my school career. They accelerated with surprising speed. Chasing any bus, I fancied myself over thirty yards, but a trolleybus was a different matter. Once, at Hammersmith on the way home, I grabbed the platform rail but could not get feet aboard and was dragged helplessly along until I let go and fell flat on my face in the road. At Ealing, I got my hand on the rail of a 607 and my cricket bag – of which more later – on its platform, but then slipped, leaving the bag to travel on alone to Shepherds Bush. (There was a tense journey on the next trolleybus before I caught up with the bag and a bemused conductor.) On a third occasion, I was actually on the platform when I was knocked off, at twenty miles per hour, by the unyielding conductor. For these were days when conductors, male and female alike, carried immense authority, over schoolboy and city gent alike.

Nevertheless, such autocracy could be fallible. There was the Saturday morning when my train hooted dementedly from Acton Town to Ealing Broadway and I alighted from the rear, to meet two officials bearing the driver away, their arms locked with his. One morning, varying my route for old times' sake and catching a 65 at South Ealing, I waited nervously while minutes passed and a very long queue formed. When the bus finally arrived I sat down immediately by the platform. Soon there were passengers standing. I leapt up and, with my accustomed gallantry, gave up my seat to a lady. At that moment the conductor thundered down the stairs, took one look and barked out, 'Only five standing. Off you get, sonny.' I looked to the lady in mute appeal. She stared straight through me.

On my first day at St Benedict's I reported and was taken to Upper Prep B. I realized immediately that this was the wrong class and went at break to point this out. Next day I was in Upper Prep A. The school was in an old Victorian house on Montpelier Avenue, divided from the Senior School by the 'black pitch', an extraordinary concoction of cinders hard enough to scar your knee if you fell or were tripped. There were chestnut trees at the entrance, so conker fights were a seasonal obsession. Coats and shoe bags were hung in the 'Ark', a long wooden structure which survived, amazingly, until 2000. We would assemble there daily for Father Philip's Assembly and the Angelus. Behind the school was the monastery church, incomplete and damaged by bombs.

I was hopelessly ill-prepared for the practicalities of life. Arriving for the first time at the playing fields in Perivale, sitting on the splintered wooden verandah, I was horrified to find that I had to lace up my own boots. Why was it that everyone else seemed to be so much more brisk and efficient than I was?

I had relatively few friends. Indeed, Jimmy Dapre was the only boy who came often to Lower Park. When I visited his house on Gunnersbury Avenue, we would go out on the paddle-boats in Gunnersbury Park. It was for me an introduction to a gentler form of Catholic piety, the kind and softly spoken mother and the father who had inherited from an Austrian father his craft of sculpting devotional wooden statues.

If you seek a memorial from my Junior School days you will not find it on Honours board but in the group photograph, reproduced regrettably in St Benedict's School's centennial history, of the cast of *Alice in Wonderland*. There I am, dough-like, as the Two of Hearts – the most significant part I was to have in the whole of my school career. I grew in confidence in my final year under our most austere and academic teacher. Mr Jenner was a converted Anglican clergyman and I suspect that he taught out of necessity, rather than preference. He lacked humour and appeal – smacking errant boys on the inside of their thighs seemed distasteful, even then – but he introduced us to Latin and I enjoyed the ever-higher mental hurdles put before us, the more so as others struggled.

This made up for my disappointments in cricket. Never has a little boy taken more seriously his debut and never was the duck more saddening. That was in the Under 10s. My first eleven career started more promisingly with 17 against Durston House. There followed back-to-back contests with Wimbledon College. The tension clearly got to me. Perhaps Worth would prove a happier experience. After the longest coach journey of my life I registered a third consecutive duck, then heard, to my utmost consternation, that my brother Michael, brought on as seventh-change bowler, had taken nine wickets for seven runs in the Under 10 match. This was too much for the solemn, self-centred, round little boy, the putative Cyril Washbrook, whose bat had been purchased at great expense from Alf Gover and the Surrey Cricket School and who had devoted all those hours of practice with his father on Seaview beach, Putney Heath and the Lower Park garden. To be so utterly eclipsed by an ebullient clown, who had hitherto shown no interest or skill in the great game, was grossly unfair.

Perhaps I had been led up the garden path by my father. There had been an earlier disillusionment when he went in to bat for the Parents against the Senior School First Eleven. It was bad enough that he too made a duck. The worst of it was that he pulled a muscle in doing so and could only hobble slowly, grimacing, to the pavilion.

Cricket brought its own peculiar encumbrance. My parents were overjoyed by that £50 Scholarship and they wanted me to know it. One day I saw them march in bearing a special gift, a cricket bag. This was not an ordinary sports bag – functional and fustian. No, this 'sausage bag' was a very svelte affair, softer, longer and droopier than any I had ever seen. Lugging it into trains and queues and, even more impossibly, into crowded buses was my summer term nightmare. I would push it into the luggage compartment of the bus or trolleybus, where it would bend double degenerately like a drunken tramp. Then, through some Freudian process, I would as often as not forget it. Every time, like a bad penny, it would surface – in trolleybus depot or lost property office. My parents became so exasperated that, in the style of modern parents, they even complained to Father Bernard. (His response, I was led to understand, was brief and unsympathetic.)

But it was through cricket that Denis and I shaped our first and lasting fellowship. Each summer we would have tickets on the roof of Archbishop Tennyson's Grammar School to watch the Oval Test Match. I would take my scorebook with me and meticulously register each ball bowled. I was too young to take in the full significance of my 1948 initiation – England bowled out for 52, Bradman out for a duck in his final Test – but sat patiently through Hutton's double centuries against New Zealand and West Indies and England's humiliation at the hands of Ramadhin and Valentine. Cricket brought out the Indian in my father, the excited enthusiasm and lack of inhibition. Together he and I would hang on every word that crackled from Australia in the winter of 1950-1. I mourned privately as Cyril Washbrook failed time after time, while Reg Simpson hit the innings of his life. I was not a good team man. England without Washbrook was not worth supporting. I was at best ambivalent when the Ashes were regained in 1953 and was positively delighted next year when Fazal Mahmood gave Pakistan their first victory over England. Looking back, I suspect that I reflected Una's and Kathleen's love-hate relationship with Britain.

On the one hand I grew up on *Our Island Story*, *Our Empire Story*, *The Wonder Book of Daring Deeds* – and G.R. Henty. Henty took me to Crecy, Agincourt, Plassey, Quebec and a score of other battlefields, instilling into me the knowledge that English pluck would always triumph over foreign perfidy, for all the pain and captivity that would obligatorily be experienced along the way. On the other there was the knowledge that we, the Catholic Tobins, did not really *belong*. Ours, the one true Church, had been persecuted cruelly by the State. A false Church occupied *our* churches and cathedrals. *Our Island Story* told me that, while Mary had burnt Protestants, Elizabeth was not cruel to Catholics. Koo deleted the 'not'. Over forty years later, when I found myself headlined for expressing opposition to education in 'Citizenship', I realized that I was expressing the insights and mindset of childhood. And when Bishop Nazir Ali opined recently that the Act of Settlement should remain in place until the Pope expressed his regret for Catholic attitudes to Queen Elizabeth I, my hackles rose and reminded me that, if and when I have to make the choice between my religion and my state, my loyalty to my religion will always be paramount.

St Benedict's served to reinforce both patriotism and detachment. The choir of the priory church had been destroyed by a German bomb in 1940, several teachers had fought against Hitler and of the many monks who had served as chaplains one had died with his men on the beach at Dunkirk. The school had its Combined Cadet Force. Father Bernard, wanting his school to be as good a public school as any, was elected to the Headmasters' Conference. We were, as he often reminded us, the first Catholic day school so to be honoured. St Benedict's was to be a preparation for public life, not for the ghetto. When King George VI died in February 1952, we were immediately assembled and sent home. That free afternoon dragged terribly, the last straw being that there was no '*Children's Hour*' on the silenced radio.

But the catechism left us in no doubt as to where our priorities should lie. 'What does it profit a man to gain the whole world and lose his own soul?' Father Casimir shared with us his disgust that a Catholic, realizing that he could not be an admiral and a Catholic, had joined the Church of England.

We encountered 'Cas' in the Middle School, then a two-year interlude between Junior and Senior Schools. It had its own house, staff and headmaster, the urbane and talented Father Gerard. For the first time we were taught by subject specialists, some better than others. Mr Wilding, an Old Boy of the 'Priory School' in its more genteel days, gave us the received version of English History. Mr Botting, red-cheeked, sloshing and sputtering, indulged us and himself with his readings of *Stalky & Co*. Mr Radford supplied Geography, Mathematics, Rugby or whatever else the school needed. (Together these three decamped shortly afterwards to launch their own school in Maidenhead.) 'Syd', once a Cambridge Blue in Boxing, could not control little boys and we learned no French for a year. Mr Fowler, who seemed to be over ninety and whose woollen underpants peeped over his shirt, taught for nothing and introduced us to Greek.

This gentle bachelor, who had, it was said, come into money in India, lived on his own in a flat near Putney Bridge. He was a great benefactor to the school and its pupils and many a university career was enhanced by his 'Fowler Leaving Awards'. He took Michael and me to see *Demetrius and the Gladiators*, the sort of kindly generosity that would today occasion the concern of the social services.

Enter Father Casimir. In his self-professed mission to restore a wasted year he insisted on teaching us for the first period in every day. Short, squat and usually bad-tempered he would tramp in and slam our books on to his desk. Then he would deliver a stream of insults and home truths. Our feet, we were told, were the most important part of our bodies. Any other part could get cold with relative comfort but not our feet. Did we know the difference between calumny and detraction? Calumny was bad, telling false tales about someone else, but detraction was worse, because you were telling the *truth* about someone and could not then take it back. 'P...l: NP&E.' – Cas would look quizzically at us for a moment – 'Nose picker and eater.' I never forgot the difference between calumny and detraction! He would lash out – 'Havery, do your prep again, come into detention and write out 5000 lines' – and then, when Havery burst into tears, would say instantly, if with very bad grace, 'All right, you don't have to do your prep again, you aren't in detention and you needn't write any lines.' I was variously 'Moonstreet Rose' and 'Back of a 65 Bus'. Poor Henry Gillette was 'Boiled Owl'.

Henry lived in Slough, one of many to join St Benedict's at this stage. Most were the 11+ Scholarship boys, the Catholic intelligentsia from Barnes, Rickmansworth and far-flung parishes. For me boys like John Anscomb and John McGrath represented a major threat to my assiduously acquired academic ascendancy. Nowhere was this rivalry more keenly pursued than in the attic after lunch where the chess ladder oscillated daily. John Anscomb and Michael Davis became especial friends. My world was slowly broadening. Years later, many us would go up together to Oxford and Cambridge. I fear that the abolition of the 11 plus examination did great damage to the cause of Catholic education and that St Benedict's was one of many schools never to be the same again.

But there was a division, even so, between those who belonged to the parish of Ealing – who served on the altar or sang in the choir – and those of us who travelled to school. Ealing saw itself then as the 'Queen of the Suburbs', very English and largely professional. Yet again, I saw myself always as an 'outsider'. The shamrock, received from Tullamore each 17 March, dutifully worn to school and watered under the tap each break to give it some semblance of life, was an emblem of Irish family attachment – and detachment.

Really, my Lower Park family was hopelessly confused as to its identity. We were educated but hardly genteel. By contrast, the unmistakably Irish Auntie Mary's offspring, the Coulsdon and Epsom Goodwins, seemed comfortably affluent. They lived in their own, capacious houses, had sideboards and garden loungers and played croquet and board games, the like of which we saw only when we visited them. On the other hand, thanks largely to the remarkable Auntie Mary, brimming like a dynamo at the heart of it all, they sustained a genuine connection with Ireland, rather than a shamrock one. They would make the journey to Tullamore each year. They patronized Aintree. Una and

Kathleen would *talk* lovingly about childhood trips, but that was as far as it went. At any rate, our reciprocal gatherings were stimulating, often riotously funny, exercises in barbed sparring, particularly between Una and her cousin Margaret. The Goodwins had a refined art in the sort of praise that encouraged indiscreet preening. 'Oh Patrick, you are so clever.' We were the bohemian intellectuals, they the owners of property. They were robustly anti-intellectual. Aggressively I once pushed some issue of religious contention. 'Oh, Patrick, that's not the sort of topic for Christmas Day.'

But these were Irish who had really suffered for Britain. Auntie Mary's son, Denis, had perished as a fighter pilot. So too had Cecilia's Australian husband. They had only just married when he was killed. She was carrying his child but she lost the baby too. So she returned to London, made a career for herself and, for the next fifty years, would be as brave and sane and smiling and warm an advertisement for her religion as it was ever my privilege to know.

Relationships with my father's side were subtly different. John, after spending the War in the Army but completely remote from any active service, had settled with Mabel in Ealing. Mabel Legge brought into the family many ingredients hitherto lacking in it, notably a love of music – her brother was the great musical impresario, Walter Legge – and the sharp and intelligent perspective of the convert who had defied her family's displeasure in making her leap of faith. She had much in common with my mother, the wit, the London upbringing and the love of words, but I suspect that Una and Kathleen were discomfited rather than attracted by someone who had no roots whatever in the Irish world. When Walter Legge was divorced and remarried, they were certainly not going to allow themselves to be impressed that John Tobin's new sister-in-law was Elizabeth Schwarzkopf. I have a horrible suspicion that they may not even have known who she was. It all compounded the Lower Park reading of the Ealing Tobins – that they were rather 'soft' and indulgent.

This applied also to the Goods, the children of my Aunt Sheila, now living in Somerset and coated with a West Country burr. When they came to stay with us, they did not kneel bolt upright for the nightly Rosary but wanted to sit. They complained that the London pavements were too hard when my mother marched us briskly around the sights. In short, the Ealing and Somerset Tobins brought out the Prussian in their Putney cousins.

And, moving now out of the background and into our lives, came Grandma Tobin. Devastated by George's death in 1942, and very conscious of the unfeeling neglect of Amy and Topsy, she decided that wartime Britain, with her children, was preferable to India and her squabbling servants. Remarkably, for she hated risk, Budgie took ship for 'home' in 1944. For a time she stayed with the Goods in Somerset, then with the John Tobins in Ealing. I doubt if Lower Park ever figured in her thoughts of accommodation. Una would surely have given the response attributed to Pat's wife, Dorothy, in rebutting our bid for asylum in Wallasey at some stage in the War – that she had 'neither the room nor the convenience'. So encounters with Grandma were limited to infrequent trips to Uncle John's and to the even more occasional 'state visit' to Putney.

Grandma was more or less of the same height as my father – just under six foot – and she had bulk. Her clothes seemed as voluminous and old-fashioned as they probably were. Like John, and to a lesser extent Denis, she had a distinct Indian intonation. She was severe in impression and slow in movement, partly because her legs were hugely swollen by elephantiasis. She would enter the flat, breathlessly ponderous, sit down heavily and then endure stoically as the conversation buzzed around her.

She had a great capacity for 'shockability' – 'Grandma,' I asked innocently, 'Are you Anglo-Indian?' – and the slightest irreverence was guaranteed to evoke its anguished reaction. This was meat-and-drink to the latent iconoclasm of Una and even Koo. Sharp in their wit, instant in repartee, crisp and clear in their diction and half a foot smaller, they seemed an ocean apart from Grandma Tobin – as indeed they were.

It was only later, when Grandma was in an Old People's Home in Ealing and I was a teacher, that I went to see her regularly by myself and came to know her as a fond and rather remarkable phenomenon, the ever dignified relic of a bygone age, a Christian lady of stoic fortitude who patiently went on expecting the whole world to wait on her.

My father, for once, exercised some influence of his own. We would all go up to Dumbarton, to stay in the house of his friend Boucher while he was away. This was a great adventure. At Euston we climbed aboard the train headed by the mighty *Princess Elizabeth*. First stop was scheduled to be Glasgow, and thus it proved to be. Many Geography lessons came alive through the pall of smoke as we sped through the Black Country and the Pennines. Scooping up water we stormed up Beattock. We arrived, on time, in a manifestly foreign country. Years later, during my eleven years as a Principal in Edinburgh, I often regretted that I had no clearer memories of the Scotland of the mid-fifties, beyond trips on Loch Lomond and the Clyde. The child rarely sees what he later wishes to recapture.

Thus emboldened, Una and Kathleen decided that this was the time to introduce Michael and me to our Irish roots. We took the old route to Holyhead and Dunlaoghaire and stayed in a seaside hotel in Bray that must once have been the focus of their dreams. Then it was off to Scrubb and a few days with Auntie Katie and Auntie Bridget, my grandfather's sisters. Their cottage was so little changed by the years as to qualify as a 'hovel'. There was no electricity nor, as I recall, even running water. At the rear, a solitary cow grazed. Katie was old and feeble now but Bridget was still a power in the land. At Mass next Sunday, the priest prefaced every other announcement with the question, 'Is that right, Bridget?' She would later learn to drive, with no other prior preparation than a single *Hail Mary*. That first night, trying to accustom ourselves to life without water or electricity, we all knelt to say the Rosary.

'*HailMaryfullofgracethelordiswiththeeblessedartthouamongwomenandblessedisthefruitof thywombJesus*' –

'*HOLY MARY, MOTHER OF GOD, PRAY FOR /*

'*HailMaryfullofgracetheLordiswiththee…*' Desperately Michael and I and Denis raced to squeeze in our 'Holy Mary's, until, at once gasping for breath and struggling not to explode, we writhed helplessly on the ground, tears of laughter spattering the floor.

Scrubb was extreme. The Tom Flanagans lived in some state on the family farm. Seamus ran the local distillery, the source of *Irish Mist* and *Tullamore Dew*. Tommy's Pat, whom we met later on our travels, was virtually the senior policeman in Ireland. He was as slow, gentle and considered in his every response – 'I tink…' – as Bridget was ferociously rapid in her devotions. But it was from Scrubb that we took the most indelible impression of our Flanagan ancestry, as well as, in my case, a gastric condition of much intensity.

I recuperated in Dublin, a far cry from today's cosmopolitan capital, yet a useful antidote to images of peasant backwardness. We went to dinner with the family of an Irish Senator. He and his household clearly had style. We acquitted ourselves quite well, I thought. Two days later, we were cycling back from our latest expedition. A car passed us and slowed down. All of us saw that it was the Senator's car, all, that is, except my father. He was irritated and shouted at the car to get out of his way. It moved away, then slowed down again. Denis became extremely agitated. He yelled, he gesticulated, he may even have sworn. The car eased away and we never saw or heard from its owners again.

In future I would be the main problem on family holidays. I do not need a psychiatrist to tell me that I was the indulged, self-important elder child of an erratic father and two doting women. Michael was a far more open and attractive character. I was scrupulously religious, dutifully wearing the scapula, purchased for me by Koo at Aylesford, that ensured that I would have the grace of preparing for my death. Once I made for the presbytery after Mass to tell Father O'Kelly that I had received communion with toothpaste still in my mouth. I was jealously possessive. I was secretive. I was manipulative. I had my favourite bus.

The RTWs, London's first eight-foot buses, had taken over the 74 route in 1949, powering past the old Daimler 93s as they lumbered up Putney Hill. One day, I caught sight, as it whooshed past, of the gleaming new RTW 427, Registration Number LLU 577. (I should explain that the number 7 had a special significance for me, blessed as I was with two Christian names with seven letters and a flat numbered 7.) 427 was divisible by 7 and 577 had two 7s. So that when, one day early in the next holidays, I saw that RTW427 was F7 for the day. I knew that it was time to strike. Yes, I told my astonished mother, I would be more than happy to go with her to see that film in Sheen. As we came out, I looked at my watch. 'Let's walk,' I said. We reached the bottom of Putney Hill. 'I'm tired. Can we catch the bus?' Into sight came a 93, followed by the familiar, broad, gleamingly red image of RTW427. 'Let's catch the 74.' And it overtook the 93, a key test of my bus' virility. I suspect that my mother saw through my plot. Afterwards I made no secret of my attachment. So that when my favourite bus did not appear in its appointed order, and I was worried about its health, I sent my father down to the garage to inquire. He returned with news that it was indeed sick, that it had been towed home but that a rapid recovery was to be anticipated.

Michael, meanwhile, was getting deeply into tug boats, but that is for later.

To this settled world there was only one threat, that we might move. One Saturday we all made the journey to Banstead in Surrey. My father had heard of a house. The remaining four of us made it clear that such a move had no advantages. I would lose St Benedict's and my bus. Michael would lose his tugs. Una would lose her second-hand furniture shops. Koo couldn't bear it. There was no need even for a decision. Putney and Ealing would remain the focal points of my existence.

CHAPTER 3

Most Difficult Boy

Back to the centre (of St Peter's)…which is the traditional site of the tombs of the Apostles, St Peter and St Paul. Here we kneel and pray as millions of Catholics, saints and sinners, have knelt and prayed down the ages and will continue to do so for ages still to come. No saint, bishop, priest, nun, layman or laywoman ever visited Rome who did not visit and pray here, and to us it is given now to do the same… There isn't anything to be said; we kneel in reverence – there is only one true Church founded on St Peter, one mystical Body of Christ of which we are members – the wealthy American businessman on one side of us, the little Chinese monk on the other, the French nursing sisters, the German Jesuit, the Eastern Bishop, the old Italian peasant woman beyond speech with tears in her eyes, the prelate from Central Europe exiled by persecution, they are all there every day in testimony of the unity of the Church of Christ.

(Dom Peter Flood, *Anno Santo, 1950*, in *The Priorian*, June 1950)

YOU WILL HAVE gathered by now that the one characteristic common to all my family was its Catholicism. This was as true of my wider family as it was of the inhabitants of Lower Park. None of the siblings of my parents ever wavered in their outward allegiance – although Pat did ask me once, when he was about 70 and I about 35, whether I really believed in it all – nor do I know of any falling away by their cousins. Among the extended Flanagan clan there were rumoured to be the odd sexual aberrant, along with one suicide, but divorce and separation were unknown on either side of my family.

Growing up in the last days of Tridentine Catholicism I was fostered, it seems to me now, more by fear than by beauty. Mortal sin was lethal because, if you died in that state, you would be liable to eternal damnation – and mortal sin was the corollary not merely of sexual weakness but also of non-compliance with the Church's rules – Mass on Sunday, Confession at least once a year around Easter, abstinence from meat on Fridays and so on. It was anathema to betray one's faith through participation in non-Catholic services.

The Headmaster (of the Junior School) ended on a solemn note. He had been distressed to find that several boys had missed Mass during the holidays and on Holidays of Obligation and many had not been to the Sacraments during the holidays. He took a very serious view of this and warned parents of their responsibility to God for the souls of their children.

(*The Priorian*, October 1950)

That is not to say that parents and priests did not emphasize the gospel of love, but in the last resort that did not seem to matter. The important thing was to avoid the clutches of the devil. It was also highly desirable to build up a fund of divine good will through frequentation of the sacraments and through assorted pious devotions. Such investment could and indeed should be turned to the account of those for whom we prayed, especially the dead. To attend three Masses on All Souls Day was to bestow great benefit on the dead in terms of remission from the pains of Purgatory. In short, it was a religion that was always at risk of being submerged by considerations of duty and calculations of spiritual benefit.

That said, it was also the last age of the Catholic mission to convert England. At Benediction each Sunday we would pray that '*Mary's dowry*' would once again find its way to home and Rome. The mongrel Catholic community – English Catholics who had endured centuries of discrimination and even persecution, the Irish millions for whom Catholicism was inseparable from ethnic identity, the Poles (roughly a tenth of the boys at St Benedict's were sons of Poles who had settled during the War), Catholics from India, Italy and so on – took heart from the remarkable growth in its numbers. New churches were built and new dioceses came into being. It was living proof that Christ's promise to his apostles was being fulfilled. In 1950, we celebrated through a pontifical High Mass in Wembley Stadium the centenary of the re-establishment of the Catholic episcopate in England.

This spiritually self-sufficient community, with its huge reservoir of Irish priests and nuns, rejoiced in the troubadour advocacy of Chesterton and Belloc. It had also acquired a more contemporary literary glitter in those more recent converts, Graham Greene and Evelyn Waugh. From time to time we emerged in our thousands to remind others of this phenomenon in their midst, as when Father Payton preached at a great rally in Hyde Park on the theme, 'The Family that Prays Together Stays Together'.

Our family prayed together every evening – five decades of the Rosary, followed by the *De Profundis* for the dead. We would normally go to the 6.45 Mass on Sunday mornings, because you could not eat at all before receiving Communion, and we would attend Benediction each Sunday evening. Abstinence from meat each Friday was a genuine mortification for me, the more so as I hated fish. The three adults meticulously observed Fast Days, the 'collations' of breakfast and lunch being weighed to the ounce. When there was a mission to the parish, as happened quite frequently, we would be there.

This black-and-white religion suited Una and Kathleen's spiritual needs very well. In a sense it governed their lives, but in another sense it did not intrude unduly. Denis was probably the most devout of the three. He would often go to an early-morning Mass before breakfast and his cycle ride up to the office in Millbank. Throughout my upbringing theirs was a religion of total conviction, but it must be said also that it was not yet tested and eroded by the material prosperity of the next half-century.

St Benedict's itself reflected both growth and mission. Monks from the abbey of Downside had established a priory in Ealing at the end of the nineteenth century and they had launched their school in 1902. Just before I joined the school the priory in Ealing was given its autonomy from Downside and in 1953 it was accorded the status of an abbey.

It was, during the 1950s and 1960s, still very much a monastic school. Each day would begin with Father Bernard presiding majestically over the whole school. Most afternoons would end with Father Rupert's mellow tones – 'O God, the Creator of all who hope in thee, without whom nothing is strong and nothing holy, increase thy mercy upon us so that with thee for our ruler and our guide we may so enjoy the good things of this life that we will not lose those of life everlasting.' I remember Father George taking us across to the abbey church to instruct us in the Mass, and in his own simple piety. Every week the whole school would walk across the Black Pitch to Sung Mass, Father Bernard manifestly ascendant within the monastic choir, and to an evening Benediction whose format never changed and where there would always be a choice of monks to hear your Confession – Father Dominic, aged and holy, who would address you as 'Darling', or Father Peter, who heard your sins with such brief despatch that you reeled out wondering whether you were properly shriven. Nowadays, it would appear, there is no time for such devotions, or perhaps they are not seen to be appropriate. For me they were formative experiences and I wonder whether my children's generation has been as well served.

I have one unanswered question from those weekly school Masses, un-answered because it was never put. Who were the old man and the old woman, black-clothed, virtually toothless, who shambled in, bent double? My friends and teachers and I never mentioned them, but I imagined, for some reason, that they must have been in Belsen. Until then I knew little or nothing of German atrocity or of the Holocaust. In the train to school a friend had passed me a paperback written by Lord Russell of Liverpool, with naked corpses piled in heaps. I think that I reacted to it with wary hostility, as if it were left-wing propaganda or pornography. What, then, of the old man and the old woman at the school Mass? It was as if they occupied a different compartment of humanity. The hardest of all truths was no more a part of my boyhood education than of my contem-poraries. In 1971, as a teacher about to leave St Benedict's and struck by the fact that 10% of the pupils seemed to have Polish names, I issued a questionnaire to an English sample and to all the Poles. It included the question, *'Do you think that man is naturally kind and decent?'* The English reply was massively affirmative. Without exception the Polish boys answered in the negative. By then I had read my Mickiewicz and I understood why Poles were like lava, dry and hard on the exterior but concealing a hidden fire.

If, as always, religion masked a multitude of deficiencies and hypocrisies. I would judge the St Benedict's of my youth as emphatically more deficient than hypocritical. Such cruelties and abuses as there were came mainly from pupil to pupil or pupil to teacher. 'Who's that ghastly old baggage that just served us tea?' 'She's my mother.' The elderly monk, Dom Meinrad, pressed into service with the 'B' stream stood no chance. Without fail he would have to send John Lindley – six foot three, ginger-haired and mighty – out of the class. This time, however – 'I can't, Father.' 'Why not?' 'I'm chained to the desk.' 'Unlock yourself.' (Key is thrown to another boy and dropped out of the window.) Whereupon Dom Meinrad hauled desk and John to the classroom door, where he collapsed, never to return. Years later, just before I left, 'Bill' Williamson, cycling out of school in the dark of a winter's evening, was nearly decapitated by a rope drawn between school building and a tree. The Mini belonging to another teacher appeared on the school roof. The Biology laboratory was broken into on the eve of the Advanced Level practical, the Head Boy being the perpetrator. When the chain was pulled in the Common Room loo, the school bell rang. In other words, the Benedictine ethos hardly touched original sin.

What of myself? Until about 1955 I was, in my way, quite a nice little boy. I had a round face (in a head rather too big for its body), fair hair, blue eyes and a ready smile. For as long as I can remember I was conscious of being rather short and tubby. Una, perhaps because of our lack of pounds at birth, was a firm believer in 'building up' her two boys, while Koo, although herself Manichean in her approach to life, competed all the way in the indulgence of Patrick. When I returned from school I would normally obtain from Una a plate of cold red beef, with tomato and beetroot, followed by Koo's treacle tart. Two hours later the family meal would, until the week's supply ran out, culminate in Una's apple pie.

If the older child was more clamouring in his appetite it was becoming increasingly evident that Michael would have the more athletic and impressive build. In height I clearly took after Una rather than Denis and Michael soon surpassed me. He was picked to play on the wing in rugby. I was a reserve hooker, being so reticent in my out-of-scrum activity that my father later took to calling me 'Gollum'. I was actually the more skilful in ball games, with a better eye in cricket and tennis. Michael was, like Una, a tennis player with no strokes but infinite tenacity and an infuriating ability to run down virtually every shot – the ball always came back. I took life very seriously. Michael had from birth a talent for reducing convention to absurdity. Although cricket was a passion shared by Denis with me rather than Michael, I always felt that he was closer to Michael than to me.

Perhaps this was because of those war-time years. Koo doted on me. Una loved Michael dearly but she saw in me the promise of academic prizes. Neither saw it as their mission to wean Michael and me away from dependence. On the

The St Benedict's schoolboy.

contrary, everything was arranged for us, including the haircuts with Frankie on the Upper Richmond Road. (My hair was habitually longer than that of my peers and for years, until I finally insisted in masculine conformity, my parting was on the right side.) My father coexisted with me, rather than brought me up. Koo bought Michael and me our first razors.

Imagine me, therefore, as a distinctly unmasculine young man as I moved up into the Senior School of St Benedict's. Never was this more apparent than on Fridays, when I travelled to school in CCF uniform – well pressed battledress, polished boots, blancoed belt and gaiters with pristine brasses, beret with polished badge and, on winter days, army greatcoat – except that my creases were never in the right place, my blanco was caked, my brasses were dull and my boot caps opaque. 'Get your 'air cut!' the veterans of El Alamein and Normandy would shout at me, as they saw this effeminate youth parodying their very recent sacrifices with his louche disorder.

During the London Bus Strike of 1955, on the other hand, I found that I was much more likely to succeed in hitching a lift on the days when I was wearing the Queen's uniform! During those few weeks, as the whole of London hitched lifts to work, I experienced more cars than in all of my fourteen years. Eventually, the strike was defeated, much to my satisfaction. I did not know then that something was dying, a public service involving *everyone*, and that the future lay with the private car rather than a proud London transport.

The main part of the Senior School of St Benedict's was – and is – a hideous 'jam factory', devoid of any charm or aesthetic appeal, but it was flanked by the red brick Victorian houses to which I had become accustomed. There was little of the modern about St Benedict's. If this was hardly surprising, given the austerity of the times, I was somewhat astonished, forty years later, to find my classrooms just as I had known them.

For a while all went well for me in the Senior School. I carried on winning prizes in my favoured subjects and dropped with indecent speed all those in which I did not shine – Art, Geography and every facet of Science. I thrived on the diet of competition and measurable success. Father Rupert, our kindly Latin teacher, once paused during a class and started drawing big circles on the blackboard, to all of which he added spikes. 'Do you know what they are?' he asked. 'They're marks, big hairy marks. Tobin DREAMS of marks.'

This was, in fairness to myself, hardly surprising in that the driving principle at St Benedict's under Father Bernard seemed to be that you took examinations as soon as it was humanly possible to do so. I was in the fast form who took all of our Ordinary Levels a year early. Dom George Brown, burly, rubicund and blessed with an arm as heavy as the rest of him, genially noted my ever more intense competition with Raymond Woolfe. He decided to steal a march on other subjects and secure the best for History by entering Raymond and me for Ordinary Level History at the end of our first year in the school. I was not yet

thirteen. My parents, it goes without saying, were delighted. They invited Father
George to join us for a day of Test Cricket at the Oval. It was drizzling as we
arrived. By 3 we were on our way back to Vauxhall Station, with not a ball
bowled.

In my experience teachers react less than charitably to presumptuous parents,
especially when they breed presumptuous children. During the Michaelmas
Term, the Mathematics department decided that they would accelerate certain
pupils so that they sat their Ordinary Level at Christmas, a year-and-a-half early,
but they limited the experiment to those likely to take Science so that they could
start Additional Maths. This blatantly discriminated against Martin Harman and
me, who normally jostled for the Mathematical top spot. (Martin, an avid soccer
pundit, was also my mentor on to the stands of Craven Cottage, Stamford
Bridge and Highbury.) Now his mother button-holed mine at a Parents'
Evening and together they protested. In consequence Martin and I were both
entered as well. Martin duly passed. I, stricken with tonsillitis, failed by a few
marks – to the undisguised delight of my Greek teacher, Gil Harrison, who
went out of his way to inform me, in public, on the first day after Christmas.
'Er, Tobin, you've FAILED,' he screeched delightedly.

At least, those Christmas holidays yielded one positive outcome. From time
to time Una would take time off from bargain-hunting in the King's and
Fulham Roads to patronize Harrods. At Christmas we would normally be taken
on a tour of the great shop. In 1955 they ran a series of quizzes for youngsters,
so Una pushed me forward. I did not distinguish myself – until the Sports
Quiz. Here, with a few inspired guesses, I proved invincible. Shortly afterwards
we received a letter from ITV. They had been impressed by my performance at
Harrods. Would I like to participate in a televised general knowledge
competition in April? My trouble was that my knowledge was never general but
intensely specific. I knew what I liked and the rest did not matter. In my bones I
must have been aware of this but it was when I met my competitor that my
confidence evaporated irretrievably. Maroussia lived in Lexham Gardens, South
Kensington. She was tall, well-spoken and immensely assured. She seemed
several years older than I was. (She was probably a normal girl!) I cannot recall
getting a single question right. 'Complete the proverb, "Make Hay When…" I
had never heard of it but suggested, "When the Sun is Out." Perhaps they gave
me a mark for that. I returned home with my tail between my legs, while the
rest of the family, who had sweated through my ordeal in the Roes' flat – we did
not have ITV – were restrained in any insincere applause.

By now I had a more regular reason for frequenting Harrods, the record
department. For our Music teacher, Mr Bowyer, our weekly classes must have
been a grim ordeal, destined as they were to become ever more purgatorial with
our massed descent into adolescence. Certainly his temper came to seem
permanently frayed. Yet I loved singing the arias and choruses he presented to us

and I would go up to Harrods to purchase those that most took my fancy. On the back of the Anvil Chorus on one such record was the Pilgrims' Chorus from Tannhauser, the beginning of a lifetime love of Wagner. I migrated from 78s to 33s, spending virtually all of my saved pocket and birthday money on my growing collection. Then, using the Shawe Taylor and Sackville West *Record Guide* as my bible, I raided the second-hand shops in Soho for old 78s, until I had several hundred. I have never played an instrument but Bill Bowyer had given me a jewel of great price. I fear that, as with so many teachers, he will have remained to his death totally oblivious of how much I have owed to him.

Failing Mathematics turned out to be a blip. I waltzed through my programme of Ordinary Levels. Maths apart, my academic diet consisted entirely of 'Arts' subjects, including Latin, Greek and Ancient History and they were all full of the black-or-white, right-or-wrong details and categories that I grasped easily. I was not correspondingly accomplished in my dealings with my teachers. Some of these had notably colourful personalities. Gil Harrison, peppery product of Oxford and the Welsh marches, was responsible by now for my Classical education. He laid himself wide open to caricature by his bombast and aggression – 'Er, don't think that I don't know what you did, because I KNOW!' – but was wise in his fashion. I responded to provocation with insolence. 'Er, hullo, it's Paddy the Putney Pud.' 'Ah, you must be Harry the Hereford Hog.' Gil Harrison at least asked for it, and probably enjoyed it, but my sparring match with Frank Hanley was less comprehensible. No boy taught by Frank Hanley ever failed French. The brother of James Hanley wrote his own most accomplished short stories in the school magazine and he had the bearing and piercing gaze of the Intelligence Officer that he had so recently been. He terrified most of my peers. 'Davis, you are frowning. Relax, boy. GRIP the desk.' When John Livesey pronounced 'Les Jardins de Luxembourg' as if to rhyme with 'de luxe Hamburg', we had no doubt that the sky must fall. John himself knew it. Under albino-white hair his cheeks flushed scarlet to the roots. In a grand gesture Hanley swept every book from his desk. This was not a man to trifle with. Which made my own behaviour so unaccountable. 'Tobin, you are an am*using* fellow.' 'I beg your pardon, Sir, did you say, "Do you *use ink*?"' 'GET OUT!' At the end, as the class dispersed, I went in. 'I am very sorry, Sir, I did not mean to…' 'Oh, Go away, Tobin.'

That was becoming the general attitude of my teachers towards a boy who was too frequently getting into scrapes. There had been warning signs in the previous year of an inability to keep clear of trouble. Mr Simister broke up my scrap on the black pitch with Michael Ryan, took us over to the gym, handed out boxing gloves to us and told us to get on with it. While I flailed, Michael clinically picked me off. Jimmy Dapre, ever kind, stopped the fight in my favour because Michael was covered in blood. It was the blood from my nose. Now I launched into another scrap, this time outside the 'B' stream classroom with a boy from that class. Father Kevin waited for no explanation. 'Bend over.' 'You can't, Father.' 'Why not?' 'I've got a haematoma.' 'Bend over,' he boomed.

Underlying everything, by then, was a friendship problem. My own 'A' stream friends were not, after all, what I wanted. Rather, I preferred Jack the Lad. This 'B' stream contemporary seemed to me to embody everything that I would have wished God to have given me – speed, athleticism, fun and the common touch. Providentially, his family moved from the far north-west of London to one of the new LCC mezzanines on the Alton estate in nearby Roehampton. I took a new route to school. I attended Mass in a different church. I became jealous and possessive, obsessed with an elusive 'best friend' status, whatever that meant. In vain did my mother incant, 'Laugh and the world laughs with you, cry and you'll cry alone.' To cut an anguished story short, I became such a nuisance that one evening there was a phone call to my parents from Father Bernard. It did not take me long to pick up the gist as I sat in the family room. In tears I ran down Putney Hill.

My hapless family reaped the whirlwind during the Easter holidays that ensued. I imagine that we would have headed abroad sooner or later in any case but the particular cast given to our enterprise derived from a chance encounter with a priest at the Brompton Oratory. He was a convert, the brother of an actor and himself witty, cultured and flamboyant. To me he gave, in succession as they came out, the three volumes of a new saga that clearly enthralled him, *The Lord of the Rings*. To my mother he gave something else, in that he seemed to embody everything that she sought for her family in terms of cultural advancement. The Blue Room was opened for his entertainment and we all hung on his every word. 'OONA' became 'YUNA' in his mouth, 'PeterSHam' 'PETER'S HAM'. It was not long before he was mapping out for us our equivalent of the Grand Tour.

It was to be a spring holiday in Florence, the first of a succession of such pilgrimages – to Sicily, Venice, Apulia, Provence and so on. Until my father bought his first car in 1962 each was by train. Occasionally we travelled by night, sleeping fitfully in crowded couchettes. Having arrived in each new centre, we would heave our cases on to buses and around towns, seeking out hotels and pensiones, sometimes booked and frequently not. In the morning we would emerge for our assault on a series of churches, in all of which my mother, Blue Guide or Baedeker in hand, would deliver enlightenment to us in her best classroom tones. I would never have imagined then that I would inflict the same experience on my own children. I suspect that they will do likewise to theirs.

But this first Italian holiday was uniquely gruesome and memorable. At our first stop we had been led to believe that we might find in the hotel a celebrated Catholic architect and his family and when we arrived it was indeed so. There was great fluttering and excitement as we were groomed and schooled before our descent to dinner. Una made the overtures, with airs and graces drawn from a convent past, but the family, though courteous, stayed disappointingly distant and there was no exchange of addresses. The scene still haunts me.

In Florence we put up in the priest's recommended pensione. The *Pensione Morandi* was suitably old and cheap. The meals were table d'hote, a test for someone who, Fridays apart, was used to dictating his own terms. As we trailed from church to church and gallery to gallery I decided that I did not like Florence. No, I positively loathed it. The trapped animal lashes out – next year, swinging at Michael, I would put my fist through the window of a vaporetto – or takes flight. I hared off along the Arno, my father in pursuit, criss-crossing crowded bridges until I had shaken him off. Now what? I trudged back slowly to the *Pensione Morandi*, and was mortified to find that the family, even Koo, seemed unimpressed and unmoved.

From this sorry year I draw two notably happy memories. The first was an evening trip on the *Charnie*. Michael had arranged it. For years now his private world had been the Thames. Every day he would cycle down to and along the river, so that he rapidly knew every tug that pulled barges from the Port of London to Brentford and Teddington. Sometimes I would barter with him a trip to the river for a game of cricket on Putney Heath, enough for me to understand something of the fascination that the river scene held for him. He enthused over the old steam tugs, like *Floresco*, that would lower their tall funnels to pass under the bridges at high tide. But his favourite tug was a sleek, low-lying, powerful, diesel tug, the *Robertsbridge*. Its master, Albert Buss, and mate, Dick, soon got to know the fair-haired boy who tracked them each day. They invited him aboard, so that it became common in holidays for Michael to join them at Putney Pier, sail down river with them and return with barges laden with timber to Brentford. My mother, predictably, expressed neither anxiety nor concern, and indeed this friendship, that would today surely be taboo, was as innocent as it was enriching. Nor was there cause for intellectual condescension. Dick's son moved through grammar school to Cambridge, where he won a Blue in Soccer.

Somehow Michael also struck up a friendship with another lighterman, the owner and operator of a small tug, the *Charnie*, that operated out of the River Wandle in Wandsworth. That is how the three of us, Michael, my friend and I, enjoyed a sunny evening of rare contentment in that bleak summer.

Father George meanwhile had seen that all was not well and asked me whether anything was the matter. 'No,' I replied brightly. I can only assume that he was not fobbed off, for during that summer term he was the author of an act of mysterious kindness. The Australians were touring England. After drawing the first Test they won the second. The Ashes were clearly in peril. The selectors met to find the winning formula, 41 year old Cyril Washbrook among them, and their answer was to pick Cyril Washbrook. On the first morning, with England 17 for 3, my hero strode to the wicket. Dom George summoned me to

On holiday in Dorset with the Good cousins and Michael (second from right), summer 1956.

his study, switched on his tiny television and left me to watch the great man (just) survive his early moments. On and on I sat, in growing excitement, as classes passed. When I went home Washbrook and Peter May were still at the crease. It was the turning point of the series.

Father George would be a friend to his death, but the majority view among my teachers was very different. At the end of the summer term of 1956 my acting Divisions Master, Mr Connolly, tersely summed up the past year. *'He is, without doubt, the most difficult boy in the school.'*

Charity demands that I attribute to this report my family's extraordinary behaviour in the middle of the ensuing CCF Camp. It was my first summer camp, the first time indeed that I had ever been away from home. It was at Stanford, near Thetford. The weather was extraordinarily wet and the landscape extraordinarily dull and flat. For the most part we were kept so busy that we hardly noticed our circumstances, but Sunday was a rest day and I was standing aimlessly in the lines. Suddenly I perceived four unmistakable silhouettes, riding high above the East Anglian horizon. My family had arrived – to take Father Kevin and me out to tea! God knows what this huge, bullish Canadian – 6 foot 6 inches and with a voice to match – made of it and I never wished to ask. (Father Kevin was never a man to mince his words. 'OF COURSE IT'S A MORTAL SIN!' he once boomed from the confessional, with the waiting queue, doubtless quaking themselves, torn between their customary English reticence and their curiosity as to the identity of the sinner.)

The irony is that I remained a deeply conventional boy. It must have been about that time that Michael and I had our only summer holiday with my Somerset aunt's family, a week near Chesil Beach at Puncknowle in Dorset. Hervey and Antony were boarders at Prior Park College and it was clear that they had a far more subversive attitude to discipline than I did. Hervey asked me if I would like to try a cigarette. I did, not knowing that I should exhale, and nearly choked myself. It was the last cigarette that I have ever had.

Father George, typically, sought a brighter horizon. Towards the end of the summer holidays I received a small card, half covered with the familiarly infinitesimal writing.

> I was away when the O/L results came out so could not phone you. Heartiest congratulations on your brilliant success. You and Woolfe were the only two to pass in all subjects, Fernandez failed Maths.

Someone still believed in me. It was to be a long time before I vindicated that faith.

CHAPTER 4

Let Us Now Praise Famous Men

'Most Holy Father,' I said, 'we had prepared a special copy for you, which was sent by aeroplane from London, but which has failed to arrive: so that all I can offer you now is this ordinary copy. But I will have the proper one sent to you as soon as it comes.' He said, 'This is beautiful, perfect, I congratulate you and I thank you.'

He then asked who it was written for and I explained to him that it was written for everyone, for priests, school teachers and scholars too, and that it was meant to be a summary of biblical knowledge down to 1950. '1950?' he said with a smile. 'Why not 1952 or 1953?' I replied, 'No, Holy Father, that was not possible because, as it contains about 2,000,000 words, the proof reading and printing took a very long time, about two years to complete.' He then repeated with emphasis, 'I congratulate you and I thank you, and I give my very special blessing to you and to all who have worked at it.'...I then said, 'Most Holy Father, may I also ask your special blessing for my own community, for the Prior and for all, and also for the School of which I am the Headmaster, the Rector?' He replied, 'Certainly, I give a very special blessing with great affection, for the Community, for the Prior and for all.'

(Dom Bernard Orchard, recalling his audience with Pope Pius XII at Castel Gandolfo in August 1953, *The Priorian* Summer 1953)

THERE WAS, indeed is, an Olympian quality about Father Bernard Orchard. Tall, athletic, aquiline, he seemed born for headship. Like many of his brethren he was a product of the Priory School, where he established a new Long Jump record in 1926. I think that it still stands! In 1946 he was despatched by Downside to become Headmaster of their Ealing satellite and there can be little doubt that it was his achievement, first to secure the future of the school and then to destine it for eminence.

On his school, as indicated by his account of his meeting with the Pope, replete with photograph of JBO taking centre stage with the pontiff and dwarfing him and all the rest of the assembly, he bestowed new notions of self-importance. We were the only Catholic day school whose Headmaster was a member of the Headmasters' Conference. When Cardinal Heenan received his red hat, 'The Priorian' printed JBO's telegram of congratulation.

There was undoubtedly an elitist tinge to JBO's initiatives. Important Catholics, like Gilbert Harding, Sir Shane Leslie or Lord Pakenham (the future Earl of Longford), were invited to address the 'Twenty-Five Club', a select group of budding intellectuals. By today's standards it all seems rather pretentious and self-advertising, but JBO was impelled by a noble aim, the desire that young lay Catholics from families like mine should not be inhibited, through lack of confidence or social ease, from playing a full part in English public life. I was soon to find, first at Oxford, and then in Tonbridge, how right JBO had been. If Catholic schools have faltered during the past forty years, it is from a deficiency of pretension rather than an excess!

We did not always live up to this image, notably when Lord Pakenham kept us waiting for our tea through his late arrival. The sandwiches and cakes beckoned enticingly. At last, Maurice Pearce flung the door open and announced triumphantly, 'He's arrived,' except that the noble speaker did not immediately materialize. By the time poor Mr Williamson, our somewhat pompous Sixth Form master, ushered Lord Pakenham into the crowded room, there was neither a sandwich nor a cake in sight. Mr Williamson raised the teapot and a single drop fell out. 'Stop, Stop, please,' shouted the peer, with a courtesy so exquisite that I yet writhe. 'Never, in forty years of teaching, have I been so *ashamed*,' rasped 'Bill' Williamson next morning.

We came close to similar embarrassment when Billy Wright was the Guest of Honour at the School Fete. Hot and sweaty, I was taking off my cycle clips, when I was accosted, told that the Head Boy had failed to materialize and hurried off to be photographed shaking hands with England's Football captain.

Such disasters never seemed to touch JBO. He had a headmaster's gift of being associated always with success and never with failure. The same assurance characterized his teaching of Sixth Form RE. If he rarely brimmed with empathy for his adolescent pupils, he made up for this by his sheer certainty. He taught us, me at any rate, not to be frightened by evolution or scientific advance. There was, as far as he was concerned, no tension whatever between Darwin and Genesis. I learned from him a sense of the Catholic Church as the guaranteed vehicle for Christ's Revelation of doctrines whose essence never changed but which would always 'develop' with man's scientific understanding.

We were quite proud of him, entitling our school newspaper *So to Speak*, JBO's catchphrase. He appeared on television where, in an uncomfortable encounter with a profoundly sceptical and hostile psychiatrist, he affirmed the virtue and value of celibacy. It was clear that there was no place in Freudian analysis for JBO's holy innocence. Humphrey Berkeley exposed a different naivety, when he inveigled JBO, along with many other famous Headmasters, into responding to one of his spoof *Rochester Sneath* letters. As I recall, Mr Sneath complained to JBO about the behaviour of St Benedict's boys on the street. JBO loftily replied that what his boys got up to, out of school, was no business of his. Today's Heads are more streetwise.

I suspect that, for his teachers, such aloofness was seen as insensitivity. The story was told, probably by Ken Connolly, that JBO had told Ken, who had lost a leg in the war, that he didn't have a leg to stand on, and then laughed. Steve

Walker's wife, Marian, once gave me a different perspective. She saw in JBO's insouciance the guileless *modesty* of a great man who never stopped to worry about his 'political' image.

Overriding everything JBO had the supreme talent necessary for successful headship, the ability (or good fortune) to attract teachers of genuine class. Some of these I have mentioned already. Others I encountered only after I entered the Sixth Form. Two, in particular, patiently nurtured the indolent youth through the successive years of underachievement. Each was a convert and each a historian, yet Paul Olsen and Steve Walker could hardly have been more different.

Paul Olsen had the craggy build and features of Scandinavia and a growling sincerity to match. He was earthy and he was 'left wing'. He could talk to us of his naval service in Scapa Flow and he would relay his conversations at the allotments – 'Sad about Old Alf.' 'Oh! Why?' 'Gassed himself.' If Frank Hanley contributed elegant short stories to *The Priorian*, Paul Olsen reviewed papal encyclicals. From the Navy he had gone to Balliol College, Oxford, and into teaching. Truth to tell, I found him somewhat intimidating and never really fathomed his expectation that I would write original and scholarly essays on the back of his densely typed paraphrases of the latest historiography. Frank Stenton's analysis of proto-feudalism in Anglo-Saxon England was not what I had expected of History.

It certainly bore little relation to the familiarly simple accounts given by Father George in European History. Part of my problem perhaps was that I was literally the only boy from my year-group to be taking Advanced Level History. The other A/L Historians were a year or two older, the type described as 'Army Sixth'. They would post me at the door of Father George's study to warn them of his approach, so that they could stub out their cigarettes. 'Bit of a fug here, Zollo!', he would quip, and on we would go regardless.

As with History I was to take History-with-Foreign Texts (HFT) at the end of my first year in the Sixth Form, in other words while I was still under sixteen. Here too I was by far the youngest member of the set but it was 'elite' in comparison with the History set. Steve Walker taught the five of us in the room which, until his marriage to Marian in 1957, doubled as his study and bedroom. The smoke from his pipe would gradually fill the room and I would remain equally hazy in my grasp of my texts – Tacitus, the anonymous *Encomium Emmae*, Voltaire's life of Charles XII of Sweden and Michelet's *Pages Choisis*. I thought that this last was a particularly odd book, in that it seemed to hop all over the place, Joan of Arc one moment, the Bastille the next. It was only very late in the day that I realized what the title meant! On one occasion I piped up with a comment. 'Oh, who wrote that, Patrick?' asked Steve. 'Ibid,' I replied brightly, to universal mirth.

From RGS Worcester Steve had won an Open Scholarship in History to

Merton College. It was said of him that he had been destined for the Indian Civil Service, only to be denied by Independence in 1947. He would have been a marvellously just and dispassionate proconsul. He filled the world of St Benedict's with his ample frame – Head of History, Housemaster of Pickering, First Eleven Cricket coach and Careers Master – and did everything with such urbane calm that, when Father Bernard once acclaimed him as the most hard-working master in the school, we inwardly laughed. Nothing, in fact, was too much trouble for this most generous of men – including the cricket nets in Chiswick.

Out of his own pocket Steve paid for promising cricketers in Pickering to receive cricket coaching from the ex-Middlesex opening batsman, Harry Lee. We would arrive on Friday evenings in CCF kit, change into flannels for an hour or so of coaching and then wearily don our battledress for our journeys home. I enjoyed my batting practice but my bowling, always a problem at the best of times, became purgatorial under Harry Lee. I spun very slow leg breaks out of the back of my hand – for some reason neither I nor my son have ever been able to bowl differently – and the consequence was that the ball ended more often than not on the top of the net. Harry Lee told me that he would fine me 6d for every time that this happened. Next week I arrived with a large fine to pay – and the next week – and the next. Finally, I mentioned this to Steve. His face turned from ruddy to blackly crimson, I got my money back and that was the end of that particular phobia.

My third A/L subject was English Literature. This was a conventional, two year course. Mr Connolly guided us capably into Chaucer, Shakespeare, Milton, Donne and Wordsworth, relying on us to digest the various novels on our reading list. The pace was relaxed. From time to time our teacher would demonstrate progressive credentials by sharing Tom Lehrer with us, while Brendan Horan, eternally mute, would for ever shuffle imaginary decks of cards. 'Tobin,' Mr Connolly asked one day, 'Give us your idea of the qualities that would make up a perfect wife.' 'Well,' I responded cautiously, 'She would have to be pious.' For such pearls have my erstwhile classmates remembered me.

That summer I gained passes in History and HFT. In those days there were no grades, only marks, so that mediocrity could be cloaked more easily. It was, however, a mediocrity shared with all St Benedict's historians, as Father George informed me:

> ...The European marks were terribly low so you will be pleased to know that yours (40%) were the highest of the lot. I am glad to say that Zoltowski also passed. The surprises are that Coles, Hawes and Yeoman all failed – luckily nothing to do with me.

Father George was kind but probably misguided. The last thing that I needed at that time was the reassurance that all was well. The young and, in our eyes, absurdly earnest Classics teacher from Cambridge, Basil Nickerson, was clearly not impressed by the work ethic of my peers. From the school's archives emerged very recently an internal report that he wrote in October 1956 on the five of us who were coached by him in Latin Unseens: 'They need to attack Latin for its own sake, not to do as little as possible. Tobin seems reasonable at Latin.'

By then I had been entered for the History Scholarship examination of Merton College, Oxford. Steve Walker sent a card to greet me on arrival, asking me to tap his old college's stones, but I was totally out of my depth and the letter of rejection was eloquently succinct. I surmise that my mother got my father to seek further enlightenment from Father Bernard; long afterwards I came across his reply:

> Dear Mr Tobin,
> Re yr request for information about Patrick's excursion to Merton College in January. They said about him, 'seemed bright enough on interview and very likeable; he talked intelligently, if youthfully: a possible recruit for PPE course.'
> His marks were all either gammas or betas: no alphas. The experience however has been valuable and will strengthen his will to get to Oxford – a very important factor. I think he must now make a very good showing at Advanced and Scholarship Level before we send him up again: a reassessment after the July results are known is indicated. I am also discussing with Fr George the question of entering him as a Commoner for a College fairly soon as part of a long term policy.
> Best wishes, Yours sincerely, J.B. Orchard

The outcome in the following July could scarcely have been more damning. Far from a 'good showing' in History, I now descended to the bare pass mark, 130/300. In English, I failed. I was surprised, even though there were set books that I had neglected to read. George Meredith's *The Egoist*, in particular, had proved much less accessible than its title had promised.

It would be an unpleasant exercise in introspection to explain such a calamitous performance, beyond the manifest truth that I had been bone idle. Circumstances in the flat in Putney were never conducive to quiet reflection. I had no room of my own. Outside there was a tennis court to while away the summer hours. In 1957 it had been a surprise to the tennis specialists at school, if not to me, when I reached the semi-finals of the Open competition. Now, Michael beat me in the quarter-finals, adding gall to that sterile summer. It must have been about this time that I took advantage of the cancellation of games to launch a foray into the West End. Surfacing from the Tube at Hyde Park Corner, I was suddenly transfixed by the spectacle of my mother, sitting on her bike, waiting for the traffic lights to turn. Hurriedly, I turned and stumbled back into the darkness below, knowing that there was a God.

'Get on your bike', my teachers must have been muttering with utter exasperation. My Coronation model Rudge merely became another form of escapism. Michael and I decided that we would have a race between ourselves to 'spot' every trolleybus in London. Every summer Sunday afternoon we would take off on our bikes – to Stamford Hill or to Poplar or to Bexleyheath – on huge journeys of ultimately total accumulation.

My mother's cousin, Winnie, ever solicitous, seems to have been the only member of my family to perceive the need for me to be familiarized with reality. By now a senior civil servant in the Ministry of Labour, she was alarmed and dismayed by the ease with which my family set themselves above and usually against everything and everyone outside Lower Park and by the total failure to get Patrick to do anything that was mildly distasteful. It was through her intervention that, in the Christmas holidays of 1956, I had obtained my first paid employment. For three pounds ten shillings a week I filed artificial insemination certificates for the Milk Marketing Board in Esher. My particular role was to insert into the card index data relating to the impregnation of Mary, Betty and Doris and their sisters by studs like Dalton Helmar the Second. I was the youngest by far in my office and the only male. At lunch time I wandered off to the railway bridge to watch the trains thunder past. Otherwise I remember nothing, except the undeodorized smell of my colleagues. You might say that the experience should have engendered in me a fierce determination never to join the ranks of the unskilled. If so, you would be wrong. It would never have occurred to me that I would have such a future. Something would always turn up.

Underlying everything was the sheer arrogance of an utterly opinionated intelligence. I was deeply uninterested in shades-of-grey scholarship that produced *qualified* judgements – and suspicious of those whose adult view of the world was less pronounced than my own. I did not want my mind to be broadened. I get an awful insight into my cast of mind when I ponder the minutes of the school debating society that I had helped to resurrect in 1957. Thus –

'Pop musicians sacrificed their integrity to remain at the top of the hit parade.' – this from someone who had no personal experience whatever of the hit parade or of any pop music.

'We have seen the results of democracy. The Trade Unions set out to safeguard the rights of the individual. Now they were to the detriment of the individual.'

'What was Liberty but a word? Absolute liberty leads to anarchy. Complete liberty leads to nothing but turmoil in the world.'

If such 'far-right' views were not far from the centre of St Benedict's opinion, they accurately reflected the bias of my family upbringing. Koo was especially virulent in her detestation of socialism. I was schooled by her in three historical truths – that the English Reformation was a tragedy, that the Partition of Ireland in 1921 was a great crime and that it was a blessing that General Franco had triumphed in Spain. Una was less extreme, but even she would let slip from time to time that her father said that we had 'allied with the wrong side' in the Second World War. I can recall going with her to the little cinema on the Upper Richmond Road to see a Russian film of the capture of Berlin by the Red Army in 1945. Watching the Russian soldier unfurling the Hammer and Sickle above the Brandenburg Gate I felt that I was colluding with the enemy.

Since then, of course, I have acquired balance and enlightenment! My Church too has sought to attune itself to the spirit of the times. The curious thing is that this 'aggiornamento' has not diminished the hatred and suspicion of the liberal media and intelligentsia for the Church of Rome. Rather, they remain baffled and annoyed by its survival, seeing in the intransigence of the Catholic claim to historic truths and values a fundamental challenge to their own facile certainties. I am the more glad and grateful that my family and school anchored me in my beliefs. Two years ago, seeking to revisit the intellectual foundations for the 'world picture' instilled in me, I was struck by the sheer topicality of Chesterton's paradox about the early Christian Church:

> It (the Church) was important while it was still insignificant, and certainly while it was still impotent. It was important because it was intolerable…it was intolerable because it was intolerant.
>
> (G.K. Chesterton, 'The Everlasting Man')

My personal paradox, fifty years ago, was that, alongside my belief in the God-given mission of the Catholic Church, I had an equivalent pride in my country. When the Suez crisis erupted in October 1956 I had no doubts concerning the justice of the British cause. One afternoon, stepping off the bus at the top of Putney Hill, I was greeted by the hoarding, 'The Troops Go In', and I rejoiced. I was correspondingly shattered by the ignominious evacuation that followed. It was the moment of disillusionment, the point in time when I appreciated, for the first time, that God was not an Englishman.

Rather, I listened impotently with my family to the News, that October Sunday lunch-time, that the Red Army had come down from the hills around Budapest to suppress the brave Hungarian uprising. The world appeared to be hardening under its crust. Next April, the Lower Park Tobins could not have guessed, as we attended the Easter Mass in St Mark's Cathedral and listened uncomprehendingly to the Easter sermon of the elderly Patriarch of Venice, Angelo Roncalli, that we were hearing the man who, as Pope John XXIII, would shortly revolutionize the Catholic Church.

In the following spring, I declared an interest in the Normans of Sicily and my parents decided that it would be prudent to give me my head. We took the overnight train to Rome, taking five of the six couchettes in the compartment.

In the morning, my father announced that he must have put his false teeth in the wrong shoe – and we left the station trying to spot a limping Italian. As we sat on the train's wooden benches and trundled slowly through Calabria and into Sicily, we played bridge and the natives gathered around, fascinatedly staring at the strangers in their midst, especially at the fair hair and peach skin of Koo. 'Che bella, bellissima,' they murmured, to the great amusement of her nephews. By the time we reached Enna, however, a family row erupted. We plodded sullenly up the steep hill to the cathedral and realized only then that we had left a suitcase in the train. So we summoned a taxi and were taken many miles to Caltanisetta, in time to meet the same train as it drew in. The compartment was exactly as we had left it. The same peasants were in the same places. The suitcase was still in its rack. So much for the Mafia!

At the beginning of the next term Paul Olsen pronounced sorrowfully that it had been his 'great misfortune' to teach me the previous year. The only redeeming feature had been my 'amazing speed of strike' as hooker for the Second Fifteen. (One hooker had been stricken with polio and another had left to get married.) I thought that this was hard and even hypocritical, in that he had never spelled out to me at the time where and why I was falling short. If there are pupils of mine who have wondered since why I was so brusque and direct about their shortcomings, here is the explanation.

Nevertheless, despite all the evidence to the contrary, some blind faith remained that I might rescue success from failure. Steve Walker and Paul Olsen sought to broaden my range and supplement what had been so superficially absorbed from medieval times by launching me into a new period in History, the sixteenth and seventeenth centuries. I was entered for two Oxford colleges, a repeat attempt at Merton, followed by a commoner examination for Oriel. Paul Olsen growled sardonically to his historians, 'Eddie King (later to be Professor of Medieval History at Sheffield University) is the only one of you who knows what to write and Paddy Tobin is the only one who knows how to write it.' Style without substance again proved unavailing during that winter's Oxford campaign. I remained a mile away from success.

By now, I was pursuing yet another 'crash' A/L course, in Politics & Economics. Mindful of recent failure, my teachers decided that it might be prudent to 'spread the risk' and enter me also for three further Advanced Level examinations under the London Board – in British Constitution, Economics and Economic History. In consequence, the summer of 1959 yielded a not undistinguished pass in English, a third, if still mediocre, pass in History and *four* passes in variations of Politics and Economics. I was compensating in quantity for what I generally lacked in quality.

If ever a boy grew up at his own, very slow, pace, it had been I. Paul Olsen had me over to his home in Totteridge, introduced me to Mary as 'my friend, Pat Tobin', and tried to walk some sense and commitment into me. Perhaps this

Two fifties in a weekend, summer 1959.

was the trouble, that too many of my teachers were inveigled by my wit and apparent sparkle into focussing on the latent talent and the turn of phrase, rather than on the actual failure to read in depth or, indeed, do anything that was not rigorously checked and marked. With their headmaster and my mother pressing for success, it was tempting, no doubt, to hope for the best. After all, these civilized and utterly Christian men saw education as a garden, not a factory, and thereby they cultivated a few who achieved great distinction. The rest found their own level. It was still a time of austerity, without the wherewithal to mediate scholarship to the masses. There was no substitute for diligent immersion in uncompromisingly earnest tomes. Failure was rife. Even so, a headmaster educated in the early 1970s in a London grammar school expresses incredulity at my tale. I can only conclude that St Benedict's, liberal and permissive to its core, was at a particular stage in its own development – laced with aspiration, circumscribed by general mediocrity, tentative in its demands and utterly hand-to-mouth in curricular design. A decade later, idiosyncratic still, it had become competitive with the best.

Yet, gradually, there came some silver linings to console my poor parents. In the summer of 1958 I played my first games in the Cricket Eleven. Next February, to my utter astonishment, I read on the Games Noticeboard that I had been picked to hook for the First Fifteen. (Again and again, I went back to that noticeboard to reassure myself that it was really true.) Then, in the glorious summer of 1959, runs flowed as never before from my bat. I was even appointed a School Prefect. Paddy the Putney Pud had arrived.

Having secured my election as Chairman of the Debating Society, I broke with all tradition by inviting the girls of Notting Hill High School to join us in a mixed debate. The choice of motion was not equally progressive – 'This House believes that the Woman's place is in the Home'. It was carried by 77 votes to 44, with 10 abstentions. My friend, Gordon Wilson, professed himself appalled at the chaos that might ensue if women took part in public affairs. Even so, I received an agreeably congratulatory letter from my counterpart at Notting Hill. When, decades later, I introduced girls to one school and then became Principal of Scotland's oldest girls' school, I reflected wryly that the debate with Notting Hill High School had constituted my sole previous experience of girls' education.

My fourth Oxford attempt, in my fourth year in the sixth form, succeeded in persuading Christ Church to accept me. I remember the two dons, John Mason and Charles Stuart, blinking at my academic trail and muttering 'extraordinary' to each other. My success left me with no further academic assignments in school, except for A/L Latin, but there was no question of leaving school at Christmas. I was determined to be Captain of Cricket.

By now I was Deputy Head Boy, I had gained my Colours in Rugby and I was even a Staff Sergeant in the CCF. Being house captain was proving to be another satisfying ego-trip. Someone, perhaps seeing in all of this the making of a future teacher, suggested that I should be offered pocket money to coach during lunch hours four boys who could not be timetabled for Ordinary Level English Literature.

The cricket season proved anti-climactic. In the wettest summer for 273 years, a series of calamitous St Benedict's batting debacles was punctuated with wins eked out through miserly bowling. If I proved reasonably adept in the management of a medium that I did not understand, I displayed less judgement when an aggressive Junior Colt was picked to open our attack. Young Chris Patten bowled 15 overs in his first game and nineteen in his second, of which the first seventeen were consecutive! When the time came for the First Eleven photograph to be taken, I was given an elaborate blazer to wear and am thereby preserved for posterity as Mr Toad. I must indeed have been insufferable. Presiding one day in the new Library created by Father Bernard I heard the familiar tones of Tom Lehrer pulsing from Mr Connolly's adjoining study. I decided not to resist the temptation to knock at his door and interrupt his 'class'. Perhaps he could moderate the sound, there were boys in the Library who wished to work. 'Grrh,' Ken Connolly exploded, 'That's a bit rich!'

At the end of it all I received the top school award, the Priorian Medal, but Bill Williamson refused to melt. 'He is far more conscious of the privileges of leadership than of its responsibilities,' he snapped in his final report. He was proved right when I failed my Latin A/L. I had not read the set texts.

I was certainly conscious of the *privilege* of having been at St Benedict's at such a time. It happened that Father Bernard's (first) period of headship ended with our departure, adding an extra piquance to our last School Mass in the Abbey church. I remember that we asked Father Bernard to lead us in a final rendering of *Christus Vincit*. He would have needed little persuasion. There was always a virtuoso element in his rendering of the great affirmation – *Christus Vincit, Christus Regnat, Christus Imperat* – and the *Imperat* with which he 'signed off' duly cascaded with gratifying power.

A group of us walked with him to that Mass. As we took the familiar route across the Black Pitch we asked him if he was pleased with the outcome to his labours. We had ourselves in mind. That year a record ten of us had gained entry into Oxbridge. These included John Anscomb, Michael Davis and Joe Fernandez, but the majority were from the year below, the group with whom I would have grown up had I gone into my proper class when I joined St Benedict's eleven years before.

Would it have made a difference had I taken a more conventional route through school? I suspect that my personal foibles and failings would in any case have ensured a less than even ride. Even so, when educationalists now speak the language of 'individual pathways' and suggest that abler boys and girls should undertake sixth form studies sooner than their peers, I reflect from my own experience that the main purpose of education should be the development of whole persons rather than the acceleration of academic attainment, indeed that the first is in many cases the prerequisite for the second.

During that final year Father Bernard had done his best to prepare us for Catholic adulthood. He laid on an early-morning Mass, cooked breakfast provided, and Pete Hubner induced me to join him in consuming the greasy bacon and eggs lovingly and unhygienically bestowed on us by the Irish maid. He sent us away on Retreat, where an Irish missionary, recently freed by the Chinese Communist government after years of solitary confinement, dwelled on the import to himself of the Mass covertly said over prison bread and a few grapes crushed into wine. I won the RE prize with an essay on monasticism, rehearsing faithfully the arguments expounded by JBO, including Christ's counsel of perfection to the rich young man. Father Bernard was sufficiently encouraged by this to invite himself round to lunch at Lower Park. While my mother made the coffee, he asked if I had thought of becoming a monk. It had never crossed my mind, nor has it done since. I knew that I lacked both the faith and courage to commit myself to such self-denial and the guts to persevere with it.

I may have turned my back on monasticism but I was far from ready for the future. At the very moment that I was leaving St Benedict's the trolleybuses to Hammersmith were replaced by gleaming new 'Routemaster' buses. The first bus lane was established and the old, pedestrian-friendly, Hammersmith Broadway became the hideously concrete one-way system of today. Childhood and magic were ending simultaneously.

'End of a Mastodon' was the headline of a half-jocular, half-sentimental leader in the *Evening Standard*. The trolleybuses had to give way to the forces of progress. Looking back, I suspect that the real mastodon was the civic pride and cohesion of London, the morale and self-belief that had united the world's greatest city during the agonies of war and the privations of peace. *I'm All Right Jack* was showing in the cinemas.

I wept as I stood alone on the platform of Ealing Broadway at the end of my final summer camp. They were tears of love and attachment, tinged with a very real apprehension. I was leaving a world that had tolerated my self-indulgent indolence. Oxford would have standards that would be distinctly un-Benedictine. Would I be up to it?

CHAPTER 5

Oxford Interlude

I AM NOT SURE that it is as good an idea to keep a diary as some make out. Forty years on, I track myself through my youth and am filled with sadness. I wince at the *lack* of enterprise, ambition, initiative and courage. I do not mourn the occasional silliness so much as the overall lack of silliness. Above all, I count the many meetings with the friends of those times and I note especially the final encounters. Where are they now? *Are* they now?!

At least a diary is a corrective to the trick whereby the memory compresses. Without it I would have thought that my years at Christ Church would have been much less varied and pleasurable than they really were. When I tell my children and pupils that I aimed at working an average of three hours per day, they look incredulous and I feel incredulous. Whatever could I have done with the remaining hours? The diary tells me.

The memory compresses because I knew then and know now that I failed to make the most of Oxford. Why? It was in part the sheer relief of getting in at all. In my studies I aimed simply at keeping my head above water. Beyond that I was a faithful Catholic and a keen enough college sportsman. That was enough for me in terms of development. My social contacts were confined preponderantly to my fellow Old Priorians and to our Catholic friends from Downside and elsewhere.

When I seek to explain to my children why Oxford was for me as much a case of opportunities missed as of opportunities taken I recall one scene and one failure of nerve. The scene is my arrival in Oxford station. I had dragged my cases on to the platform, as on so many previous Italian expeditions, but this time I was surrounded with the aggressively confident baying of men from the public schools. I had never met them en masse before. I felt small and inadequate. They clearly knew that they belonged.

The failure relates to the Union. I had 'shone' as a debater at school and I at once became a member of the Union. In my first year I attended every debate. Each week I would wonder whether this would be the occasion for my intervention from the floor. It was not that the words froze in my mouth before I could move. No, the problem was far more serious. I never had an idea to contribute before the moment had gone and the next speaker was in full flow. Decades later, my former pupils from Stewart's Melville College would thrust their way to notice and eminence. The Putney Pud, from the essentially similar background of the city day school, remained eternally mute.

I have but one excuse. I belonged to the first generation absolved from National Service. My intake to Oxford divided between boys like myself and men from the Army, Navy or Air Force. In rugby and cricket, with school credentials as strong as in debating, it would take me a year to become established in the College team.

I had graceful, ground floor rooms in Peckwater Quad. For the first time since 'Balcombe' I had a bedroom of my own. The sitting room I shared with a fellow Catholic. Lawrence Boyle was a Scholar in Natural Sciences from a local maintained school. It did not seem to trouble him that he was even further removed than I from the boarding school background of most members of 'The House'.

Not for Lawrence or me the extravagances of 'Brideshead' or any shoulder-rubbing with future luminaries like Jonathan Aitken. We never missed breakfast, indeed took all our meals in the timbered magnificence of the Christ Church Hall. Whereas Sophie, my youngest daughter, fended for herself in terms of meals and laundry, ours was more the existence of a boarding school, with personal service added. Clifford, senior scout of The House, woke us each morning, washed crockery, cleared up after parties and gave us the comforting feeling that we were in a great tradition.

I never presumed to ask Clifford what he *really* thought. He probably loved his job and found Lawrence and me exceedingly boring and conventional. One party excepted, there was little bacchanalea in Peck 2.1. Rather, there were teacups galore as our rooms became the social magnet for the Old Priorians of Oxford. Seven of us had come up from St Benedict's that term, making thirteen in all, and I looked first to them for my friends. Many evenings I would play table-tennis with Brian Burns. Chris Mulvey and I invented our own 'decathlon'. I cycled once with John Anscomb to Woodstock and we went for a long winter's walk through the estate. Michael Davis sought to raise his own and my cultural sights. Tony Ford, in particular, usually wended his way, ostrich-like, into Peck in the course of his socializing perambulation. Tony was relatively aged when at St Benedict's and he passed few examinations. The Ruskin College of Art provided his passage into Oxford.

'Artist extraordinary, representative of seven societies, member of ten, this doyen of O.P.s fascinates all by his empty conversation.' Thus wittily did I prattle about Tony in my letter to *The Priorian*. It was through him that I got to know Jacqueline Geldart from the Ruskin School and from him that I inherited my digs in St John's Street. He would be an Usher at our wedding. Of all my friends he would (probably) be the first to die, disappearing about ten years later from the world which he loved, from which he craved affection and recognition but with which he was unable ultimately to conform. I grieve for his gallant gaity. I deplore my callow sense of superiority to him. *That Was The Week That Was* would soon impart a more savagely satirical note into the last days of

Harold Macmillan – a Prime Minister after Tony's heart – but that does not excuse the ease with which I subordinated a friend's feelings to my need to cut a dash before my St Benedict's readers.

It was a very good time to be going up to university. Macmillan had won the Election of 1959 with the slogan, 'You have never had it so good.' That was certainly true for the happy few who were university students. Our tuition fees were fully met. We received generous maintenance grants from local authorities. We would leave Oxford free from potentially crippling debt, although it must be conceded that our taste for overseas holidays was frugal compared with today's undergraduates and even sixth formers. And we would, in the main, be well rewarded for our degrees. By the late 1960s the 'marginal revenue productivity' of a first degree was measured as far in excess of that of other qualifications. We were the 'lucky' generation, certainly in comparison with our parents who had endured war, austerity and the loss of personal opportunities.

For a month after I arrived it rained, literally, every day. As the meadows drowned I scurried under my umbrella to tutorials and lectures, regretting the cloisterless expanse of Tom Quad. I felt inundated too by the work. In one term we had to pass muster in Bede's *Ecclesiastical History*, de Tocqueville's *Origins of the French Revolution*, Unseens in French and Latin and, most memorably, a course in Historical Geography. I would raid the staircase loos for transparent toilet paper, then trace maps from books, shade the back in pencil and render on to my essay. At least I became master of one skill! De Tocqueville evoked memories of previously skimped set texts, but somehow I passed. From then on I was guaranteed survival!

The Catholic chaplaincy was my second home and the saintly Father Michael Hollings my spiritual mentor. My diary surprises me with the number of weekday Masses that I attended and Newman Society talks that I graced. Father Michael kept open house in the Old Palace, tolerating whimsically the 'chaplaincy mice'. He told us that, unless our faith *grew* and became more challenging during our time at Oxford, it would diminish in relation to the rest of us – and that is surely a profound truth. In my second year he told me that it was time that I did something for someone else. I should join the Society of St Vincent de Paul. He probably saw in me the rich young man wedded to his pleasures and, although I dutifully did what I was told, I have sadly to admit that this would have been a fair assessment. We would often pass in the night, I returning hurriedly to get back into college before Tom struck midnight, Father Michael moving with brisk guardsman's stride to catch the post before the midnight collection. He was a wonderful priest.

I suspect Father Michael of another, equally unsuccessful, attempt to broaden my horizons. I was invited to a Catholic Dining Club, the Effingham Club, to meet its members. I went back to London and Harrods for my first dinner jacket. The diary records, 'Very enjoyable dinner and atmosphere. Suffered from after-effects.' I was not invited again.

Tea rather than dinner was my chief social medium, with Fuller's layer cake the habitual delicacy. Occasionally, however, I would be plucked from this petty bourgeois world. One evening I had 'port and conversation' with Colin Matthew. After Mass very early in March, we sunned ourselves and drank sherry on the roof of the Meadows building, before lunch in the college garden. Later I was violently sick.

Most weeks I would see some way-out film. On a day trip to the Bath Festival we heard a song recital, a concert given by the Menuhins and a solo revue by Joyce Grenfell. For months *Anna Karenina* was each evening's prelude to sleep. In the Summer Term I played some College cricket, watched the university side in the Parks and learned to punt. On each of my first two outings I fell into the river at the identical point under Magdalen Bridge, emerging on the second occasion to find that the Jesuit in our punt was climbing out also – with my umbrella. I expressed profuse thanks for his generosity, all the more striking in a Jesuit to a Benedictine. 'You pulled me in!' On 4 June 1961 there was an unforgettable rendering in Tom Quad of the *1812 Overture*, replete with cannon and the bell of Tom Tower.

That summer, I had a narrow escape. Dom Edmund Flood of Ealing Abbey was at the time studying in St Benet's. He took it into his head to put on at the Playhouse his production of *The Taming of the Shrew*, with me as the Shrew's father. Even an audition in Peck 2.1 failed to put him off. My relief when I heard that the project was off was unqualified.

My tutors seemed content with me, in an uncommunicative sort of way. Daniel Bueno de Mesquita was a tall owl of a don. He had a deep booming voice, sparingly used. The story went that, shortly after a tutee had begun reading his essay, Bueno fell asleep. The young man tiptoed out – and returned next week with the same essay. As he sat down, Bueno stood up, went to the door and locked it. 'Now we can begin,' he beamed. John Mason tutored me in medieval English and European History, as well as lecturing on the Crusades and on the Normans in Sicily. Very like Father George in his Englishness – he has never visited Sicily or the Holy Land – and in his wry humour, John Mason has loved and still loves the House with all his being.

The lectures that made the biggest impact on me came from the fiery furnace that was K.B. McFarlane, expert on and champion of the fifteenth century aristocracy. As he trumpeted and fulminated in his weekly anti-Cambridge, anti-Social History, tirade, he sowed in me a particular historical interest that I would one day pursue, to lengths of excess of which he must surely have approved.

So there was some development in that first year. At home, however, little had changed. I continued to go with my family on Easter holidays to Italy and life generally still revolved around family and old friends. We often saw Winnie

Coombes and Eva Flanagan, my grandfather's second wife, both of whom had moved up to London from the 'country', as well as Grandma Tobin and the Barnicots, friends of my parents in their first married days on the Upper Richmond Road. At Lower Park there was an endless round of tennis, now involving girls from Kings Keep, the next block of flats up Putney Hill. School continued to hold me in its embrace. At Christmas I attended the funeral, after just one term, of Dom Gerard Hayes, Father Bernard's successor. Father George now became Headmaster and he invited me to do some teaching – for a total of twelve guineas – during the Easter holidays. I returned in the summer to invigilate public examinations.

I was saving money faster than I could spend it. At Christmas in each of my three years at Oxford I worked for the Putney Post Office. Now my father informed me that he had a contact in Shell, the Head Messenger, and that he could arrange a summer job for me. As with the Milk Marketing job this was, above all, an insight into the tedium of an office job. Occasionally I would be sent into the City on some errand. For the most part, I was confined to base in the old Shell headquarters in St Helen's Court, the most interesting task being the operation of the oldest lift in London. How many times did a bowler hat brightly say, 'Life is full of its ups and downs!'? Why, Oh why, did I not use my lunch breaks for walking the City and seeing its churches and landmarks? It was typical of me that I didn't. By 1962 Shell had moved to its new Centre by Waterloo and I became a full-time liftman during my second stint with the firm.

I also broke new ground for the Lower Park family by taking driving lessons. They were arranged, it need hardly be said, by Koo. At the Ministry of Transport she had investigated the success rate of local instructors and Mr Reynolds in Kingston was the best. To Kingston, therefore, I went, passing in November after just eleven lessons and despite the fact that I turned a corner with one hand on the gear stick and the other signalling out of the window.

It is a truism that the second year at Oxford is the most relaxed, back to the known and far from the terrors of Finals. For most it offers also the promise of new accommodation, preferably with friends of one's choosing. I was different. I decided to stay in my rooms and take my chance with the new room-mate. This was, almost by definition, a freshman.

Colin Miesch could hardly have been more the opposite of Lawrence Boyle. He was a Modern Linguist. He had been a boarder – at Blundells. He was an agnostic. He was a cheerful, extrovert and gregarious 'bon viveur'. He was a prop forward, sixteen stone and built like a tank. He did as little work as possible, indeed not enough, for he would ultimately fail his Prelims and this would be his only year at Oxford. It was a privilege and an experience to share it with him.

We had rugby in common, indeed the front row of the scrum. With Colin at tight head and Hamish Ritchie at loose head, few college hookers could go wrong and we encountered only one scrum that season that beat us in the only score that mattered, the tight head count. Colin and I would cycle to the ground on Iffley Road or to foreign fields bellowing *Moon River* – I had taken Kings Keep Mary to *Breakfast at Tiffany's* – and Colin would then grunt and harrumph his path of destruction from scrum to scrum, wearing down his opposite number until he was gasping for mercy. It must indeed have been an ordeal for them, in those scrum-ridden days. My diary has its meticulous record of each scrum count. At the end of term it stated a satisfactory balance of 76 tight heads won and 35 loose heads lost. In 1989 the school doctor would ask me in my medical if I had played in the front row of the scrum. When I questioned his question he replied that the lump on the top of my shoulder blades was the give-away.

My normal diet for the week was two games of rugby and two of squash, a game admirably suited to my competitive instincts. It was not a year of intense academic effort. I did enough. As always I did least for those tutors who left me to my own devices – as did the young Theodore Zeldin, perhaps because Tudor England was some way from modern France, and young Mr Littleton of All Souls, who steered me too tentatively into Political Theory.

Rather, I sought my own car. In November Brian Burns, Michael Davis and I considered the purchase of a BSA three-wheeler, but for some reason it was not ready for inspection. We arranged to take it out on New Year's Day and duly turned up at Westbourne Park. The roads were thick with snow and we left frustrated. It was at this point that Chris Cook, full back in the House fifteen and a member of the RAF Squadron, let Colin and me know that the barman of the Squadron wished to sell his 1939 Morris 8 Series 'E'. It had been garaged throughout the war, was in excellent condition considering its age and was ours for £100. So we bought it. I stabled it in the drive of the Chaplaincy, Father Michael supplying both his permission and his blessing – Colin grumbling about the rust – and there it lived for the next year and a half.

HFC 750 was one of the best acquisitions that I ever made. Yes, it was constantly causing trouble – a series of punctures, a tendency to break down at the end of every return journey from Stratford, failure to pass its first test. With a petrol capacity of only four gallons, it tended to run dry whenever garages closed. In cold weather it had a reluctance to start and the elements wreaked havoc on the paintwork. After one particularly cold snap, when I had swung the handle to exhaustion and friends had slithered unavailingly to push-start me, I was towed by Charlie Tucker's Vandenplas. My engine fired, Charlie swung left into a garage and my bumper alone followed him. The poor barman wept when he saw his old vehicle so sadly ravaged.

My little Morris gave me some more acutely hair-raising moments, as when it ran out of steam overtaking a lorry near the crest of a hill, but it added much to my university life – excursions to Cambridge and Stratford and places nearer to Oxford, lunches out with friends, the 'celebrity' that came to one of the very few at that time to be running a car at Oxford – and in time I acquired a certain resilience in responding to the latest crisis thrown at me by my machine. On the first occasion that I took my parents from Putney to Oxford, they were as impressed as they were staggered when, after HFC 750 had given up the ghost on Denham Hill, I calmly lifted the bonnet, thumped the side of the petrol pump hard with the bonnet key, depressed the pump a few times and re-started the engine.

My favourite outing was to 'Dudley's', The Lamb and Flag at Kingston Bagpuize. Dudley himself was a publican of massive girth, his belt more like a saddle. He had a St Bernard of equally impressive stature. The meals were copious, there was no bill, you simply went up afterwards from the cellar and told Dudley what you had consumed.

It was a small world. If I owed my car to Chris Cook, my introduction to Dudley's derived from Father 'B' from the Oratory, who happened to have been a generous and good friend to Chris Cook. Perhaps it was for this reason that, when my three attempts elsewhere had failed, he had suggested Christ Church to me as a college large enough to include me. Colin Miesch, from the first time he met him, referred to him dismissively as 'Your queer friend'. I had known, ever since one fleeting and mercifully insignificant episode, that Father 'B's orientation was indeed odd – I had told my mother and she had reacted calmly, telling the priest that I was going through a difficult phase and opining to me that many men only became priests because they were that way inclined – but Chris certainly did not. We both enjoyed our lunches with this somewhat extraordinary man, who knew his food and wine and zoomed around happily in his flashy MG Magnette. Our last lunch with him was after he had moved to become chaplain of a new Catholic boarding school near Basingstoke. Years later he was dismissed because he had grossly abused that trust. He is dead now. I believe that he knew that his inclinations were sinful. I heard him once preach a Lenten sermon, in which he inveighed against those who wished to downplay the sinfulness of sin. To me he was generous.

Why was Colin so much more 'aware' and wary than we were? In part, it was probably because such men were the occupational hazard of boarding school education – although Chris too had attended a boarding school. Was the Catholic Church, as Colin would have implied, another zone particularly inclined to such deviance? As it happens my diary records meetings with another Catholic whose proclivities were undoubtedly awry. He was an aging New Zealand roué, Roger S., who had, according to the Oratorian priest, changed his name for some reason or other from the original 'Gordon George'. He wrote unreadably pretentious books and haunted Oxford. When we were boys he had invited Michael and me up to Oxford for the day, I had had a splitting headache and took refuge in the station waiting room and Roger S.

made an unsuccessful pass at Michael near Parsons' Pleasure. In other words, he was a dirty old man. Yet the family went on making him welcome and we saw it as expected of us that we should do the same. Truly the past is a foreign country where they did things differently!

The only 'date' that I can recall from my school days had been to join John Anscomb in making up a party with Rollo Rumford and his sister, Melanie, at a New Year's Ball in The Bull at Sheen. I fear that my utter incompetence in dancing must have made it an agony for my partner. I was gauche and I was prudish. For 13 January 1962 my diary reads: 'Saw *Irma La Douce*. Amusing and saucy – perhaps excessively so.' I reassured myself that the problem at Oxford was that there were so few girls. This was self-deception. I remained on the touch-line as Michael Davis typically aimed high, paying court to the most elegant Catholic girl in Oxford, a double-barrelled member of St Anne's. I was waiting for someone to turn up – and I would go on waiting.

It must, I suppose, have been equally difficult for the few girls, albeit for the opposite reason. Surrounded by herds of circling men, effortlessly the object of platonic devotion, an attractive girl like Jacquie Geldart could hold court at the Chaplaincy without much danger of real contact with her subjects. I was one of the many who chatted with her over lunch. One day, she announced that she was off, heading for her home in the Black Forest. Why? The Cuban Missile Crisis had triggered a parental summons. My stunned amazement remains a stronger memory than the crisis itself. Why on earth would anyone want to survive a nuclear holocaust? It never crossed my mind to do anything other than await developments. And everything would surely be all right.

So my little circle in Christ Church, confined more or less exclusively to two staircases and three schools – Blundells, Downside and St Benedict's – whiled away hours at pontoon and I was an invariable loser. Even longer hours were devoted to conversation. After the rugby club dinner I sat up to 3.30 in the room of a freshman, with me as earnest on religion and Catholicism as only I could be. He survived the experience and is now Senior Censor of The House.

Life in Peck 2.1. came to a somewhat lurid climax when the House boat came Head of the River and we were informed by the grapevine that an act of collective pillage was the least that we could do to celebrate. Normally such activities were confined to the 'Brideshead' brigade, who would hunt in an inebriated pack after dinners, looking for intellectuals to cast into Mercury, while the timid middle classes sported their oaks. This was different. Every window in college was smashed in an orgy of destruction which, as far as I recall, met with no censure from the authorities. Next morning the college labourers were out in force and we all had the gratifying sensation that we had brought employment to the dependent classes.

My holiday world continued to revolve around my St Benedict's friends, like Pete Hubner, Chris King and the floridly ostentatious John Groser. At Easter I stayed two nights with Chris in his new home in Hindhead. It was the first time that I had been away from home in a friend's house. I remember him expressing perplexity that my parents did not own their own house. At the end of the summer vacation, I went with Chris on our own form of mini-Retreat, a few days in Quarr Abbey on the Isle of Wight, walking, swimming and drinking, as well as attending some plain chant. This very virtuous impression of myself and my friends should be stood against my sorry performance six months later. I was with Pete Hubner and John Groser in a pub in Leicester Square when I noticed that a youth at another table was wearing Pete's Middlesex Hospital scarf. I challenged him. He leapt up and started half-slapping my face, so I thumped him. He went down, he got up, I hit him again. Once more he went down and came up. In desperation I hit him a third time, whereupon the landlord stormed across, saying that he was calling the police. 'I would have you know,' interposed John Groser in his fruitiest tones, 'that I am a qualified lawyer and that my friend here was *assaulted*.' We beat a quick retreat.

At the beginning of the summer vacation of 1962 I celebrated my new independence with a solo car trip to East Anglia, but for the first time I was beginning to sense a shortage of money and the next few weeks were spent at Shell Centre. I had a reason by then for cycling home quickly after work. Hardly an evening passed without tennis with Kings Keep Mary. Afterwards we would walk up to the pub or drive in my car to Wimbledon. She was the youngest but one of a huge Catholic family who had come over to England from South Africa. Her English mother taught PE in a Catholic girls' school in Kent, her South African father was a psychiatrist at Wormwood Scrubs. The whole family was good at games. Mary had been a rebel at school and was doing temporary work in the West End rather than going to university, but she was iconoclastically intelligent.

She had offered little or no encouragement to me in the previous autumn. Once I stood for hours at Piccadilly Circus and never received apology or explanation. I persevered and took her to *Breakfast at Tiffany's*. On her eagerly awaited Christmas Card, she wrote, 'With love (of the Christmas kind!)', and that effectively dowsed my hopes. Now, however, we seemed to be getting on really well. For a fortnight or so life acquired a delicious regularity. I drove her one weekend to St Albans, then took her to *West Side Story*.

Looking back I think that I can see that a somewhat short and rather overweight young man needed at the very least to exhibit some passion if his attentions were to be worthy of consideration. I did not feel passion, only a growing attachment. I certainly did not intend to suspend my normal life on Mary's account. She knew that I was about to set off on a car tour of northern monasteries with Michael Davis and Brian Burns. On the previous evening she led me down a side road, then firmly took my hand. This was when I should have kissed her, or done something. I was numb. She dropped my hand, said brusquely that the family was moving next week to Richmond and that would be that. Her only worry was the harm that it would do to me. In my diary I wrote simply, '*La Fin*'.

The Yorkshire holiday at least forced me to think of other things. Michael and I made it to Ampleforth in HFC 750. We spent two nights in the monastery, with generous measures of beer each evening, and visited Byland, Mount Grace, Rievaulx and Castle Howard before meeting Brian at York Station. That afternoon the car failed gallantly in its attempt on the Buttertubs Pass from Wensleydale to Swaledale. Next day, as we drew into Leyburn for Mass, it expired. A piston was broken. We walked to Jervaulx and returned next day to pick the car up, only for it to develop fresh problems. Eventually, late at night, we set off down the A 1. The car petered out near Grantham, then sputtered back to life and we hared off, leaving behind us an enormous pall of dense black smoke. I got back to Putney about 3.30. Brian had not had much of a holiday!

I took the car to Ken Shaw for repair. He was a mechanic at the Duke of York's barracks in Chelsea, never out of overalls or clean of oil, and Mary's father had found in him a reliable and wonderfully cheap answer to every mechanical problem. Ken restored HFC 750 to fitness and assured me that it had many years left in it – and I tried to console myself that my friendship with Mary had yielded one positive outcome.

I had not quite abandoned hope of Mary. My 21st birthday party was looming, in Lower Park, and Mary was invited. My diary sugars the pill of a bitter evening. '21st Party – went off very well. 18 men, 8 women.' In fact the hours passed and Mary did not arrive, while Michael endlessly played and replayed my Buddy Holly record. About midnight I was asked to say a few words. 'I did not know I had such nice friends,' was all that I could mumble, to a stunned silence, leaving unsaid all my feelings of love and gratitude to Una and Denis and Kathleen. Mary then turned up, presentless, for the most perfunctory of appearances.

'If you knew, Peggy Sue, you would know why I feel blue…' I went round to see her a couple of days later to plead my cause, got nowhere and drove on to Oxford for my final year. HFC 750 broke down, sympathetically, on the way.

At Oxford, there were big changes. I was out of college and into Tony Ford's old room in 36 St John's Street, where Mrs Roberts presided over a household that otherwise consisted of two Young Conservative contacts of Tony. Colin Miesch too was gone, having failed his re-sit of Prelims. He lingered for a while in the Talbot Arms in Eynsham, pondering a come back, and I drove out from time to time to see him before he gave up and we lost touch. He bequeathed to me his half-share in HFC 750, having repainted it from Maroon to French Blue. Next year he would claim to have shaped the outcome of the General Election. Regarding Rottingdean as safely Conservative, he and all his friends decided not to leave their party and cast their votes. The Labour candidate won the seat by less than ten votes, contributing a substantial share of Harold Wilson's wafer-thin majority.

By way of compensation I could now enjoy in Oxford the presence of my brother. In his early years in the Senior School, Michael had taken eccentricity to unimaginable lengths. In particular he took to tormenting Gil Harrison, now his Divisions Master. He would ambush Gil on his route from home and then crawl behind him on all fours across the Black Pitch. He was frequently caned by Gil for his sins – until he demolished even this sanction by repeatedly knocking on Gil's door, interrupting his class and asking to be beaten. At this stage an Oxford place for Michael would have seemed absurd. But he came under the towering influence of Frank Hanley and he succeeded where all others had failed. Michael achieved distinction at Advanced Level and duly arrived at Wadham College in October 1962. He settled down happily and eschewed his St Benedict's notoriety – until Eights Week in my final month at Oxford.

Michael had decided to take a girl punting. A sequence of press photographs recorded the disaster as, with ghastly inexorability, it unfolded. First the eights are in the distance, with Michael parallel to the shore. Then they are nearer, but Michael's punt is heading into the stream! Now the first boat checks, to avoid collision with Michael, and the second crashes into it. Finally, there is mayhem in the river, with boats piled into one another, but Michael continues to punt, serenely, to the far shore. That night, the lawn of Wadham College was dug up.

For me the final year had a monastic regime. I went on playing rugby until Christmas, although, shorn of my two great props, I found hooking a much tougher battle – too tough against Jesus where an opponent, Welsh I assume, gouged my eye. I went to few lectures that were not relevant. One, by Peter Levi on unfamiliar poets, stands out in my diary, in part for its rarity, in part on account of our later association through Prior Park. By then I had completely forgotten that our paths had ever crossed.

Perhaps the most portentous entry referred to my meeting in November with 'the Christ Church representative at the Treasury', the opening shot in Charles Stuart's bid to get me into the Civil Service.

Charles Stuart turned my mediocre academic career into something better. He was a scholar, the editor of the revised Oxford History of the Whig Supremacy, but he was above all a brilliant teacher. Under him I suddenly 'got the knack'. At the same time I was also discovering unexpected pleasures in my Constitutional History option, documents relating to imperial history in the nineteenth and twentieth centuries. Here too, in tutorials at Mansfield College and lectures at Rhodes College, I had superb guidance from Dr Madden. By Christmas I was moving fast, so that I was not deflected by the more casual style of J. Steven Watson. He was the prototype of the media don, an occasional performer in *That Was The Week That Was*. We waited for tutorials as his voice

Christ Church Rugby XV 1962 – Harry Shutt tallest in back row,
Taff Fairman cross-legged to left.

boomed through the door, briefing the *Daily Mail* by phone on the historical differences between 'snubs' and 'quasi-snubs' – this following the cancellation of Princess Margaret's visit to Paris following de Gaulle's exclusion of Britain from the EEC.

Gratifying, if belated, though my academic advance was, neither I nor my friends were prepared for the bombshell on 14 November 1962. I bumped into Lawrence Boyle in Kilcannon. He stopped me. 'Eh, Paddy,' he said in his flat tones, 'I see you've won an Exhibition.' I don't think that I said anything, my confusion was self-evident. 'Eh, go and look, it's on the College Notice-Board – a Boulter Exhibition.' And so it was! I remain unclear as to the criteria for the award, but could only assume that it reflected the House's satisfaction with its hardworking student. The repressed fury of my friends can only be imagined. Years later, a young teacher at Stewart's Melville happened to be sitting next to a Christ Church contemporary of mine. He asked him what I was like. 'Keen on sport, went around smiling all the time, incredibly idle,' was the much quoted response. My friends and I remain puzzled to this day.

In the longer term I extracted great benefit from the Boulter Exhibition, especially on cvs. Immediately, it created a problem. I would clearly have to do some work if I was to avoid embarrassment all round in the following summer. Evidence for this is not apparent in my diary entry for the holidays. There was tennis virtually every day before Christmas, even when the weather was so cold that the car froze. I went to a number of shows. After Wesker's *Chips With Everything* I noted, 'Difficult drive through the snow – one bump.'

1963 opened with my examinations for selection for the Administrative Grade of the Civil Service. I did a little work before returning to Oxford in mid-January and there is then a record of many lectures and some application. Brian Burns, Michael Davis and I possibly established a new record when we attended a lecture by Max Beloff in Schools one Saturday morning, in that we were the only three present. Was there, we wondered, a previous occasion when everyone attending an open lecture came from one school?

Even so, my motives were not always simple. It took me a while to work out what was meant by an obscure entry for January 22nd – 'Farce in the Camera' – but then I remembered.

At the end of the previous term I had gone to a second round of lectures by K.B. McFarlane. Another devotee was a very beautiful girl, with long dark hair and pale complexion. She came and went by herself, took notes sparingly and, in the style of courtly love taught to me by Ken Connolly, I worshipped her hopelessly from afar. Then, on 22 January, as I went to the Camera to read Gash's *Life of Peel*, there she was. I spent the morning wondering whether I had the nerve to speak to her – I hadn't. I hurried back from my lunch at the Chaplaincy. She hadn't moved. I went on reading, or at least half-reading, Gash. Tea time approached. Then I hit on my stratagem. I had missed one of McFarlane's lectures. I would ask if she had been there and if she could possibly lend me her notes? It was an uncharacteristically courageous initiative and it was well rewarded, if not in the length of the notes. Yes, indeed, would I like to come round to St Hugh's for tea next day?

Every night for weeks afterwards I went to sleep thinking of Evelyn. Now I look back at my diary for those weeks and wonder what on earth I was playing at. I can only assume that I was so shy that my first and only priority was to avoid a second rebuff that year, so I played it cool. Next week I return the notes. A week later, I take Evelyn out to dinner in Iffley and we go on to a party together. Then five weeks elapse before she comes again to tea.

I suspect that at some stage Chris Mulvey told me that she was the girlfriend of Jonathan at Magdalen and that I was 'hanging in', hoping that something would turn up. A few days later Chris himself gave a party in Magdalen. There was Evelyn, with Jonathan. I slipped away and took myself to the all-night Lenten vigil at the Chaplaincy. Hours later we pious few sang 'Lead Kindly Light Amid the Encircling Gloom'. It was a hymn that I loved but, in that cold, passion-drained dawn, they even played the 'wrong' tune.

There was a postscript. Just before Finals next term, I found in my pigeon-hole a little package. It was a bottle of cherry brandy from Evelyn. I don't know why I never thanked her – I did feel very grateful. We never met again. I hope that she is happy.

At the end of term there followed in quick succession the two events that would determine my future career. On 1 April I drove over to Ealing to see Paul Olsen. He was leaving in the summer to become the first headmaster of a new Catholic school in Birmingham. He thought that I might like to take over from him as a teacher of History and as the only teacher of Economics. At St Benedict's this was then taught only to Advanced Level. It was flattering and very tempting. I told Paul that I was being interviewed the next day for the Civil Service.

I like to think that I underperformed grossly in these interviews because my heart was really set on teaching. In truth I did not compete in the 'group' situations for exactly the same reason as I had not spoken at the Union – I was too callow, immature, narrow and inhibited. When questioned one to one, I soon exposed my essential lack of interest in the actuality of government. I went away knowing that I had failed, as indeed was the case, and learned only later that I had managed to undo a very considerable advantage established previously during the examination, when I had been in the top ten of a group of several hundred.

My mother was heartbroken and went to see Paul Olsen. 'Don't worry, Mrs Tobin,' he growled, 'Pat will be a Head by the time he is forty.'

If Patrick refused to be a civil servant like his father, Una was not prepared to allow Denis to remain a cyclist when Patrick had his own car. First she sent him out to learn to drive. Then, before he had passed his test, she instructed him to buy a limousine to make others stare. SUV 233 was a 1953 3.4 litre automatic Armstrong Siddeley Sapphire in dark and light grey. It had soft leather upholstery, into which Denis would sink when driving, so that only his head would be visible above the dashboard. From now on trains were out and the Tobins would tour Europe in style.

By the summer term of 1963 I had become a disciplined workaholic – the Camera from breakfast to lunch, Mass and a salad at the Chaplaincy, back to the Camera in the afternoon, dinner in Christ Church, then a final stint in the Camera until it closed. All the while the sun blazed. It was still shining as we drank champagne in the High after the last paper of Finals. By lunch next day the sun had gone. In any case, I was back in the Camera, 'winding down' via Warren's *King John*.

Finals had gone as well as could have been expected. There were areas where no patchwork could effectively disguise previous neglect. On the other hand, in two of the papers covered in my third year, I obtained touches of alpha. I cannot realistically say that I went to my 'Viva' with the slim possibility of a First. My ignorance of the direction of bread prices in 1647 ensured that the Viva would be a brief formality.

It was in Italy that I would learn the outcome, along with Brian Burns and with two of my Christ Church fellow historians and rugby colleagues, Harry

After Finals – with Chris Mulvey and Brian Burns.

Shutt and Taff Fairman. Taff, like me, went straight into teaching. Harry and I had been run in tandem for all our tutorials during the first year and more. I think that it had amused John Mason to juxtapose the narrow Catholic with the scoffing agnostic. We are friends still.

Harry's father supplied the car for the trip and Harry was our leader. We took just over five weeks to drive down the west coast of Italy and return up the east in his Austin Somerset. It boiled over every time we got stuck behind anything on a hill, but survived. On its passengers Harry imposed an 'iron ration'. We camped virtually every night, the most memorable site being a refuse tip near Florence into which we had been attracted in the dark by the unwonted pliability of the soil. We would then search for food, Harry limiting us to 800 lire, so we would wander past trattoria after trattoria until we at last found spaghetti within our range. In Rome we heard *Tosca* in the Baths of Caracalla. In the municipal gardens of Palermo, having just read in a *Times* at the station that we had all gained Seconds, we were half way through 'Nessun dorma' in *Turandot* when the clouds opened and the natives fled. In Agrigento, our cheapest spaghetti meal went on for many happy hours as we chatted and sang with local students. On our way north, in Lanciano, a family known to the Shutts gave us what was by any standards a handsome supper. Starved as we were it seemed almost unbearably sumptuous. What was more, to me at any rate, the youngest daughter, fair and grave, was beauty personified. Sadly, our hosts had arranged for us to stay in a local convent. As I had already persuaded Harry that it would be appropriate for us to stay in the Pontifical Seminary in Venice he became more than usually caustic about papist peculiarities. On our return journey, pitching tents in the Tyrol, we were accosted at gunpoint by the carabinieri on suspicion of being terrorist separatists. And we celebrated our safe return and Wagner's 150th anniversary at a special Promenade concert, of which Birgit Nillson's Brunnhilde is the only and indelible memory. Thank you Harry!

My prevailing mood when I left Oxford was still one of relief. In 1960 I was relieved that I had got in. Now I was mightily relieved that I had come out of it with a good Second. I had been put to the test and emerged with the one thing necessary. That Oxford degree would be springboard and foundation for my career.

Nor is that all. As I read my diary and write these pages, I realize the more what a huge privilege those three years were, how much I had savoured and enjoyed, even how much I had gained in human experience.

Yes, but...!

Underlying the wasted opportunities, or at least associated with them, was that sense of being an *outsider* that I had taken from Una and Koo and would retain in all my non-Catholic posts. Nothing expresses this 'ghetto' mentality more eloquently than the fact that I was three years in the only college to have its own cathedral, in which time I never set foot in it – not for any religious services, because that would have been apostasy, not even as a cultural tourist. Like a future Congress leader coming to Oxford from India before 1947, or the working class boy determined not to be seduced from his roots, I supped with the Establishment, because it was there, but I was not in communion with it. It was not the fault of Christ Church that I co-existed with it rather than truly belonged to it.

Seventeen days after returning from Italy I went back to St Benedict's.

CHAPTER 6

Marking Time, Driving to Byzantium

'Don't you think that I ought to be trained?' 'My dear Paddy, teachers are born, not made'.
(Dom George Brown, before I decided to go back to St Benedict's to teach.)

I ASKED THE question and I got the answer I wanted. If, deep down, I felt that I should be resisting the siren call to return, untrained, to my old school, there was no hesitation in my acceptance. Conventional wisdom insists that there is no worse way into teaching. Yet two of the very best teachers I would myself appoint also began their careers in their own schools, one without a PGCE. They are now Headmaster and Deputy Head of two fine schools. In that sense Father George was undoubtedly right.

Father George was one of many familiar faces. Steve Walker was my infinitely obliging and tolerant Head of Department. Frank Hanley and Ken Connolly were now colleagues, and I was a guest to parties at their homes. Basil Nickerson still taught Latin, coached the Second Fifteen and imparted a fanatical zeal to everything. But there were new faces too. Dom John Main had recently joined the Abbey after a distinguished career in the Colonial Civil Service and as a Law Lecturer at Trinity College, Dublin. He had style.

So too did John Bogie, for whom St Benedict's was a first teaching post after his Education degree at Strawberry Hill. He had been educated by the Irish Christian Brothers at Prior Park (along with my Good cousins), he had played rugby for Bath and cricket for Ealing and he was as different from the Putney Pud as could be imagined – fast bowler to my batsman, centre threequarter to my hooker, man's man to my introspection. John offered me a passport into clubbability – we were playing the fruit machines in Ealing Cricket Club with him when news broke of the assassination of President Kennedy – but it was not really for me.

As always I took everything far too earnestly. Nobody ever accused John of that. 'I know that I am facetious,' he replied when chided by Cecil Friedlander, the CO of our CCF. 'Facetious, John, you're bloody outrageous.' It was a great shock, at the end of our first year, when John announced that he was entering the monastery. A few months later, there was a phone call, 'I'm OUT,' but he moved away from London. Our paths would cross again.

The first year's adrenalin and fatigue will be familiar to all teachers – every face has to be identified, every class prepared, every course planned – but at least today's probationers will have been trained, observed, criticized and improved. I could draw only on instinct and on memories of my own teachers, good, bad and indifferent. Poor Simon Codrington, desperately asking a question, had nodded off by the time I finished answering it. A Scottish student teacher named Canavan, having watched one of my classes, passed me a book entitled, *How to teach History*.

Apart from a single History class with younger boys, all my teaching was to the Sixth Form or on the games field. Throughout my time at St Benedict's I was timetabled to teach rugby and cricket on two afternoons a week, with the remainder of my timetable spent preponderantly on Lower Sixth and Upper Sixth classes in History and in Economics. There could be no doubt as to where the greater challenge lay. In medieval History I dictated notes, handed out typed notes, set essays and marked them in much the same way as I had been taught. In Economics, there was a daily struggle to keep ahead of the class. There was no colleague to whom I could turn, no reservoir of knowledge on which I could rely. At least I empathized, all too fully, with my pupils' difficulties in comprehending economic theory. In this respect I became a better teacher of Economics than of History.

What I lacked in gravitas and know-how I made up for in commitment. I seem to have gone down quite well with pupils, to the extent that parents worried that such a novice held sway with their sons. Walking down a corridor I passed two parents, then, returning immediately, heard one of them say to the other, 'But he is so *young*, isn't he?' I bored the pants off Chris King and his guests at a dinner party as I enthused about the joys of teaching. As my friends advanced into adulthood I was regressing.

Not surprisingly, the euphoric excitement of those first terms alternated with moments of bleak self-analysis. 'Dom,' piped Graham Balfour to Dominic Ingram after rugby training, as I walked ahead of them in the enveloping dusk, 'Do you *like* Mr Tobin?' My first Oxford Sevens tournament was a purgatory of migraine, gloomy introspection and numbing chill. I was ill at school after sitting up to hear the first fight between Cassius Clay and Sonny Liston, then stayed up even later to watch, disbelievingly, the fiasco of the return fight.

My first Advanced Level results, even in Economics, were satisfactory. From his school in Birmingham, on a small piece of paper and in the familiar italic type, I received Paul Olsen's congratulation. His letter says as much about him as about me.

> I was lucky enough to get a copy of the GCE results from the office and I really do feel that you have made an awfully good job of your first year! I had expected a lad like Steve Jay to do well – but it's the likes of people like G which are the true test of teaching ability. How well old J has done after all his battles and dissatisfaction with the beastly grind of Modern Languages. I'm glad to see a lad like Mn coming up – it might give him something to look happy about after all. Mh is a mild grief – he had better things in him – but poor fellow I suppose he was always at home. If I

remember him R must be a rank outsider too. W, last of the trio, is simply out of this world. My only real sorrow is old S who really had good stuff in him. – the most reflective mind of his year. How these goofs can give a better account than he I know not. Perhaps after all it is the Examiner who should be examined.

Steve Jay's success created a problem. He was going to apply for Oxford. Together we went up to Foyles to hunt for books on macroeconomics. On a Saturday morning I recall nervously going to his house in Barnes to provide a 'tutorial' on Keynesian theory. Somehow he got in.

My heart, however, was in the Oxford attempts of three young historians. When I had been a prefect they had just entered the Senior School in a 'B' stream that brimmed with fun and goodwill. Now, sitting in Steve Walker's study, surrounded by attentive, responsive, friendly faces, I immersed myself in their cultivation as if they would be the only pupils whom I would ever teach. In my first summer term I drove them up to Oxford and enticed all to aspire to the glittering prizes. One made it and will presumably have been grateful since for my amalgam of affection and ego-trip. I felt very guilt on account of the disappointment that I had brought on the others.

I did not know then that life does not end at 21 and that there are more important things than entry into Oxford, or even academic success. At my first Parents' evening, the most waywardly erratic member of my History set was denounced, first by his mother, then, more fiercely, by his elder sister. Tony seemed incapable of settling to anything – other than the pursuit of Buddy Holly. It was said of him that he possessed every photograph ever taken of the star, including the one without glasses, and that he had once telephoned his way into the hotel bedroom of 'The Crickets', they assuming that his unbroken voice must be that of a woman. Tony is now reputedly a millionaire.

My passion for sport eased my entry into teaching but I was only moderately successful as a coach of rugby and cricket. After all, I had little to offer except enthusiasm and my own very limited experience. I knew next to nothing about threequarter play or bowling and was decidedly shaky as referee or umpire. John Bogie's Under 15 Seven had reached the semi-final of the Llanelli Sevens. Year after year following his departure I made the annual Easter pilgrimage along the A40, slept on the hard boards of the Llanelli Grammar School classrooms and returned empty handed.

As an officer in the CCF I was even more amateur. I enjoyed my forays in Land Rovers and Champs and my first summer camp saw me clambering into the cab of a three ton lorry. There was, of course, no preliminary HGV training and nobody seemed to mind when my first turn of the wheel took the lorry into collision with the roof of a nissen hut. A year later I very nearly backed a lorry and a full complement of cadets over a precipice.

I did, however, receive formal training for Her Majesty's commission. After a few days of officer training at Frimley, I was attached for a scorching fortnight in

August to the 'Buffs' Regiment in Canterbury. By now I had replaced my Morris 8 with a MGB in British Racing Green and this made an instant impression on the Officers' Mess. My arrival coincided with the Canterbury Cricket Festival, where the Buffs had their own tent. I took the Colonel's daughter to *Mary Poppins* and for a drive along the coast. My attachment ended as Duty Officer for the Adjutant's parade. Sword in hand, I had to march out in front of the whole regiment. Heaven knows what the massed ranks behind me were thinking.

I can add a telling footnote to that exotic week. The Buffs marched as a regiment to Canterbury Cathedral for a Remembrance Parade. It was, as I recorded, 'very impressive'. Who should be there to watch but my parents? Afterwards we all went out together to revisit Tankerton and Grandad Flanagan's bungalow.

The family had indeed reclaimed me. I was back to Lower Park and back to the family holiday. I should have savoured that holiday more, for it was to be the last time that all seemed well. In the previous September my parents had enjoyed a Silver Wedding party in the flat. Michael was doing fine at Oxford. But I found it harder than ever to cope with my father, the Armstrong Siddeley misbehaved and the weather was hot. There was a brief respite at Lourdes and then a general descent into the abyss in the hotel that had once been the medieval monastery of Escaladieu.

This should have been an idyllic stay. On our second day there, however, we set off up the Pic du Midi, the highest point in the Pyrenees. I was driving. On reaching the car park, I reversed carelessly and scraped the bottom of the car on a boulder. Hydraulic brake fluid poured on to the ground. 'Chewing gum, get some chewing gum,' yelled Denis, at his most Indian. I suppose that we should have taken more seriously the advice of the only engineer among us, but the thought of taking a car weighing several tons down the longest and steepest slope in France with our lives hanging on threads of chewing gum did seem risible. Instead we summoned help, waited at the top for six hours and were then consigned indefinitely to the delights of Escaladieu. These palled. My father, when not swimming in the river, flirted with the maid, Solange, to the utter fury of Koo. The wasps previously manifest in the old abbey metamorphosed into a plague of hornets. It was late in the second afternoon of our life in the country that we learned that our limousine awaited us.

There was to be no family holiday in 1965. Instead Michael returned from his year in Rennes speechless and clearly ill. It was diagnosed as depression. Later the doctors changed the diagnosis to schizophrenia. Michael would never be well again. He would be in and out of hospitals for the rest of his short life. There would be occasional shafts of his intelligence and wit. In April 1968 *The Times* published his vigorous response to an article by A.P. Herbert about the Thames. Years later, old friends told us that they had just been to Crete. 'Oh, did you see the minotaur?' asked Michael. 'No, we didn't have time,' came the reply, and Michael turned towards me and silently rolled his eyes. The Old Priorian Cricket team always made him welcome and he is fondly remembered by them. But as the prospects for him became bleaker and as his illness removed him more and more from fun and friends, Una fought indomitably for Michael and railed bitterly at the family and the world for failing to do more for him. Denis was the chief casualty. For a decade or so he continued his cricket, often to amazing effect. How many sexagenarians have averaged over 60 with the bat? In the end, however, she hounded him from his umpiring and his company in the bar, driving him too into depression. Koo, meanwhile, had one hip operation after another, while the family for which she lived disintegrated around her. It was tragic. I alone would survive, because I was selfish enough to survive.

All that lay in the future. By the mid 1960s my teaching life was settling into the pattern that would endure until a generous providence shook me out of it. I managed to detach myself from the CCF in 1966, having convinced myself that I was not suited to military discipline or to things practical. Not every officer bends and snaps his wireless aerial through his lorry window in an attempt to improve the signal. I played for the Old Priorian Cricket Club during the summer holidays, having presented myself as its saviour from extinction. In 1965 I succeeded Maurice Pearce as Secretary of the Old Priorian Association itself. For the next five years, I more or less single-handedly ran the Association, organizing dinners and dances, busily recruiting leavers and diligently sustaining them in the card-index, recording the deliberations of the Committee and the formalities of the AGM and producing annual reports in the *Priorian* including a miscellany of latest individual news. I even arranged the Old Priorian Retreats. Michael Hollings came down from Oxford and Archbishop Roberts from his retirement after Bombay. Over lunch the latter told me of his belief that in Heaven we would all have our jobs to do, like teaching the infants who had died in their mothers' wombs. Dom Victor Farwell, shortly to become Abbot of Worth, returned to his old school. He must have wondered what it was coming to when, airing a lifelong prejudice, I challenged him to explain why the Church did not regard smoking as a more sinful abuse than masturbation.

The reader may wonder whether the Secretaryship of the Old Priorian Association is worthy of note. The odd thing was that, out of all of my activities during those early years of teaching at St Benedict's, it was the only one that specifically rehearsed some of the 'competencies' required for headship.

My diary for those early years of teaching continued its laconic way –

24 January 1965 *Death of Churchill.*

30 January *Churchill's funeral – Shooting in morning, in afternoon Emanuel.* How remarkable it seems now that schools should have been carrying on their normal Saturday activities when the greatest man in British history was being

buried – a far cry from the hysteria of a later age. After the rugby match at Emanuel we did stand alongside the railway line in the hope of seeing the funeral train. Alas it took the 'Putney' route from Clapham Junction.

14 July 1965 *News that Father George is to be succeeded by Father Bernard* – the second coming of J.B.O. as Headmaster of St Benedict's.

9/10 January 1966 *Visited Olsens.* Paul had invited me up to Birmingham in the hope of inveigling me into joining his Common Room. I was not attracted by the austerities of maintained school education.

13 March 1967 *Helped adjudicate Prize Debate – Ackroyd the winner.* It remains a regret that I never taught Peter Ackroyd. This prize was my entire contribution to the education of St Benedict's most eminent man of letters.

22 March 1967 *Went with Brian (Burns) to see Fulham v Man Utd – 2-2 draw, ground very full 47290 – biggest since 1938.* Best, Charlton & Co. in their pomp were held by Johnny Haynes, Bobby Robson, George Cohen and the less illustrious.

29 April 1968 *History Society outing to Winchester (St Cross and Cathedral), Old Sarum, Stonehenge and Avebury. Rather wet. John Dodd sick.* Just recently Edward Fennell told me of one life-shaping experience during that visit to Winchester Cathedral. We never know what impact we are having on our pupils.

9 October 1968 *Publicity in the 'Evening Standard' about Mary Wilson.* One of my first pupils, Denis Matyjaszek (now the Government Minister, Denis MacShane) had telephoned from Oxford to ask me to add my graduate's endorsement to the nomination by Richard Ingram and others of Mary Wilson, the Prime Minister's wife, as Regius Professor of Poetry.

11 October 1968 *Visited Grandma after school. She seemed low physically but more resigned.*

October 12th 1968 *Grandma died during the night.*

I had gone to see Grandma quite frequently. This time she begged me not to leave her but I made my excuses. I was the last member of the family to see her alive. My father wept at breakfast, the only time I ever saw him cry.

18 November 1967 *Watched Fulham beat Nottingham Forest 2-0 – 1st goal in 20 seconds! Devaluation.* I was actually more interested in the politics and economics than in the football. Week by week I had read my *Economist* and traced the ignominious descent of the Wilson administration from the brave aspirations of 1964 to the casuistry of the 'pound in your pocket'.

The years were passing and I was putting on weight. Every now and then a girl appears in my diary, for a page or two. Tennis with Common Room colleagues was my most frequent diversion. Two colleagues had me home to their very different backgrounds, Alan McNamee for a couple of nights in Burnley, Rodney Bomford, soon to be an Anglo-Catholic vicar, for a gracious tea at Sutton Courtenay. Alan was replaced by one of the most inspirational teachers to grace St Benedict's, the red-haired and appropriately passionate

Philip Lawrence, and I was right to sense a challenge. Basically I was stuck in a rut.

In one respect only did I show a flicker of adventure. During 1965 I began to entertain the idea of a camping expedition in the steps of the First Crusade. I even met a BBC television producer in Ealing to discuss the possibility of making a film. John Bogie and Father John were briefly interested, only to fall away. In the summer of 1966 I hired a brand new Volkswagen camper van in Roehampton and four of us set off on the long road east. Brian Burns was the other veteran of the Shutt expedition to Sicily. Michael Davis and Maurice Pearce made this journey an entirely Old Priorian venture.

The project lacked nothing in scope. We would drive overland through Turkey into Syria, Lebanon and Jordan, before crossing into Israel through the Mandelbaum Gate. Then, because it was impossible to return from Israel through an Arab country, we would take ship from Haifa on a voyage via Cyprus, Ephesus and Rhodes to Piraeus, whence we would drive homewards through Greece.

For over a week all went well as we made our way through Yugoslavia and Bulgaria into Turkey, marvelled at the Byzantine and Ottoman splendours of Istanbul and headed past Seljuk Konya into the centre of Asia Minor. Just after Nigde Michael was driving down a long hill when we saw a dolmush (taxi) reach our road from the side. As we raced down the dolmush slowly pulled out in our direction. Michael pulled out to overtake but the dolmush, steering a very wide bend, now filled the left half of the road. Michael cut inside. The dolmush came back to close our space and we cannoned over quite a steep bank and down into a field. One moment I was reading H.V. Morton. The next I was drenched by our entire water supply. But the vehicle, miraculously, remained upright, while Brian, sitting in front, hurriedly jotted down the number of the disappearing dolmush.

We stumbled out. The front tyres were flat. The gear box was wrecked. The great Anatolian plain was empty, vast and silent. And then there appeared, as if from nowhere, scores of little boys, with crew cut hair and brown faces, excitedly chatting about and to the strangers in their midst. Next we heard tramping feet, as of soldiers, and we turned to see that there were indeed soldiers marching towards us along the road, rifles at the ready to deal with looters. They motioned to us to follow them along the track out of which the dolmush had so recently materialized. And there was a Roman bath, a jewel hidden in the middle of Anatolia. We put our tents up cooked our meal and awaited the morning.

It was decided that I would steer the van as it was towed into Nigde. The garage was literally on the pavement. How was I to get back? The mechanic pointed to a lorry. It stopped and I climbed in, sitting between the driver and his mate. As we drove out of town, in what I hoped was the direction of our camp,

Anatolia 1966 – after the accident.

the mate produced a gun and asked what I thought of it. I wondered if I should jump out of the lorry and roll on to the road if the lorry failed to stop. It stopped.

On the next morning we were all taken into Nigde for our interview at the local Army Headquarters. Lieutenant Cetin Haspisiren was smart, businesslike, 'western' and young. He sat us down in the shade while orderlies brought us drinks and watered the dust in front of us. The questioning was in French. Brian, Michael and Maurice affected complete ignorance of the language, while I secretly blessed the memory of Frank Hanley.

Next day I was driven into Nigde. The van was ready. Somehow the pavement mechanics had hammered our Volkwagen back into shape. So we continued our fantastic tour – Crusader castles, Aleppo, Byblos, Baalbek and Damascus – and reached Jerusalem as planned. We walked the Via Dolorosa, heard Mass in the Church of the Holy Sepulchre and visited St Anne's church. There, at the reputed site of the Pool of Siloam, we met a young musician, a putative composer. Next day we drove David Fanshawe out to Petra, missing by a few minutes the dawn that makes rose-red the city half as old as time. In what was still Arab Jerusalem we inspected the Dome of the Rock and the Wailing Wall, then drove out to the Jordan and Jericho. Only then did we make our way into Israel, perceiving very soon that the Israelis were much less friendly to English visitors than the Jordanians had been. Even so it was thrilling to visit

Nazareth and Capernaum. We stood on the Horns of Hattin and imagined the parched Crusader knights vainly charging the army of Saladin that stood between them and the Sea of Galilee. Our affection for Israel was not enhanced when the dockers lifting our van on to our ferry damaged the gearbox repaired at Nigde.

The rest of our journey passed without incident. Michael decided that he had to get back to ensure that he was ready to start work and that he would return by train from Athens. When he saw that the main line from Greece was no more impressive than a wayside halt he must have wondered whether he had made the right decision. We arrived back less than a day later than he did. Then we went our separate ways – Brian back to Arthur Young, Maurice to the Dental Corps, Michael to the Inland Revenue and I back to the classroom.

There was a final twist in our dispute with the dolmush driver. Before we had left Nigde and its charms the traffic police had interviewed us. It was a far cry from the Raj-like ambience of our meeting with Lieutenant Haspisiren, but we pressed through our inquisitors our claim against the perpetrator of our misfortunes. Shortly after our return we received a letter in Turkish and I asked Alex Ohrnial, an Armenian pupil born in Turkey, to translate. It transpired that we had been awarded damages of about £100, but there was a snag. The account was frozen in a Turkish bank account, to be collected in person. The only immediate consequence of our unlikely success was that our own insurers deducted the £100 from their own liability. I decided that there was nothing for it but another expedition.

By now I was beginning to 'strike gold' with some of my pupils. Richard Gordon, now a leading barrister, had successfully masked his genius from his teachers during a leisurely progress through the 'B' stream. For some reason he was excited by my teaching and, fired by his own manifest progress, he duly won an Oxford Scholarship. Next year I was confronted with two 'A' stream youths of star quality. Richard Wells was quick, feline but wise beyond his years. Edward Fennell was Danton to Richard's Robespierre, an exhibitionist in prose who alternately beamed approval and boomed dissent. They too would win their scholarships to Oxford.

I imagine that I first floated the idea of a school expedition to Byzantium during a Lower Sixth History class. In the end six came on board. In addition to Edward and Richard there were two other members of their History set, Stephen Dempsey and Tony Ginty. Jim Armstrong and Chris Garety had taken the 'B' stream route through the school and were in that sense a year behind.

The expedition was months in the planning. In January 1968 I exchanged my handsome MGB for a pale blue Commer dormobile. This purported to be new. In the light of what followed I came to the conclusion that it must have been a refit.

We commandeered plenty of 'compo' rations from the CCF. Otherwise our dried food was purchased for us by Jim Armstrong's mother, Joan, a wonderfully feisty Australian. (Joan Armstrong was totally loyal to the Church and scathingly critical of it. Half-way through the expedition we would pick up from her our first news of the Pope's prohibition of artificial contraception, *Humanae Vitae*, along with her own anathemas against the encyclical. My friendship with her would endure until her deathbed.) Jim, unfailingly calm, benevolent, courteous and willing, assumed the role of expedition chef, a role that no-one thought or wished to usurp. Chris Garety, who emerged as expedition mechanic, had a family mission to perform. He had to collect in Istanbul his sister's wedding present from her future father-in-law. This highly valuable silverware proved hardly suitable for transit in a dormobile and a nightmare as we neared British Customs.

I look back to the afternoon when the six first loaded their equipment into my minibus as an occasion when my nerve froze. What was I thinking of, embarking for weeks into the Middle East without any adult assistance? Now the same question screams at me. The trip would take us over 7,000 miles, in the heat of the summer, at a maximum speed of 55 mph. – say, 140 hours on the road. There was no relief driver. Any personal incapacity, or serious affliction to any of us, would create a major crisis. By no stroke of the imagination could I see myself as a mechanic nor did I know anything of first aid or even of the dietary needs of adolescents on such an expedition. Today, regulations alone would prevent the trip – and I suspect that the sheer risk would deter most parents. Yet it happened.

The six coped admirably and were astonishingly good company – in circumstances that must have been very testing. I drove the van and the itinerary forward with relentless determination, allowing my companions and myself too little time and space for genuine relaxation. One consequence is that I had largely forgotten most of what we did and what I felt and where we went until I dug out after retirement the fading typescript of Edward Fennell's diary of our progress. This remarkable document, a vivid record of our expedition, was an early demonstration of journalistic skill by the future mainstay of *The Times* Law Section. It was also a detailed and telling appraisal of the conduct and leadership of the expedition.

My 'new' Commer soon betrayed its weaknesses. By Day 3 Chris Garety was having to secure the exhaust pipe with wire and by Day 5 the generator had packed up. We spent hours slogging round the sights of Vienna while it was fixed. The campsite in Vienna was more than usually full, as hundreds of Czechs were taking advantage of the 'Prague Spring' to have their first trip to the West since 1948.

As we crossed into Hungary the boys were sobered further by their first experience of the 'Iron Curtain'. After Budapest, the rain set in and we passed garage after garage in a fruitless and increasingly desperate search for petrol. On our very last drop, we spluttered into a garage able to supply us only with 72 Octane fuel. The Red Army, we later surmised, had commandeered all supplies for its imminent putsch in Czechoslovakia.

In Belgrade next morning, it being Sunday, we asked a young man where we could find Mass. He dismissed the question scornfully. 'We are Yugoslavs, wine, women! NO RELIGION!' So we headed out towards the mountains. The rain lashed down and the road degenerated into a slippery track, before, at last, we came upon the monastery of Manasija, protected by its castellated walls. Mass just beginning. The priest seemed young enough, but his small congregation was exclusively female and evidently aged. Yet the interplay between the intoning of the priest, the haunting responses of the black-clothed women and the frescoed richness of the interior seemed, as Edward put it, 'to transcend time and convey us back through the last eight centuries.' After about an hour I felt embarrassed that the boys had stumbled upon a religious marathon and asked if they wanted to leave. Without hesitation they all shook their heads.

Such interruptions to our journey were rare, but it was not until Day 8 that we reached the border between Bulgaria and Turkey. A phalanx of cars, vans and lorries stretched before us. Hours passed before we reached the Turkish customs post, its cheery message, 'Bon Voyage', dissonant with the surly officials who shut up shop at the least hint of impatience. It was our introduction to the Turkish guest worker, returning from Germany with his refrigerator, washing machine and television. My abiding memory of this otherwise fraught scene is of Jim Armstrong, his head clearly visible above the surrounding hordes, walking calmly forward to investigate, the very model of British composure and dignity. We crossed the frontier into Turkey five hours after we reached the queue.

We spent four nights in a campsite on the London Road to the west of Istanbul, driving into the city each day through those wonderful walls that have defied the passage of armies and ages. In four visits I came to know my way round Istanbul/Byzantium better than any other city but London. I even loved driving through its narrow streets and up and down its seven steep hills. For me Istanbul was a 'dodgem ride' without equal. For my party, as Edward remarked, it was hell to be a back seat driver.

We enjoyed one particularly happy stroke of fortune. The Ealing monks had given us an introduction to a Mr Lister, who had for decades been the British Consul in Istanbul. We met him in his club and he entertained us all to an excellent Turkish lunch in his house. He had many a story to tell of his friendship with Ataturk. From time to time the great man would call on him and issue his challenge, 'Hey Lister, you and I are going to drink each other under the table,' and so it would be. Lister's wife was Turkish. When Ataturk decreed that all Turkish men should abandon the fez in favour of western hats, Lister's friends flocked to his house to ask if they could wear Mrs Lister's hats!

Eventually, after a leisurely cruise along the Bosphorus, we wrenched ourselves away from Istanbul and headed into Anatolia. The boys were overwhelmed by the lunar landscape and magnificent frescoes of Goreme. Then on, through Nigde and past the scene of the accident, to the Cilician Gates, through which, as Edward recalled, Alexander the Great had pursued Darius, King of the Persians, and the leaders of the First Crusade had ridden to their various destinies.

It was here that I gambled and won. Robin Fedden, in his account of the Crusader Castles, included the Armenian castle of 'Lampron'. Seeing a roadsign, 'Namrun', in roughly the right area, I offered the boys a detour of about 20 miles in pursuit of a hypothetical castle. We soon found ourselves driving through valleys so deep that their pine trees descended hundreds of feet below the road as it snaked around the mountains. Their scent wafted through the open windows. After hundreds of scorching miles, we felt ourselves refreshed by Mediterranean temperateness. Then, suddenly, we came upon the castle, set on its own natural fortress of sheer rock, and up this we scrambled, in the heat of the afternoon, to find a hall, a storeroom, a few arches and a magnificent view over many valleys. As at Nigde two years before, out of the seemingly barren terrain there had emerged an improbably large crowd of children. We gave them small cakes before departing in a flurry of waving arms. An experience to savour!

Tony Ginty had less happy memories of our assault on Anavarza. This was the second of two great Armenian castles that we climbed. Extending for a mile at the top of its cliff it is a stupendous site. Local children took us to the 400 steps – huge, rocky and uneven, with no handrail up the face – up which we must climb. An old peasant volunteered to show us the way and up he flew, leaving us panting and perspiring in his wake. By the time we descended we were all exhausted and Tony was none too well. I suggested that he drink some salted water and he was promptly sick, perhaps my most inglorious memory.

During the next week or so every member of the party was to some extent the victim of sunburn and sickness. We kept going, among the temples and beaches of the south and west coasts of Turkey and up towards Greece, passing lines of camels and convoys of armoured vehicles. What was happening in Czechoslovakia?

By now the appetite for cultural tourism had lost its edge, but the boys gallantly coped with Athens, Daphne, Delphi and Epidauros, although they derived more pleasure from the beaches of the Peleponnese. Day 34 saw us heading into the mountains out of Greece. The road was literally being blasted before us as we progressed. An impatient German in a wide Mercedes did his best to force us off the road. The van's engine began to splutter ominously. We staggered on. The last sixty miles before Pec were a three hour purgatory along a dirt track. The boys cheered when, just as we entered the town, we at last hit tarmac.

Next day, the tarmac expired after 100 metres. The ride into the mountains of Montenegro was bumpy and grim with anxiety, the more so as the van stalled many times on its climb to the pass and it proved ever more difficult to coax the engine back into life, but the panoramas were stupendous and at last we began our descent towards the Adriatic, in the illusion that all was well. Then, suddenly, the engine gave out, with evident finality. I authorized a number of attempts to push-start us down the mountain, then pulled in within sight of a pull-up for lorries. The nearest garage, we were told, was 25 kilometres away.

Two lorry drivers strolled up. Other drivers stopped, looked and moved on, but these two were determined to help. For over an hour they probed. At last, they motioned to me to press the starter. Nothing. Then again, and this time the engine surged into life, evoking loud cheers and clapping from the rear. Until then there had been hardly a word and definitely not a smile, but now one of the drivers asked, glumly, 'Deutsch?' 'No, English.' It was then that the smile emerged. 'Ah, Eengleesh, good! Deutsch, Italiano, Americano, Francesi, INferior! Eengleesh SUPerior!' It was worth having the crisis to enjoy such a moment of national affirmation. (We did not reflect that it was the anniversary of the outbreak of the Second World War!)

We thought when we reached the Adriatic that our problems were behind us, and indeed the vehicle saw us home without further hiccup. At Zadar, however, in a most attractive camp site on the sea shore, long, flickering tongues of lightning across the sea heralded the advent of the 'Bora', the Adriatic's own very fierce, indeed hurricane-like storm. Two of the tents were blown from their moorings and their inhabitants spent the rest of the night in the van. Edward recorded with ill-disguised satisfaction that the only tent to brave the storm was that which belonged to PFT and himself.

Day 43 saw us back in London. Edward calculated that the party had passed through 12 countries, camped out 42 nights, and travelled some 7,633 miles. We had also inspected 172 mosques, churches, ancient sites, castles and temples. It had cost each of the party £102.

> It had cost each one of us nearly £102 – money well spent. We had seen sights that will always remain with us, and it had broadened our outlook on life so much. We had all enjoyed the tour tremendously. We were pleased to be back home again.

In the *Priorian*, Richard Wells penned a typically graceful reflection.

> During its eighteen-month period of gestation, our Near Eastern expedition became permeated by the aura of the History essays between which its details were settled – infinite procrastination. When, however, this mythical, long-awaited, never-expected event materialized, it proved not so much a holiday, more a way of

life. For six weeks we slept in tents, rose between six and seven, drove off with a gentle purr of Commer power, and bathed in the sun and sea. Cut off from the restraints of civilization we yet defied the Golding thesis, and refused to descend into primeval savagery. Religious, political and trivial argument was incessant: acrimony was there none.

It was the bravest, most reckless, probably most questionable, arguably best thing that I undertook as a teacher.

CHAPTER 7

Leaving St Benedict's

THE BEATLES and others have ensured that the 1960s have become one of those epochs when it was bliss to be alive but to be young was very heaven. The down side of such ages is that they are peculiarly *miserable* for the legions of young who do not know the password into heavenly bliss.

As a 1950s adolescent I belonged to the last generation born before the 'youth culture'. There was no teenage market as such, only a sense that times were changing. The Valliant coaches taking us to away fixtures pulsed to the rhythm of Bill Haley and Buddy Holly but it was only the few, like Gordon Wilson, who made it their business to be expert in tomorrow's mores, with 'Fab' as the favoured adjective of approval. I knew that I was 'square' before I went to Oxford and that was how I chose to remain.

I was square without being cultured, conservative rather than Conservative and conformist without being especially principled. Being the young teacher in St Benedict's was one way of achieving this synthesis, but even here I was challenged. The Second Vatican Council was transforming my Church and Dom John Main was doing his best to rally me into the ranks of the reformers.

John Main was a natural leader, positive, resilient, cheerful, articulate and entertaining. 'My dear Paddy,' he would not infrequently announce around mid-day, 'We owe ourselves a sherry.' Like Bernard Orchard he could be brusquely authoritarian in his dealings with the teaching staff. 'Paddy,' he said suddenly one day, 'I think it's clear that x has to go.' And 'x' did. I was flattered that he appeared to see me as a likely member of the liberal avant-garde. In truth, he had limited success with a religious lightweight who never read any of the key documents of Vatican II. Patiently he explained that the Mass was an 'action' and that reception of Communion was its essence, not the worship of the consecrated Host in the tabernacle. Hence Benediction was obsolete, a convenient doctrine indeed as Benediction subsided under the 24 episodes of the BBC's *Forsyte Saga*.

I read Hans Kung and took on board the message that the Church, being human, was always in need of reformation. Even so I offered pragmatic objections to the pace and scale of reform. 'How,' I asked Father John, 'could we expect the "average" Catholic, so long used to a regime which not only laid down rules relating to fasting and abstinence, fasting before Communion, Holy Days of Obligation and so on but taught also that failure to obey them was a matter of mortal sin, how could we expect our fellow Catholics to adapt so fast to a "new" theology?' Were we not adopting the distinctions made by Thomas Cranmer and Thomas Cromwell between 'adiaphora' (matters indifferent) and the essentials of Christianity? What price the death of our martyrs when so much of traditional Catholicism was being jettisoned? We were even 'going Protestant' in adopting the vernacular for our liturgy. In short, how could we expect the Catholics of England, loyal as they had been to the 'ghetto', to retain their sense of allegiance when so much that they had accepted, lock, stock and barrel, was so casually set aside? Why should one go on believing in the teaching authority of a Church that was, in effect, admitting that its previous teaching was so far short of infallible?

And it was at this very point, in the revolutionary year of 1968, that Pope Paul VI ignited civil war within the Church with his encyclical, *Humanae Vitae*, banning artificial contraception. Was it or was it not binding on Catholics? It was not technically an 'infallible', 'ex cathedra', document, but the conservative ideologue within our Common Room pontificated that it was an exercise of the Pope's ordinary 'magisterium' and should as such be obeyed by loyal Catholics. I have to admit that I was not personally involved in the debate! Two years later I took the trouble to read it and found myself baffled by the papal distinction between 'natural' and 'unnatural' (i.e. artificial) methods of contraception. If it was in order for Catholics to *plan not* to have children through the use of natural means and cycles, why was it wrong to use a pill? Aspirins had not been forbidden. It seemed specious to talk about each act of intercourse being left 'open to the transmission of life' when every care had been taken by the couple to ensure that this would *not* be the outcome.

For the moment I took my lead from Dom John. To him it was a 'tragedy' that the Pope had come out against artificial contraception as such. The real enemy was a *'contraceptive mentality'*. The social wreckage of the next three decades suggests that both he and the Pope were in their different ways correct.

Now that the dust has settled it is hard to deny that the Catholic Church, in England and elsewhere, has paid its price for the 'aggiornamento' of the 1960s. It was certainly necessary, indeed long overdue, but the very centralization of the Roman Catholic Church meant that the 'few' could dictate to the many without reflecting that the many might no longer identify with the new teaching handed down by the 'few'. A more disabling consequence was that, while most of the many continued to practise their faith, they could no longer pass on that faith with the dogmatic certainty in which they had been reared, nor could they buttress their own parenting through the support of an authoritarian Church. 'A la carte' Catholicism had arrived.

It is difficult to exaggerate the sharpness of the divide between authoritarian conservatism and the new liberalism. A non-Catholic Sixth former was caned for repeatedly failing to take his school prayer book with him to the School Mass. I was inwardly appalled but within the St Benedict's Common Room I kept my reservations for my chats with Father John. To more conservative colleagues like Basil Nickerson I affected the radicalism of youth. 'I am not a theologian,' he replied to one blast from me. 'You ought to be,' I snapped at this devout convert, with an arrogance that still makes me wince. I went to see Father Bernard to share with him my reservations about the compulsory school Mass. I cannot remember what these were, but I suspect that they related to the 'scandalously' low participation in Communion. While the fasting laws applied, it was virtually impossible for any pupils to receive Communion. Now that the Church's rules were being relaxed, or so it seemed to me, windows were being opened into adolescent souls in an utterly unedifying way and with a bland disregard for the collective spirituality of the school community. Soon afterwards the school Mass was ditched and the Catholic school lost what should have been its focal point.

I suppose that this sad tale – of 'reform' producing outcomes the reverse of what was intended – simply reaffirms de Tocqueville's dictum that the most dangerous time for any autocratic regime is when it seeks to reform itself.

So the Putney Pud was developing into something of a 'Young Turk', albeit very part-time in his radicalism. It was a contest between conscience and the MGB. In the latter I would zoom happily between pubs, hoping to cut a dash. During a lunch break I drove Kris Bragiel, the attractive Biology teacher, down to Chiswick and back, then, demonstrating batting to my cricket team in a classroom because Games had been cancelled, flourished my off-drive hard into a table leg. I was stopped by the police as I sped up from Perivale to the 'London Apprentice' before closing time, explained that I was hurrying to an appointment and was warned that, at that time of night, there were many dangerous drivers around. I accepted a challenge from Alan McNamee to race him over a mile, chugged around behind him, sprinted past him 100 yards from home and tripped ten yards from the line as I heard him breathing at my shoulder. I did run the length of the field to score a spectacular winning try for the Common Room against Steve Dempsey's First Fifteen – 'I have never been so annoyed,' Steve commented, gratifyingly – and I heaved a number of fifties over square leg, but I was running to seed.

So I made some feeble efforts to 'take myself in hand'. I joined North Surrey Squash Club. And I became a member of NACRO. It was after Mass one Sunday that I saw a notice asking for volunteers to visit prisoners. I was trained at Toynbee Hall and was soon meeting my first 'case' in Wandsworth Prison. 'MF' was a young man. He had been adopted and he was homosexual. Since about 15 he had not spent a Christmas at home. I had to make arrangements for him to go into digs after leaving gaol and I dutifully toured London looking for digs that he could afford. Shepherds Bush seemed to meet the bill in that its rent were low, doubtless on account of its proximity to Wormwood Scrubs, but this connection escaped me at the time.

MF emerged and we met a few times. After a drink in the 'Sun' in Barnes he was clearly depressed. 'Courage,' I said to him as we parted, in my best public school French accent. Next week he did not materialize and I soon heard that he was back in Wandsworth. I saw him there on a number of occasions and also visited his mother in Balham before leaving London and my voluntary social work for ever.

I did something else that was possibly idealistic in intention. 'Why don't you ever take Michael?' was my mother's oft-repeated and accusatory question. In the summer of 1969 I drove the whole Lower Park tribe in my Commer to Turkey. It was a scaled-down version of the previous year's epic. We followed a more southerly route to Istanbul, taking in the magic of Lake Ohrid and entering Turkey from Greece rather than Bulgaria. There was a droll episode in Yugoslavia when three peasants invited themselves aboard as we drove up to the monastery of Studenitsa and became involved in vigorous conversation with Michael, the latter speaking fluently in Russian. As we all got out, I said to Michael, 'That was splendid. What were you talking about?' 'I haven't the slightest idea.' Once again the Balkans did not agree with my van. In Komotini the carburettor fell off. As we waited, a Greek priest, who certainly understood nothing of Michael's language, did seem to understand his predicament, exuding a sympathy and patience that have lingered in the memory.

This time we spent only a day in Istanbul, as we were booked on to the Turkish Maritime steamer which was to sail along the west and south coasts of Turkey. Passengers shared the main deck with flocks of sheep and goats. I immersed myself in *Black Lamb and Grey Falcon*, Rebecca West's heroic and passionately pro-Serb account of her travels through pre-war Yugoslavia and into Yugoslav history. The ship stopped at Bodrum, where Una swam in the harbour, Kas and Anatalya before putting us ashore in Alanya. I remember above all the 45 minute climb by Una, Denis and me to a site called Alahan. There we stumbled upon a completely unheralded gem – an early Christian basilica whose white walls and Corinthian capitals had somehow survived in pristine condition despite being completely open to the elements. None of my photographs from that holiday was any good, save only of this one church. It is thrilling even now to look at the ancient squinch and arches resting on the slim columns and acanthus leaf capitals, all brilliantly white under the bluest of skies, a typically extraordinary Turkish experience!

We took an easy route home, boarding a car ferry in Izmir and arriving in Venice nearly three days later. This time I had to drive a mere 4,725 miles. Of all the participants in the trip, Denis enjoyed it the most. He loved the camping, the feeling of 'roughing it', the freedom. For a few weeks he had escaped the pressures of Lower Park without the concomitant guilt. The Commer had done well and it would have another expedition ahead of it, but in very different circumstances and company.

Alahan 1969.

By now Father Bernard's return to headship and, in particular, Father John's appointment as Deputy Head had brought me closer to the centre of power in St Benedict's. So many boys were opting for Advanced Level Economics that a second teacher was appointed and I was formally appointed Head of Economics. Soon afterwards, my friend Denis Costello and I were given joint custody of the Upper Sixth as their Divisions Masters. In February 1969 Father Bernard had me in and formally offered me a 'permanency' on the staff. A month later he and Father John had resigned.

To this day it is an obscure business. JBO had apparently concluded that St Benedict's must either diminish or develop. A fourth stream was necessary if the school was to enjoy the economies of scale necessary for a Catholic Dulwich or St Paul's. The new Abbot, supported by his Council, rejected these proposals as unsafe. Father Bernard then resigned. The Abbot reportedly told him, 'Benedictine monks do not resign,' but accepted the resignation nevertheless. It was only last year that I heard Father Bernard's typically candid and humble observations on the affair. He said that, whereas he was ready to 'retire' in 1960, he felt that it was a disaster that he resigned in 1969. The Abbot should never have accepted his resignation. The trouble was that the Council was packed with his opponents. He made the further mistake of copying his letter of resignation, which was heavily critical of the Abbot, to all members of the Council. It was hardly surprising that they closed ranks behind their Abbot.

We in the Common Room were given no explanation. I led the Young Turks in pressing for one. What was more, as Secretary of the Old Priorian Association, I worked closely with Dr Joe Kearns, the President, in insisting that the laity had a *right* to be consulted, let alone informed, about a matter which affected them. Surely the proper involvement of the laity was the central message of Vatican II.

The Abbey tried to fend off criticism through the promise, not of a Governing Body which, we were assured, would have been uncanonical, but of lay Advisers. Otherwise the Abbey proved immutable. In my diary I compared our questioning of the Abbot to 'fighting a rice pudding'. Although dear Father George would again be Headmaster, with Basil Nickerson as his Deputy, my loyalties were all with Father Bernard and Father John. I felt that I should look elsewhere for employment and, with due regard to my eminence, thought that the post of Head of History at Bristol Grammar School would suit. I 'broke the news' to Steve Walker, who shook me rather by saying that, as I was so much opposed to the central direction of the school, it was probably right that I should go. I was further deflated when I received no response from Bristol.

At the time, of course, I would have argued that there was no conflict of loyalties. I was loyal to St Benedict's and that entitled me not only to my opinion but to its unbridled expression. Even so, an awareness that I was trying to ride two horses comes through in my report on the Old Priorian Association in the *Priorian* of Spring 1969:

> The Council of the Association has, of course, been deeply interested in the future, as well as the present state of, the School, and has pushed hard, if not very successfully, to be consulted and to make its views known on the events of the last few months. In the whole spectrum of interested lay opinion, an Old Boys' association is probably unique in the permanence of its interest in and sympathy with its school, and the present Council is determined to continue to give the School its loyal and candid support.

How do I feel now? As a Headmaster I would certainly not have accorded the Old Boys the importance I claimed for the Old Priorians in 1969! Old Boys' associations tend not to be at all 'permanent' in their interest – and there are times when even their 'sympathy' can seem doubtful. Looking back, I see that I was astonishingly naïve to imagine that I could both hold high office in the school and lead the public opposition, in the Common Room and among the old boys, to the authority of the Abbey. When, a few months later, the post of

Upper Sixth Divisions Master was abolished in favour of a myriad of tutorships, I took this 'reform' at face value, rather than as the cutting-down-to-size of an overweening and subversive young man.

Nevertheless, I would still maintain that the palace revolution of 1969 was a major and avoidable tragedy for the school that I loved. I am also with Father Bernard in viewing it as an event that blighted the school for the next three decades. The Advisory Governing Body, incidentally, came to little, but was reborn about 1989. Last year I felt enormously honoured and proud – and a certain wry amusement – when the current Abbot invited me to be its first lay Chairman.

So did I leave? No, I was far too comfortable. I could not, for one thing, abandon my quest for the holy grail at Llanelli at the very time when success seemed to be beckoning. The great tournament at Stradey Park had by now become an annual ritual. Every Easter holidays would be dominated by several days of intensive training. When the cricket squares at Perivale had to be prepared, I would evacuate my men to the nearest available municipal stretch of green. Then, in heat wave or through snow, I would drive about 17 boys to compete against the best in Wales and the North of England, most of them teams from grammar schools on the eve of their dissolution. By now, I had abandoned the floor boards of Llanelli Grammar School. Instead we stayed overnight in the North Western Hotel in Llandovery, a remarkable establishment where the licensing laws did not apply, as the publican had previously been in the police. (His luck and licence expired not long afterwards.) Arriving one afternoon, we were greeted by the sight of two men in jock straps firing soda siphons at each other, the rearguard of the rugby team from Barking College of Technology. The natives were altogether more congenial. Of all the 'regulars' in the pub our favourite was Ivor, a small Welshman of indeterminate age. He had not himself attended Llandovery College but he had seen every one of the annual fixtures between the school and Christ College, Brecon, even though this had for long involved a forty mile cycle ride every second year. I little imagined then that I would soon coach one of those teams for this fixture, still less that it would be Christ College, but the seeds for that were undoubtedly sown in the North Western Hotel by men like Ivor who loved rugby for its own sake. I was desperately sad when I did return to hear that he had died after a violent assault, probably by men working on the nearby dam.

By 1969 hours of pub planning of tactics with Bill Twist had evolved our agreed formula. In that year our Under 15 Seven won the Middlesex Sevens and were the width of a rugby post away from winning the final of the Llanelli Sevens. Two years later, I asked Andy Kemp whether he remembered that moment. 'Yes,' he replied, 'I wake up in the night thinking about it.' Next Easter, a far weaker Seven lost again in the final. And the best Seven of all would reach Under 15 level in 1971. They won the Middlesex Sevens without conceding a point, were deprived of their two star threequarters at Llanelli, but in 1972 showed their class by winning the Under 16 Oxford Sevens, the premier British tournament for that age group.

Of all the attempts on Llanelli, that of 1970 lingers in the memory. It had been the least successful Under Fifteen XV that I had coached, to the extent that two Under 14 players were chosen on merit, and they knew that were following an incomparably stronger Seven. My pep-talk on the night before the tournament gave more than one player a sleepless night. But they got through the first day, won their quarter-final and then, in the semi-final, faced Neath Grammar School, whom their predecessors had met in the final. Down 6-5 in injury time, Richard Cooke won a third consecutive tight head, Piers Cooke broke blind and drew their winger and Chris Westby got over with hands grasping at his legs. 'How did it feel Chris?' 'I could not see the line for tears.' The boys lost honourably in the final. By then, they and I were utterly drained.

In the *Priorian* I paid them a deservedly warm tribute:

> In each of their first five matches they rose to heights that only became conceivable after their performance in the previous one, and for sheer guts and character they were unsurpassable. 'A bunch of tigers,' murmured the Llanelli coach, and he repeated it time and again; 'like a lot of little terriers' was another Welsh comment (Ivor)…They gave everything and for both of us it was one of the most emotional experiences.

But I am leaping ahead of myself. It was during the previous holidays, in December 1969, that an improbable sequence of events changed the direction of my life.

My 'deus ex machina' was Denis Costello. He had joined the St Benedict's Common Room while I was in Oxford and he took me under his wing, urging me, for instance, not to teach in my smart new suit. He got married about that time to Eileen and, as is the way with newly-weds, saw it as his mission to end the bachelor state of poor Paddy. I humoured these efforts on my behalf, once bringing to a Costello party a girl whose father was unknown to me but was, to everyone else at the party, a famous DIY celebrity in television. Denis teased me often about this encounter. He was less amused by *William Wilberforce MP*. This 'Moral Rearmament' play, was, admittedly, a somewhat extraordinary choice for my Sixth Form club, 'The Humorists', but I honestly thought, when I was unable to go, that he and Eileen would relish their trip to the theatre with the boys. 'Did you enjoy the evening?' I asked innocently the next morning. Rage spat out of those normally twinkling Irish eyes. One of the Garetys, an elder brother of Chris, had arrived drunk in the theatre. From the front row of the stalls he had heckled the cast until the attendants finally took him by the arm and eased him out of his row. Then, as a final gesture, he had vomited over the barrier, down on to the audience below.

I absolve Denis from any suspicion that the Caribbean Cruise of December 1969 was his revenge for that unfortunate affair in the theatre. In good faith he had arranged for about 20 Sixth Formers to join the four week educational cruise organized by the Commonwealth Institute in collaboration with the British India line. Yes, with one exception, the party was notably non-academic. 'D', the cousin of a renowned Ulster Civil Rights activist, was almost certainly alcoholic, but Denis would not have known that. No, Eileen had developed complications with her third baby and I was told, a week before sailing, that Father George would like me to stand in for Denis as one of the two party leaders.

We sailed from Southampton in the old ex-troopship, SS *Nevasa*, on a grey, unfriendly afternoon. There were about 1,000 Sixth Formers aboard. They had fairly primitive quarters below decks, while their teachers shared the cabin accommodation with scores of pensioners. The teachers travelled free and the pensioners cheaply, the bulk of the income being generated by the students. It was a formula that had worked well for many years, but this was the most ambitious enterprise to date and it was never to be repeated. South of Madeira, as the weather warmed and the dormitories became more foetid, tensions mounted. The journey across the Atlantic dragged.

For every one boy on the cruise there were over five girls. A battery of outfits and sun lotions proclaimed expectations that were doomed to disappointment. The male minority clustered gingerly together for comfort and security. In terms of social inadequacy my crowd was hard to beat. They scoffed oafishly at the deck games provided for them and rapidly became notorious for their smoking below decks. A regular feature of the morning announcements over the ship's tannoy was the request that the Party Leader of Party HH should report to the Director of Studies, the appropriately named Mr Case.

If discipline in Party HH left much to be desired, blame might fairly be attached to its liberal leadership. This was not my idea of an expedition, nor were the boys the sort who would normally have enlisted under me. My companion, Dom Vincent Cooper, a monk who was not a teacher in the school, was evidently in reaction against the severities of his Scottish upbringing. As we headed south across an absurdly still Bay of Biscay and then west into the Atlantic, he introduced me through his little tape recorder to Judy Collins and Leonard Cohen. *Suzanne* was my signature tune for the voyage.

We knew beforehand that a party from Ealing Grammar School for Girls would be with us. On the dance floor every evening and drinking bacardis during the day, I seemed to be getting on very well with Margery Sluce and her companion, Gill Bulley, although it took me a while to appreciate that the shimmering angel of the evenings was the dragon who sustained Prussian discipline on the quoits deck.

For me it was all a rather wonderful escape. Each day I attended the Mass said by a tall Dominican, Father Paul Foster, who otherwise strode incessantly around the main deck. He was the ship's travelling expert on voodoo. There was an army of such experts, all very impressive, and pupils, teachers and cabin passengers alike were systematically informed about the history, geography, economics, steel bands and other customs of the West Indies. The old ship rode the waves as if wafted by the trade winds, flying fish leapt alongside us and I imagined myself as Columbus – until the familiar announcement, 'Would the Party Leader of Party double H please report to the Director of Education?' dragged me down again.

This time I coincided with an incoming message from Trinidad. Could the *Nevasa* provide a rugby team to play the island team? 'I'll do that,' I said instantly, trying not to notice the scepticism of men whose opinion of my capability had been considerably tested, and by the following day I put together my team. Its nucleus consisted of the Protestants of Portadown and the Catholics of St Benedict's, with the odd reinforcement from South Wales and Yorkshire. Each morning we would train until the decks were washed and the sun became too warm. I was doing something to restore my credit with Mr Case and his colleagues.

First port of call after Madeira was Bridgetown, Barbados. Before we reached land there was a sad and striking event, the burial at sea of an Indian seaman. All the menial duties on ship were performed by Indians who, one assumed, had spent their lives in the service of the British India Line. We heard that there had been a death and that the nameless seaman was to be buried that afternoon. The pupils were not informed, so that only a few of us stood by as the ship slowed, the body wrapped in tarpaulin was gently lowered and released, the corpse slipped away into the depths and the ship then resumed course as if nothing had happened.

In Bridgetown each school party was met by its own guide, a pupil from the local school. Party HH was greeted by an incredibly smart young man and we set off at a spanking pace round Bridgetown. Within minutes a gap opened between the guide and me on the one hand and Father Vincent and Party HH on the other. I was deeply ashamed. Here we were, the representatives in Barbados of Queen and Country, and my 'shower' was letting the side down. At lunch Dom Vincent accused me of behaving 'like the Raj'.

Mr Case joined us for the coach tour in the afternoon, which was just as well, for Hubbard soon got bitten by a dog. This caused consternation and such delay that the ship was late in sailing, involving considerable expense in harbour dues. Our bad luck continued into Trinidad. Having enjoyed the massed steel bands that greeted us, our coach broke down. With trepidation I awaited the rugby match next morning.

Trinidad scored immediately, running through our defence as through butter, but then all those pre-breakfast sessions seemed to pay off. An hour later we were winners by 53 points to 5 and I savoured the prospect of Mr Case's applause as I sipped my drinks in 'The Pelican'. I was to be disappointed. It transpired that *winning* had not been the purpose of the exercise. I got the impression that the scale of our victory had probably set back by decades the cause of rugby in Trinidad.

The ship sailed on, past the Grenadines and St Vincent and reaching St Lucia which was supposed to be the next port of call. The ship was not due to dock until the morning but it was announced that the lifeboats would be lowered so that teachers and cabin passengers could put ashore for a few hours. Into a lifeboat descended Margery, Gill, Father Vincent and I. 'Have a good time, Father,' some wag shouted, as we were rowed away. We had drinks at 'The Reef', then lobster and planter's punch at the Malabar Beach Hotel, courtesy of a resident American – 'Gee, I'm the third richest industry on this island.' As the palm trees rustled over the white sands of the bay and the evening sun descended into the waters dividing us from *Nevasa*, delicious fantasies briefly surfaced.

We dutifully returned to our ship, expecting to return to St Lucia the next morning, but the winds got up and the main landing was cancelled. That evening, after we had passed an impressively volcanic Martinique, there was a mass sit-down, 1968-style, on the main deck. As we approached Antigua, Father Vincent and I decided that 'D', the occasion of so many of my visits to Mr Case, represented a risk too many and Father Vincent gallantly volunteered to be his custodian while the rest of us went ashore.

So when we all assembled that evening for the Son-et-Lumière performance in Nelson's Dockyard, I was somewhat dismayed to behold Father Vincent and 'D' taking their seats. The lights went out for an enjoyable evocation of British naval history. When they came on again at the end Dom Vincent was in his seat but 'D' was not. It was several hours before he was found, adding further harbour dues to the ill-fated voyage.

Worse was to ensue. The ship ran out of water and, to add further humiliation, there was none to be found in a Commonwealth island. Instead we would have to make for the French island of Guadeloupe. But this offered the authorities the chance to make amends for St Lucia. This time the lifeboats would take pupils and their teachers ashore, with the cabin passengers entering on the tide a few hours later.

It proved to be yet another mistake. No-one had warned us that the rum in Guadeloupe was of a singular intensity. Dom Vincent and I each drank a planter's punch, before buying our respective souvenirs. I acquired a sinuous crucifix, Dom Vincent what he deemed to be a statue of the Virgin Mary but later surmised, on account of the horns in its belly and the sleeping sickness that afflicted him, to be a voodoo symbol. As we left the shop to walk along the main street to the quay we encountered horizontal bodies in varying states of consciousness. The cabin passengers lining the decks of *Nevasa*, men who had risked their lives so that the young of 1969 would have a future, were greeted by a spectacle of debauch. Crucifix in one hand, Aberdeen girl slung over the other shoulder, I climbed the gang plank and descended into the infirmary, where the Irish nurse barked fiercely, 'We're an infirmary, not a police station.'

Dom Vincent and I mounted guard during the night to ensure that our casualties did not swallow their tongues. As I entered the dormitory for my stint, there on the floor, with one arm round a comatose 'D' and the other around 'H' who was blathering, 'I remember the day that I was born,' was the equally paralytic Director of Education.

The return journey was relatively uneventful. There were lifeboat patrols at night to prevent sexual enterprise, but the only couple discovered was a pair of teachers. My most challenging assignment was to assuage tensions between Party HH and its neighbours from Portadown. This was not a sectarian dispute. Rather, the cause of the Ulstermen's request that I should 'pour oil over troubled waters' was Grant's ringworm. I solved the problem by asking Grant to spend the rest of the trip sleeping on deck.

Christmas was spent on board, a couple of days out from Lisbon, and there was a Carol Service, followed by Midnight Mass. There were vast numbers of non-Catholics present. Party HH had, it seemed, developed unforeseen powers of missionary attraction. David d'Avray, the only scholar on the trip, threw his own wine-and-cheese party. On 29 December, four weeks after we sailed, we docked in Southampton.

Margery and I were engaged on 20 April and married on 25 July. We had teaching in common. We also shared backgrounds in Ealing and Putney. She had been brought up in Ealing and gone to school in Acton. Then, when she became a teacher, she had taught in a school on West Hill and lived in Putney, before spending two years in Istanbul. I calculated that she had been there during each of my most recent visits. It was as if the good Lord had finally lost patience and placed us together on a ship for four weeks to assure the outcome that we had so often missed.

Otherwise we were so different that a long relationship would almost certainly have scuppered our romance. Margery swept me into a regime of plays at the Aldwych and concerts at the Festival Hall, together we saw *Adalen 31* and similarly radical films and, for the one and only time in my life, I patronized the 'progressive' section of HMV to buy the records of Judy Collins and Leonard Cohen. That left little time for her to get to know my family too well – and much of that was spent visiting Koo after her latest hip operation. Auntie Mary died in June, the last of my grandparents' generation. Any spare time was filled with my frenzied efforts to finish a history of the relationship between the Byzantine Empire and the Normans of Southern Italy, a quixotic enterprise that ultimately came to nothing.

Margery was the proud owner of a new flat in Ealing. She had shared this with Sally Lowe, a colleague in Istanbul, so that I was marrying into property

July 25th 1970 – a very happy couple.

and evicting a tenant. Mickey Rooney, one of the newest recruits to the St Benedict's Common Room, gave me a crash course in power drilling and together we put up shelves so that I would be ready to move in with my books.

Throughout our brief engagement there were tensions over religion. I was sure that Margery would come to see the attractions of Catholicism and she was sure that she could wean me from it – neither of us, it has transpired, was right. Dom Vincent was realistically undemanding in the 'instruction' that he provided to Margery and it so happened that a short-lived loophole in canonical procedures enabled him to marry us through a full nuptial Mass in Ealing Abbey. We left the altar and passed through the ranks of the friends and relations who had been our respective lives before we all lined up on the Abbey steps for a grand photograph of the moment in time when we moved from one state to the next. Then, after a reception in the St Benedict's School Art room that was, by today's standards, absurdly modest in scope and cost, we set off in the Commer for a 'Tobin tour' of Sicily and Southern Italy.

We returned just before the beginning of the new academic year. It was to be our last in Ealing. After a lunch in the flat when Basil Nickerson and I had talked rugby non-stop Sally told Margery, 'You've got to get Paddy away from St Benedict's.' In fact I knew that too. In a belated attempt to inject foundations for a career I had signed up with London University for an external PGCE course. For the first time my teaching was professionally observed. For the last time I

Margery in Dalmatia.

had to sit examinations, desperately walking round Russell Square in last-minute revision. Meanwhile, I applied for various posts. I was interviewed at Rossall as a potential Head of Economics. I thank God and Roger Ellis that he spared me from building the next stage of my career on that false pretence.

Instead, lured by sentiment and rugby, I applied to be a Head of History in Wales, both at Llandovery College and at Christ College, Brecon. Margery accompanied me to Llandovery and clearly feared that I was taking her from the bright lights of the metropolis to the gulag. Her headmistress did not allow her a second outing to Wales, so I came alone to Brecon.

I nearly missed the appointment, having failed to ascertain in advance that I needed to change trains for Abergavenny at Newport, but then, by a fluke, finding the same train waiting for me at Cardiff. John Sharp, emerging like the squire of the manor as my car drew up, was none the wiser about the incompetence of his new head of department. He offered me the job before I left.

I was shown where we would live, a semi-detached dwelling of council-house style on the far side of the rugby pitches. 'What's it like?' asked Margery. 'Oh, a house,' I replied. The formal letter from Brecon arrived at the same time that I received an offer from Llandovery, but I had no problem in deciding between the two nor did I hesitate in accepting Christ College. I was determined to make my first foray into a new school and a different environment.

With marriage I had at last escaped Lower Park and ceased to be a Putney Pud. After 1971 I would no longer even be 'Paddy'. We made our farewells to Ealing and shot off in our new yellow Mini Clubman to Yugoslavia, Brecon and the unknown, unforeseeable journey together through life.

CHAPTER 8

How Green was our Valley

IN JUNE 1998 a very pleasant consequence of my chairmanship of HMC was
an invitation to present the prizes at Christ College. By then Brecon had
become almost as distant and exotic to us as it had been in 1971 when we first
arrived, Margery and I and our mustard-yellow Mini – three Londoners in rural
Wales. Now I was an 'Establishment' figure, a seasoned headmaster, a veteran
who had accumulated 18 years of experience in four boarding schools. Then we
felt like diffident novices, far from confident that we would 'fit in', and I had the
more fundamental anxiety, was I capable of teaching anywhere other than St
Benedict's, Ealing?

Before the beginning of term, we received our first invitation, from the
Bishop of Brecon, to an 'At Home' at his residence. And as we parked our
Mini, the first colleague to greet us, with typically Wykehamist politesse, was
Quentin Cavenagh. We did not know then that this episcopal hospitality to the
Christ College Common Room was the first of its kind and would, in our time
at least, also prove to be the last – nor that very few of our new colleagues had
brought to Brecon any more experience of the 'public school world' than we
possessed.

Even so, the teachers' pronunciation was decidedly more 'received' than the
South Walian accents of most of their pupils. The father of one head boy, the
owner of a local business, voiced his indignation. 'Now look 'ere, Mr Tobin. I
spend all this munney sending my boy to Chri-ist College, Brecckon, to be
educcated, so that 'e can learn to speek Eenglissh propperly, why doesn't 'ee
speek like YOU?'

The school, on the far side of the Usk from the castle, town and priory, had
been 'founded' by Henry VIII in 1541, shortly after he had dissolved the small
Franciscan friary on the site. All that remained of the religious community was
the gracefully severe thirteenth century chapel (now the school chapel) and
some precincts, although, on the rare occasions when there was prolonged dry
weather, other foundations would mysteriously surface. The main school
building was intimidatingly Victorian. In addition to dining hall and Masters'
Common Room it contained the whole of two boarding houses, with the
welcoming names of 'School House Red' and 'School House Blue'. Another
house, 'Donaldsons', overlooked the cricket square. I was its House Tutor,
under the benignly traditional mentorship of Walter Greenwood, the Deputy
Head. At the far end of the main cricket ground was the fourth senior boarding

Christ College, Brecon – walking home.

house, Orchard House, and a row of staff dwellings named Orchard Gardens, of which ours was Number 4.

Most of the school's teaching took place in a three-sided, prefabricated, wooden block, the centre line of classrooms being flanked by projecting wings at either end. This 'temporary' building had already displayed a remarkable capacity to endure – and was indeed to survive for a few decades yet.

Such new building as had occurred since 1960 – the Headmaster's house and office and the Junior boarding house – was to be found at the 'town' end of the campus, close to the Usk. (This had indeed flooded the Sharps' house on the day that they moved in.) The school boasted an open air swimming pool. Dependent as it was on solar heating, it was never open for more than a few weeks during the school year, but came into its own, as a significant 'perk' for the resident staff, during the long and frequently hot summer holidays.

Christ College had never been large. For a few years in the 1850s it had existed without any pupils at all, a veritably scandalous situation which eventually demanded the intervention of the Archbishop of Canterbury, but it had settled by 1971 into a fairly stable population of about 270 boys, mostly boarding. It had been roused from torpor by John Sharp's predecessor, Duncan Macallum, a Scot who had announced his zeal for reform by terminating the employment of three teachers who between them had accumulated over 150 years of service to Christ College. When he moved back to Scotland and the headship of Strathallan, John Sharp had sustained his predecessor's ethic of vigorous and authoritarian leadership.

Rugby was probably the school's chief passion, even though for years it had to play second fiddle to Llandovery College and its famed Lions' coach, Carwyn James. Schools as small as Brecon and Llandovery were never likely to produce as many natural athletes as St Benedict's, but they made up for this in the toughness and commitment engendered by their Spartan environment. Even in the relative warmth of September I found four afternoons of rugby each week somewhat excessive. By November, as the monsoon intensified, I was suffering more than the boys.

Our three-bedroomed, semi-detached house opened straight on to the playing fields. To the rear, beyond our not unimpressive array of vegetables, raspberries and gooseberries, were the school tennis courts. From our bedroom our view was of the hillside and its sheep. Only the smoking hearths of Llanfaes spoiled the clean mountain air. To such pollution we happily contributed, lacking as we did any form of central heating other than the antique night storage heaters supplied by Margery's brother when he at last achieved domestic comfort in his own home. The 'back boiler' heated by the fire warmed the water so that it tumbled orange-brown into our bath. I sought comfort in whisky, fortified by the example and encouragement of John Sluce, Margery's father, whenever he and Evelyn came to stay. Happy days!

Rugby and house tutoring apart my main job was to teach and organize History. In a small school the department consisted of only two full-time historians, with some assistance from the school chaplain. Teaching eleven-year-olds was a new experience. I tried to interest them in Roman history, walking them up to the Gaer, the Roman fort above Brecon, but realized anew that I was not a 'natural' teacher of the young. Timetabling needs also dictated that I should teach English to one set each year. I fear that I learned far more about Wilfred Owen and W.B.Yeats than I ever imparted to my pupils but it was nice not to feel as responsible for the outcomes as I did in History.

I assume that this attitude of mind was responsible for the hidden scandal of my time in Brecon. At the start of my second year, I had, for some reason, assumed that I would be teaching just four periods each week to my English set. The first two terms passed and the time came in the summer term for the annual cycle of class plays. Gareth Jones, Head of English, suggested a time. 'I don't teach them that period,' I objected. He looked puzzled. 'Yes, you do.' And I did – or, rather, didn't. The boys had tumbled rapidly to the possibilities offered by my strange absenteeism and the 'strong man' of the class had impressed on his peers the need for total silence on each occasion. In consequence, although the classroom was overlooked from two sides by other teachers in their classes, no-one had spotted that the boys were never taught. I can only hope that the boys benefited more from their unlicensed reading than they would have done from my teaching.

'I don't mind you making mistakes,' John Sharp had barked at me when I started, 'I do mind if I am not told.' I had no alternative but to tell him when I found out that, for the best part of a year, the two Ordinary Level History sets had been pursuing an incompatible combination. Until that year the particular combination had been entirely acceptable. For some reason I had not spotted the change in rubric. John Sharp was magnificently as good as his word. There was never a word of blame. He contacted the Board and a special paper was set for our historians, presumably at the school's expense.

Otherwise I made out. It seemed to be established practice that the Head of History should be the school's Librarian. If nothing else, it offered an unrivalled opportunity to build up the department's store of reference books. In a gaunt classroom next door I taught the Upper Sixth historians nineteenth century English and European History, plus their Special Subject. I decided that this should be different in period and chose the reign of Henry VIII. I had taught none of these syllabuses to A/L at St Benedict's, but had at least studied the whole of English History at Oxford – an education denied to today's undergraduates – and taught modern British History to Ordinary Level. The European History, however, was completely new to me. So for my first year I was 'treading water', frantically reading up each new topic and typing out piles of gestetnered notes for the Headmaster's Secretary to run off. At least the boys had come to me with a foundation in eighteenth century English and European History from my colleague, Don Jackson. Some, in their second campaign, had been taught by my predecessor. When I came to mark their 'mock' exams, however, I found that the less ambitious boys as usual fell back on to the topics they had most often regurgitated, the eighteenth century, and that I had little or no means of knowing whether they were talking fact or fiction, let alone of telling them how to improve on them. Yet the eventual outcome was stupendously reassuring, with a large proportion of 'A's and a delighted Headmaster. I was never to do as well at Brecon again.

In truth there was an extraordinary range of ability among the Christ College boys. If some seemed to have little ambition or aptitude for culture or intellect, others were steeped in the best traditions of Welsh academe. Thus the Davies brothers probably owed their 'A's more to their father at Cardiff University than to any teaching I provided. Joe Davies, having read History and gained a rugby Blue at Cambridge, would a few years later begin his teaching career in my department at Tonbridge. He is now a headmaster.

I would have my seventh term historians back to our house for their Oxbridge tutorials. It is no reflection on the individuals but on their tweed jackets and on the austerity of the boys' existence that Margery could smell immediately when the boys had been in our living room. Physically and, I suspect, emotionally theirs was a hard life. In comparison with St Benedict's the atmosphere was cold, harsh and rather Prussian. Peter Ackroyd and Julian Clary would have had a rough time. The lunches in the old dining hall were of the 'no frills' variety, though rarely as awful as the occasion when the boys picked up the fish from their plates, banged it on the thick tables and watched as the tables rather than the fish quivered. Most of the teaching staff were committed after their fashion – 'This is a life of total commitment,' John Sharp has incanted to me on appointment – but many were bachelors and the bachelor Common Room had a corporate psychology peculiar to itself, descending progressively from sanity to rancorous and potentially murderous venom as the seemingly endless succession of weeks unfolded. The worst afflicted could not resist his little 'digs', at boys and at colleagues. Walking away from my table one day, past the ranks of boys and acknowledging one of them with a smile, I caught him engaging the boys on his table with a mimicking simper, or so I thought.

On the other hand I saw my departmental colleagues as friends. Don and Anne Jackson had Margery and me round for dinner shortly after we arrived and they were soon confronted with the social inadequacy of the new Head of History. They had a bitch, who took them on daily long walks across the hills, and for about half an hour I learned all there was to know about the reproductive complications arising from such ownership. There was a brief pause for some other topic – then my brain, addled perhaps with alcohol, was invited afresh to wrestle with the 'on heat' challenge. 'Oh! Do you have a dog?' I heard myself asking, while Margery looked aghast and the Jackson jaws fell in unison. Anne clearly thought that, with no children and a fancy little car, we were very spoiled. 'It's all very well for Patrick,' she would say to Margery, but I suspect that she was envious of us both as we led a charmed existence exploring Wales, the Marches and their pubs.

I don't think that Anne Jackson would have been right or fair to blame me for the state of her husband after our beginning-of-term binges. Margery and she would telephone each other the morning afterwards to ascertain which of us was in the worse condition. Hangover apart I always enjoyed those evenings. In addition to History, Don and I had rugby and cricket in common, he had a talent for vivid hyperbole and he was always very generous to me. Being housemaster of Orchard House and the passionately enthusiastic coach of the first fifteen, he wore his historical scholarship lightly with his pupils but he will have left the best with something of his taste for the rustic world revealed through the diaries of Francis Kilvert and James 'Parson' Woodforde. He was probably at Christ College too long for his own good but the school owed him a great deal. Meanwhile, the Reverend Philip David, the first Anglican clergyman I really knew and a latterday Kilvert in his virtues, supplied a timely challenge to my Catholic arrogance. Here was someone who was genuinely Christian in the living of his life. I, by contrast, was hanging on to my religion via Canon Brady's austere Sunday Mass in the church where, improbably, Adelina Patti had been married.

Adelina Patti had made her home at Craig-y-nos and it was there, at Breconshire's imitation Glyndebourne, that Margery began to miscarry our first child. We had assumed that she would conceive immediately, but the months passed and we had eventually sought help from Q's brother, Dr Sandy Cavenagh. So the miscarriage was the harder to bear, especially for Margery, whose courage was extraordinary. There was no driving tour to Yugoslavia that summer. Instead we went to Paris and a friend's flat. Soon we were expecting Matthew, the child who could not have been born had our first baby survived. We took ourselves to the Gower for a brilliantly sunny last holiday on our own. Matthew was born in May 1973 in the Royal Gwent Hospital in Newport. That heady drive across the Beacons, in the euphoric, incredulous knowledge that I was a father, pulses still in the memory.

And in a more mellow haze I remember Margery pushing Matthew and his pram along the circuit that led around and behind the playing fields to the Usk and back to the school. 'Ritchie', the school's veteran and gentle handyman, murmured his praises of our 'bundle of joy'. Denis, Una, Michael and Koo, not to mention Uncle Pat, came to celebrate with us and Margery's family the christening of the next generation. Brian Burns was a godfather and Canon Brady descended like a black spectre from his hill over the river to lend his blessing to the occasion. At last, to Anne Jackson's satisfaction, we exchanged that Mini Clubman for a proper family car, a hideous Morris Marina. When I went to buy the weekend meat next day, the butcher's daughter asked me how I liked my new car. It took me a while to find out that her brother had bought my Mini. There were no secrets in Brecon.

That summer, John Sharp left the rains of Brecon for the Atlantic blasts of Rossall. Unlike some of my colleagues I had warmed to this most English of headmasters. I empathized with his determination to be his own good headmaster – even if I was never to emulate the singlemindedness with which he taught himself italic handwriting for public consumption. There was a Yorkshire dourness about him, but from time to time he would emerge and trumpet spectacularly like a bull elephant at boys who were not where they should be. Otherwise he would stride around the campus, with a curiously idiosyncratic swinging of one arm, never without his suit. I was given a brief insight into private passion when I asked one of my St Benedict's historians, Henry Cleary, to talk to my History Society about railways. John Sharp ensured that I invited Henry to have dinner with him and we took away with us the

Exultant dad – with Matthew summer 1973.

picture of the young trainspotter who had spent happy hours on Keighley Station. He never courted popularity and I was secretly pleased that, even at his ultimate chapel assembly, he lived down to his image and eschewed any sentimentality. 'He didn't even say, "Thank-you"', hissed a Welsh colleague. I arranged for his photograph to be taken as he made his final magisterial exit from the chapel.

It did not take long, as is always the case, for the eternal critics to canonize him. In his place the Governors had chosen another very tall doctor of science – I never worked for a headmaster who was less than six foot in height – but there the similarity ended. John Cook loved sport, had been, indeed, a county tennis player. He was Gloucestershire easy-going and informal. Like so many headmasters of the 1970s he saw Prize Days as an elitist waste of money. John Sharp, one felt, had laboured mightily to acquire his qualifications and develop his philosophy. John Cook seemed to 'get there' immediately and had the hyper-intelligent man's problem that he could not see why others failed to reach the same point with him. Worst of all, he was only 32, thereby plunging most of the

Common Room into their menopause. I could afford to be relatively sanguine in this regard, being a mere 31. Even so the new man provided a sharp reminder that I was myself no longer a young man and that I had better begin thinking about where I wished to end up.

John Cook clearly wished to 'soften' the austerity of Christ College. I suspect that he saw me as a potential ally. 'Patrick, as a head of Department, wouldn't you *know* that xyz was expected of you?' I, lacking any coherent philosophy of my own, was pretty unhelpful, for instance by airing unanswerable questions during the Common Room discussion that he encouraged. 'What is the *point* of it all? What exactly are we trying to *achieve*?' Nowadays 'Mission Statements' are all the rage. In 1973 the Christ College Common Room did not want to indulge in such quixotic pursuits.

Had John Cook read his de Tocqueville he might have hesitated before seeking to relax an authoritarian regime. As it was, he survived a fairly torrid time after my departure and went on to great things, whereupon, of course, his ex-colleagues, without any sense of irony, duly installed him on his pedestal. I suppose that I took from all of this the lesson that, however right a headmaster may be, he can never count on support from the Common Room when the going gets difficult, that you can be as nice as you like but should never give the impression that you are seeking approval, in short that headship, whether you are old-fashioned or new-fangled, is a lonely job. Walter Greenwood at least was tirelessly loyal. Over whisky after house prayers he would growl menacingly, 'Patrick, what the school needs is a few *sackings*.'

Whether Don Jackson prevailed on John Cook or whether it was the other way round I do not know, but it was to my considerable surprise, I was invited to become first fifteen rugby coach for the 1974-5 season. Don elected to be the Under 14 coach, thereby ensuring young Robert Ackermann would acquire the good habits that would lead him on to fame in a Welsh shirt, but I imagine that he and John Cook also hoped that boredom would not drive me away from Brecon and that this was a way of keeping me hooked. In this they were surely right and I accepted without hesitation.

There had been signs that I was being groomed for greater things. In 1973 I had moved up with my Under 15 team and their unbeaten season had included a rout of Llandovery. I had even been drafted in at the last moment to referee the inter-county final of the Welsh Young Farmers Cup, a clear case of fools rushing in where wiser men feared to tread. But was I really good enough to coach at first team level? It was one thing to hook for your college, the summit of my own proficiency on the field, quite another to guide and inspire young bucks, threequarters especially, most of whom were far more gifted as rugby players than I had ever been.

I began that season hoping that I could compensate through youthful vigour for what I manifestly lacked in savoir faire. It would have helped if I had been fit. I recall desperate, panting runs in which I led my new charges, if not from the front, then at least from the middle. I consoled myself with the hope that, as often in my life, it would be all right on the day. In the first minutes of the first match, Ian Davies, my talented fly half, broke his collar-bone and was out for the term. Before half-term we lost every match.

All would be well, however, if we could beat Llandovery. We took a big pack along the A40 and for 75 minutes we clung tenaciously to the success that we had never previously experienced. Keith Gibson, replacement fly half, kicked a penalty from our own half of the field to the disbelief of the home crowd. Llandovery drew level shortly before full time. Then they drove us back again, to a scrum in front of our posts, but it was our put in and the whistle must go. We duly heeled, Malcolm Palmer passed to a centre who was no longer there, an opponent dropped on the ball and all was once again ashes.

But the second half of term was better, much better. John Sharp returned to open the new staff Common Room that he had initiated and he brought with him the Rossall first fifteen. I knew how much it would mean to John Cook if Christ College could win this particular contest. We did so with something to spare. At the very end of term we were hosts to another touring team, whose pedigree was unmatched. Mata Mata, from the North Island of New Zealand, had gone 65 matches without defeat before this opening match in their Welsh tour. By now the monsoon had been so prolonged and intense that our first pitch was flooded but our second pitch was deemed adequate. Malcolm Palmer kicked a penalty, then put 'Arnie' over in the corner. That 7-0 win was my supreme achievement as a rugby coach – and Mata Mata went unbeaten through the remainder of their tour. When Don Jackson and I turned up at Cardiff Arms Park to watch them play a representative team from Welsh schools, another school coach turned round. 'Come to gloat, have you?' We had.

It must have been about now that two seminal events occurred, the birth of Emma and a life-changing conversation with my old sparring partner, the man who did not like me. Emma was born in December 1974, in Brecon Hospital. She took her time and I was sent home. Roused about 2.30 I made it to the hospital in time. 'You're doing fine, Margery,' Sandy Cavenagh drawled, 'Patrick, are you all right?' Emma entered the world with her father slumped in a faint on his chair. Eileen Costello, without whom nothing, was her godmother. And the whole of Brecon, or so it seemed, congratulated us on our 'pigeon pair'.

The man who did not like me accosted me one morning, after chapel. Didn't I realize how obscenely lucky I had been in my life? That I had never had to struggle to make out when others experienced difficulty? A bigger man than I might have paused to reflect whether he had a point. Instead, I stomped angrily over to our house in Orchard Gardens. 'I don't see why I should have to put with this sort of thing,' I grunted to Margery, as I opened *The Times*, and there was a large advertisement for Head of History at Tonbridge School.

Thus did chance determine that I would turn from 'schoolmastering' and set up my stall as an academic. I had toyed with this image occasionally, as around 1970 when I had tried to assemble a book that focused on relations between the Byzantine Empire and the Normans of Southern Italy. It was a good subject and it still awaits its adequate historian.

And in my final terms in Brecon I had stumbled on what seemed to be a more promising subject for research and authorship. The source for this inspiration was *The Marcher Lordships of South Wales 1415-1536*, documents selected by the Cardiff historian, T.B. Pugh, a disciple of K.B. McFarlane. It centred on the extensive Welsh lands owned by the Stafford Dukes of Buckingham. Their estates included Newport and Brecon – and, by strange coincidence, Tonbridge – and Duke Edward had been born in Brecon Castle. McFarlane had taught me already that the duke was very far from the anachronistic mastodon of Tudor propaganda. By now I had been drawn far into the biography of a man whose father had led an unsuccessful rebellion from Brecon against Richard III and who would himself be beheaded on Tower Hill at the behest of Henry VIII.

On top of this I had an ability to engender in others a wholly unfounded confidence in my powers of intellect. Very recently a *Times* article jerked me back to a particularly farcical instance of this talent. It was entitled, 'MI5 warning about Cambridge ring agent was ignored'. The spy was James Klugman and I met him in 1971 through Dom Edmund Flood, the monk who had earlier seen in me the latent potential to be a Shakespearean actor. Dom Edmund had hit on a scheme whereby the Abbey would market to aspiring young intellectuals tapes of debates between experts in their field. My subject was to be Marxism. Far from being an expert, my knowledge of Marxism was confined to one of the slimmest and most perfunctory of my Oxford essays. James Klugman was Marxist to his aging core. I hope that I did not have the gall to list this tape in the c.v. that I sent to Tonbridge.

Robert Ogilvy interviewed me and I got the job. I was mildly disconcerted when his letter made me Head of Geography rather than History – was I his last mistake? I had actually applied for two jobs in Kent, the other being that of Head of Humanities in a Canterbury comprehensive, but they were less impressed.

Thus was my future determined. I would not stay in Brecon, where we had known such happiness. I would not have to coach a first fifteen doomed to lose every match next season, nor would I glory in the successes in the following years of Ackermann and his heroes. Nor would I be Housemaster of School House Red, as John Cook had planned. Nor, on the other hand, would I step clear of the Independent and boarding school world and into the more demanding maintained sector. Rather, I would be going to a bigger and 'better' Independent and boarding school, where the only success that mattered would be measured in Oxbridge places and A/L Grade 'A's. And louder asked Plato's ghost, 'Are you good enough?' I actually expressed surprise to Geoffrey Parker, my predecessor at Tonbridge, that I had been appointed. 'Oh,' he replied loftily, 'I think that we all knew what you were up to.'

The final terms passed in a blur. The first fifteen reverted to losing ways but we had a good Seven. They won the Herefordshire Sevens and ran very close the eventual winners of the Oxford Sevens. For once the cricket season was blessed with sunny skies and dry pitches. My Under 14 opening batsman even scored a century. Captaining the Common Room against the school on my final day at Christ College I signed off with my first fifty since leaving St Benedict's. It would also be my last.

We had been in Brecon for only four years, but as the removal van drew up to take our belongings away to the South-East, tears and a huge sense of Paradise Lost welled up and I hurriedly took myself off to stand alone. Little did Margery and I imagine, could we have imagined, that we would be back 23 years later as guests of honour. My ambition and my inner discontent had driven us away. Returning we knew how much we had experienced and gained since 1975 but we recognized also that we had all paid a price. We retain a deep and abiding affection for Christ College, now a thoroughly humane and progressive school for the twenty-first century, then a rather severe and narrow little school to which, nevertheless, we owed a very great deal.

CHAPTER 9

Good Enough?

TONBRIDGE SCHOOL was almost as old as Christ College. Cardinal Wolsey, when he dissolved Tonbridge Priory in the 1520s, had offered the townspeople the grammar school that they had never had – and they had declined, opting instead for a restored priory. But there had been no such restoration. Tonbridge School was founded in 1553 by Sir Andrew Judde, a member of the Skinners Company.

It was the very point when the English Reformation teetered in the balance. Mary Tudor battled her way to the throne and hung on against intrigue and rebellion. There can be no doubt as to where Judde and his founding head-master stood. Judde rallied to the muster opposing Sir Thomas Wyatt. The Reverend John Proctor wrote an account of the defeat of Wyatt's rebellion, along with a number of learned works against heresy. It is one of history's little ironies that a school as strongly Protestant as Tonbridge should have com-menced on such a positively Catholic note.

For me, far more than in Brecon, arrival at Tonbridge was an initiation into Establishment Anglicanism. I dutifully attended the dedication service for the new Headmaster, Christopher Everett, and was at once impressed and chilled by the aura of massive assurance, the Houses paraded along the flanks of the long, brick chapel, the triumphant final hymn, *Glorious things of Thee are spoken, Zion City of our God*. It was the chapel service from *If* – and, indeed, the prototype for the History beak who rides his bike into the classroom was, allegedly, my predecessor but one.

Christopher Everett himself was hugely impressive. A Wykehamist with a distinguished career in the Guards and in the Foreign and Prime Minister's Offices, and without any experience of teaching, he had reputedly gained his headship of Worksop by answering the 'Why' question, 'I thought that it would be rather fun.' He exuded enthusiasm and intellectual power, words cascading in torrents, on any subject and in any situation, from brain and mouth far above those of any of his staff. Of all my headmasters, none was so tall or *seemed* so tall as he. The Putney Pud had ended up working for a giraffe!

I remember nothing of our first conversation, other than a huge sense of my own prosaic and pedestrian inferiority. I suppose that I entered the study feeling that he and I were newcomers in the same boat and that I left it wondering if and when I would ever prove to him that his predecessor's choice of Head of History had been a wise one. Nor do I recall any detail of the first Common

Room meeting, except my admiration of the confidence and mastery that he expressed with every word and point.

This was no time for introspective hesitation. Stepping into Geoffrey Parker's shoes involved three separate crises. I had to master Seventeenth Century European History sufficiently to teach the Second Year Sixth. I had to tutor for Oxbridge a bevy of Geoff's star historians. And, perhaps worst of all, I had for my first term to give a weekly lecture in 'Big School' to about 140 'Novi' – fourth formers fresh to Tonbridge from their triumphs in Common Entrance or Scholarship exams. Fifteen years after my Prelims course in Historical Geography I was back with Columbus on his journeys of exploration.

Today's historians would use Power Point to enthral their audiences. Then, thank God, public expectations had been shaped by the unadorned dryness of A.J.P. Taylor rather than by the entertainments of David Starkey or Simon Shama. Pupils, in Tonbridge at least, were still expected to listen unaided. Even so, I rapidly obtained the agreement of my colleagues that there should be no repeat of this terrible ordeal.

There were three other members in my department. Terence Vardon was the bright young thing. Mike Bushby and David Walsh saw themselves as the unintellectual schoolmaster cricketers. That both were fine schoolmasters and exceptional cricketers was certain. It took me a while to persuade each that there was nothing in history teaching that was beyond them, certainly not the teaching of an Advanced Level Special Subject. Schools like Tonbridge are great because of their 'Bushby and Walsh' – they surface as two officers in Jonathan Smith's *Wilfred and Eileen* – because their loyalty is unconditional and unequivocal, if never uncritical. To me they were at all times magnificently supportive.

Jonathan Smith was Head of English. We were of the same age and I think that he felt protective towards me as, by one of those coincidences that typify HMC schools, he had been a pupil at Christ College, Brecon. Gifted, fastidious, stylish and generous he was at once Anglo-Saxon in his reserve and Celtic in his moodiness. You never knew whether it would be the effusive, hyperbolic Jonathan or his glum and lugubrious alter ego. His neat handwriting betrayed the painstaking craftsman who was to fashion so many novels of delicacy and radio plays that were gems of wit and observation, but to his pupils he offered the face of laid-back 'Sixties Man' and they loved him for it, taking his initials of JBS to signify 'John Bored Stiff'.

Jonathan was a curious mixture. He had resisted the 'erastian' suggestion of Michael McCrum, whose headship had made the modern Tonbridge as surely as it was even now shaping the modern Eton, that he would promote his own career the better if he were seen to be more supportive of Chapel, and he quietly mocked those aspirant housemasters who had dutifully embraced Confirmation. Yet he was really as much part of Tonbridge School as they were. He sensed the limitations of the boarding school world – 'Never forget, Patrick, that in boarding schools the boys are *tribal'* – but he appreciated and loved its strengths more than I could or would ever do. After a few years at Loretto, where he had taught the young Michael Mavor, Jonathan was destined to spend the rest of his career at Tonbridge, the antithesis of Michael who, after beginning his teaching career under Jonathan, would leave at 29 for the first of (to date) three headships. As for myself, I had not totally forgotten Paul Olsen's promise to my mother but I certainly did not yet see myself as a likely Headmaster. Even so it was unsettling to be told by one and all that Head of History at Tonbridge was the threshold to headship, the last three incumbents having made this progression.

It was, for all its sociability and its charm, an unquestioningly conservative society. There were Common Room cricket matches in lovely Kent villages and Common Room dinners during which the best wine flowed, but the young man who vomited his inebriation was given notice to leave. When you read Jonathan Smith's *The English Lover* and enjoy the scene after a Parents' Evening when the teacher tells the mother who has brought her son into the pub that she has created an embarrassing situation and must therefore remove him forthwith, you can rest assured that fiction was actually fact. Margery turned up in trousers to her first coffee morning and realized too late that she was the only one not wearing a skirt. On that occasion she and the other new wives were given a choice by Billie Everett, did they wish to do the chapel flowers or polish the silver? (Margery chose the silver, little realizing that one day she would be organizing chapel flowers.) At the end of dinner parties, it was still the rule that the ladies should withdraw. I was there when one wife refused to oblige and sat on doggedly with us. Lynne Reekes did likewise, after a black-tie House dinner – she wasn't going to miss the fun! There was an abundance of such hospitality, with the houses competing to lay on the most enjoyable Christmas feasts, but the Establishment was resistant to new ideas. When Randall Stephens, Tony Little and Andrew Reekes constituted themselves as a social committee and organized a Common Room party, with a crèche, there were references to October 1917 and the Bolsheviks. The party happened, but wives had to supply the food. Through it all, and behind the mannered accents, you sensed occasionally the private hurts so stoically hidden – the handicapped child or, in the case of one housemaster's wife, the parents from whom she was marooned throughout the duration of a war.

The boarders, living in their imposing Victorian houses to the north of the school, felt superior to their day boy peers. The day housemasters strove manfully to create the illusion of parity. It was only when I left that I appreciated that it was a rule that no day boy should go out anywhere on Saturday evening without the permission of his housemaster. (Then as now it seemed incredible.) Boarders and day boys alike ate lunches in their houses. The Common Room normally purchased lunches for themselves in the 'grubber', but could obtain indoor relief through the invitation of a housemaster, the only price being the conversation that you had to sustain at the end of a boys' lunch table. Afterwards the Housemaster's wife would graciously provide coffee and you tried to convey an impression of equally civilized ease. At times pretence was strained, as when dear Jack Ind commented, 'People like you and me, Patrick, with generations of education behind us, find it difficult to imagine what it must be like to lack such advantage.'

Around the school and extending over many acres and in most directions the playing fields of the school were manicured to perfection. Only my mother could be unimpressed. When I showed off to Una the vista of the school from the 'Head', the sumptuous cricket square, she paused for a moment, then, 'It's rather pretentious, isn't it?'

There was a honeymoon hue to those early weeks in Kent. I would come back to Margery and the children at or after lunch, enthusing about the sparkling conversation in the Common Room. What a joy it was to work with such stimulating and intelligent people! It was true that I was struggling to keep up with the work. Even so, it was flattering that young Ken Fincham should pop round so frequently to seek my opinions on nineteenth century history and a delight when he won his award to Oxford, where he is now a don. He was one of a number who won Oxbridge Scholarships in History but he was the only one for whom I felt any measure of credit.

Circumstances, however, were making it difficult for us to settle. The school did not have a house for us, so the Skinners rented for us instead a little flat very close to the school. 11A Bordyke was on the first floor and was accessible only via an outside staircase, hardly ideal for Margery with a child of two and a baby of nine months. By winter we realized that we would have to seek a house of our own. We managed to sell Margery's flat in Ealing at nearly twice the price that she had paid for it but our comfortably large house in Hildenborough would cost us almost as much again. The Skinners Company were generously enlightened in one respect, advancing £3,000 as an interest-free loan, even though I was breaking the rule by living more than five minutes' walk away from the school. I invited Margery to bear the brunt and put to her the question that has never been forgotten, 'Do you think that we can live on £15 per week?'

Part of our trouble was that we had been spoilt in Brecon. We had let the Ealing flat to a delightful Maltese couple and we had tended to spend rather than save this extra income. So I had extravagantly replaced the Morris Marina with a Volvo 245. This clearly would have to go. We crashed to a ghastly, green Vauxhall Chevette and I cycled each day to school on my museum-piece of a Rudge. That did not solve the fundamental problem. My pay was too low.

When I was appointed to Tonbridge I never asked about salary. I had simply assumed that it must exceed Brecon's. It turned out to be smaller. A long common scale rewarded seniority rather than responsibility. At Tonbridge it had not been the 'done thing' to discuss pay. Within living memory, gentlemen of leisure had given their services free to the Common Room and morning coffee had been taken in the 'Rose and Crown' in the High Street. When I aired my concerns, however, with colleagues like Jonathan Smith, Peter Commings and Fred Marsden, we found that we were of one mind. It was time to have a properly constituted Common Room, elected by and representative of the teachers, rather than a body which mimicked the attitude and opaqueness of the old-style Tory party. I drafted a new constitution which, to my surprise, was broadly accepted.

The Skinners' Company began to take notice. The four of us were invited out to Brasted to meet their Common Room representative in his handsome abode. Famously I observed that I was too poor to buy my wife a coat. The results were spectacular, a major pay increase, plus a 100% discount in the fees of all sons of teachers educated at Tonbridge School. There should be a plaque to us in the Tonbridge Common Room. But the nation's economic failure, culminating in the winter of discontent of 1978-79, would force us to go on worrying about our salaries. When a major increase in the pay of maintained school teachers was followed by galloping inflation and a general pay freeze, we were again at a relative disadvantage. I asked Brian Burns, by now a partner at Arthur Young's, to advise us as to whether there were loopholes. There were none. The best that could be said for this otherwise demoralizing syndrome was that it very rapidly devalued our own personal debt, while the money value of our house as rapidly appreciated, but we had little sense then that we were en route to personal prosperity. Our time at Tonbridge coincided with the failure of a particular approach to the government of Britain. That was hardly the fault of Tonbridge.

As so often, I fear that I imported too many of Una's genes into Tonbridge. In retrospect, I wish that I had approached the august school with greater humility, with a readiness to wait, listen and learn, rather than with such a strong instinct that I must 'fight my corner'. Had I been more secure I might have been wiser and have attached less importance to competition and more to incorporation. But, operating for the first time in a school where I was at best equal to the average intelligence of the Common Room, I was insecure. It was, I imagine, important to me that I should affirm my own self-respect by articulating the values derived from my own personal upbringing and experience.

In all sorts of ways Tonbridge remains the best school I ever taught in. Everything about it was 'Rolls Royce', including and especially its teachers who, almost without exception, were sound in their scholarship, steady in their teaching and unstinting in their general commitment and esprit de corps. They took Tonbridge School very seriously. It followed that the Common Room was more 'aware' and competitive than any others in which I have taught. It was a double-edged compliment when Peter Commings asked, over a beer that first

Christmas, how I was going to follow up the History department's spectacular bag of Oxbridge awards. How indeed?

Good Enough?, the title later given by Chris Cowdrey and Jonathan Smith to their tale of the joys and travails of a Test cricketer, was the question that drummed within me as I fought to sustain for my subject its place in the sun. I strove mightily to impress and to educate, running off tens of thousands of photocopied pages of the very latest scholarship – and the more that I sought to impress my clearly talented Lower Sixth, the more they sat back and let me make the running. Richard Kitchen would very occasionally betray an acute intelligence and an otherwise hidden interest with a 'snapping' of his eyes, like the shutter of a lens, when he registered a particular irony or paradox. Otherwise the rewards were few and I only had myself to blame. I weighted down my teaching and my pupils with mountains of information and snuffed out the spark of inspiration. Peter Dodge expressed the general opinion with cool brutality. 'I hear that History is a bummer.' (I was the more pleased when he ultimately defected from Classics and entered Cambridge through History.)

I confided my disappointment to Jonathan, who said that he was really upset. Meanwhile, sitting in judgement on the sidelines, were the various house-masters, much closer to and more supportive of their charges than had been the Brecon housemasters. One such was Geoff Allibone, a gaunt and not unfriendly Classicist, albeit decidedly his own man. (He remains the only man I know who depresses the lavatory flush with his foot because everyone else has touched it with the hand.) One day, shortly after the Oxbridge triumph of 1975, he came up to me and wheezed, 'Patrick, we've just received a very nice letter from Chris Andrew at Corpus about Hooper (who had won a Scholarship in History at Corpus Christi College, Cambridge.) Geoff Parker knew Chris Andrew well. Why don't you write to him and say that you would like to meet him?'

So I did – and as rapidly got a letter in reply. He had never met Geoff Parker but would be delighted to meet me. Would I like to come up to Corpus and stay the night? I at once sought Christopher Everett's permission and had a most enjoyable and useful excursion.

But that was not the end of it. A few weeks later Anthony Wilson, who was responsible for providing advice on universities to pupils and housemasters at Tonbridge, was appointed to a post in the Science Museum. Who should replace him? Who else but the new Head of History with his impressive contacts in Cambridge? I suppose that I could have declined, on the very good grounds that few if any of my colleagues knew as little as I did. Once again I plunged in at the deep end, learning the language of the pellucid flow charts that had emanated so impressively from the calm and logical Dr Wilson.

It was my first whole-school responsibility and, as such, a marvellous training for headship. Housemasters badgered me for advice and information from the day I was appointed – and I learned that, as soon as you are a designated 'expert' in a school like Tonbridge, colleagues will ask you questions, *in the expectation that they will believe what you say*. In the long run that was to be a very helpful insight. Once again I had to address a whole year group in Big School, but this time I was praised by Barry Orchard, that kindly and much mourned Tonbridge institution, for the humane style with which I briefed the boys about their A/L choices. Perhaps I had strengths in this area. Not long afterwards, attending a conference and discovering that I was the only non-Head present, I would be staggered at how ordinary and 'small' they were. If they could do it, why was I not applying for headship?

Beware of classicist headmasters bringing gifts! Christopher Everett now asked if I would mind if his daughter, Victoria, joined the History Sixth for one term so that she could attempt Oxbridge. Then, for good measure, he added a further girl, the daughter of a well known TV News presenter. It was a pleasure to teach them both, even though I judged that the odds were against success, but the tensions mounted as the Entrance Examinations approached and their first day turned out to be unforgettable.

One of the responsibilities of the Master i/c University Entrance was to manage the Oxbridge Entrance Examinations. I had systematically filed away the papers for each day and made all necessary arrangements for the examinations. The morning of the first examination dawned piercingly cold, with several degrees of frost. As we assembled in the old chapel that served as the examination hall it became immediately clear that the heating had failed. Calmly I gathered together my flock and ushered them over to Old Big School which was warm and empty. I sat them down in their respective desks. Christopher Everett, meanwhile, whether as headmaster or father, was pacing frenetically up and down between the rows. I turned and went to pick up the papers. But where were they? Cold though I was a grim sweat moistened my brow. Feverishly I rummaged. And there, Oh Thank God, were the papers, nestling under a boy's coat casually discarded on a table.

The professional tensions of the autumn of 1976 were as nothing with the cumulative anguish of the previous summer. As the sun shone remorselessly, we shrivelled in crisis, arguably the worst in all our married life. The work was troubling me. I was worried sick about money. But I also wanted our house to be right for Margery and the children. We installed costly French windows and the putty beneath them would not set. I put up shelves in my study, the one household task in which I was not totally unskilled. I tried to lay a patio. And dig a sandpit. And plaster a kitchen wall. Every job was more or less botched. Meanwhile the weather became hotter and hotter, unprecedentedly so, and during that long hot summer huge cracks began to open across the dry clay that was our front lawn. The door into the dining room ominously refused to shut. Clearly our white elephant of a house, which we alone had been foolish enough to purchase, was subsiding into oblivion.

Then the rains came. And the door miraculously shut. And we took ourselves off to St Mary's, the idyllic house in Chideock where Margery's parents had lived since 1970, and we swam every morning and afternoon while Evelyn minded Matthew and Emma and we read and slept and drank and I recovered. Life was never to seem as pressurized and impossible again.

Further relief came in the form of our first 'Senior Student'. A safety valve had been created for Sixth Form boarders whereby those who felt most claustrophobic in their prolonged House residence could opt instead to live with a 'beak' and his family. So in term time our guest bedroom became a useful money-spinner and, with luck, we were acquiring a baby-sitter into the bargain. In four years there were no disasters; on the contrary Margery and I gained a useful insight into the psychology of the long-stay boarder.

However, the most significant step towards liking Tonbridge came with the arrival of Andrew Reekes in the History department after Terence Vardon had moved onwards and upwards. Andrew was and is a born teacher, with huge and infectious enthusiasm, pleasantly sardonic humour and considerable personal appeal. He and Lynne, his splendidly feisty and bright lawyer wife, became great friends, adding a new dimension to our lives at Tonbridge. And in Andrew I had obtained a wonderfully accomplished recruiting sergeant for the History department.

At the start of his and my third year at Tonbridge, Christopher Everett did an amazing thing. He took the whole Common Room to Oxford for a two day conference in St Catherine's College. Launching it the Headmaster noted that history was not on the side of schools that took their local superiority for granted. Thus Uppingham had once felt superior to Oakham. We knew that we had a higher standing than Sevenoaks, but they had gone coeducational and we might miss the tide if we failed to respond to market forces as they had done. The young Turks read the signs and were eloquent in support of change. The housemasters were as eloquent in their silence. We returned to Tonbridge, the weeks passed and that was the last we heard of St Catherine's or of coeducation. There had clearly been a 'non fiat' from Skinners' Hall.

Four months later Christopher Everett imparted a more personal spin to my existence. We were down in Cornwall with the masters and sixth formers who made up the annual A/L revision Reading Party. This was a thoroughly civilized affair. We would read collectively in the mornings, embark on bracing walks in the afternoon, pack in some more reading before and after dinner and end most days in the pub. It was in a hostelry in Rock that I unguardedly shared with the Headmaster my experiences of going overland to the Middle East. 'But Patrick, that's super. We must do it here. You must take a party of Sixth formers. I will come with you!'

I advertized the trip and awaited responses. Andrew Reekes gallantly agreed to be co-leader but Christopher backed away, frightfully sorry. Soon afterwards I went to tell him that Margery was expecting our third – testimony to the life-giving force of a royal Silver Jubilee – and that I thought that I should cancel the expedition. 'When?' 'February/March.' 'Oh, there's nothing you can do when they're that age. Tell Margery that you've got to go.'

Lucy was safely delivered and the expedition went ahead. Margery was not very impressed, although Lynne was a great support to her while we were away. In some ways it was a much less risky enterprise than in 1968. This time I would have a co-driver, plus Martin Francis, the school chaplain, who came with us as far as Istanbul. We avoided the Balkans by taking the car ferry from Ancona to Istanbul and from Izmir to Venice. And our Ford Transit minibus was a far more rugged vehicle than the Commer. Even so I am aghast when I think of the gallons of petrol that we carried aboard from Syria across Turkey as we successfully circumvented a Turkish petrol strike and I remember only too well my alarm when Johnny Redford went missing for two hours in Lattakieh. The only sickness was in Damascus and it was short lived. It was impossible to like Syria, with every other person an armed soldier or policeman. Nothing epitomized better the demise of a once vibrant tourist instinct than when I led my 14 into a seaside restaurant and was summoned to choose my fare. Twenty minutes later it arrived – for me alone. But the castles were spectacular and the campsites frequently idyllic. Andrew and I shared one tent, my head in, his out. 'Oh God,' he exclaimed one morning, after a dog had urinated over his head. His main complaint, however, was shared by the boys. The Harry Shutt regime of austerity only suited those who were previously well endowed. Our party returned looking like survivors of a concentration camp. I alone looked healthy in the extreme. I also had a thick brown beard. 'Take it off, Daddy,' rasped Emma, and that was the end of that.

Christopher Everett was warm in his praise, Andrew Reekes mounted an exhibition in the new History accommodation that I had acquired for the department and there was every reason to settle down and be content with my lot. Instead the demons drove me on.

I had convinced myself that History would never get a fair crack of the whip at Tonbridge unless and until it was given more time with pupils so that they could discover its magic before they made their O/L choices. Christopher Everett loved hearing an argument and delighted even more in rehearsing it. Decisions, however, were so slow to emerge that one suspected that he could not bear to make a decision because that would end the discussion. Eventually I wrote him a letter, more or less to that effect, and received back a very sharp note in which he stated that the tone of my letter had far exceeded the normal bounds of courtesy. Jonathan Smith, who had a very good relationship with Christopher, intervened and all was smoothed over. The Headmaster (very rightly) resisted the pressure of his importunate Head of History, but the latter found a way around his Fabian tactics by entering into an alliance with Jonathan

The Tonbridge party at Goreme, Cappadocia, 1978.

Self scrambling down crusader castle.

113

Bearded PFJT and Andrew Reekes, flanked by Tom Yarker and Patrick Thom.

Smith whereby all boys in their first year would be taught English and History by the same teacher.

To me the cautious hesitation of the Headmaster in this matter was symptomatic of a more fundamental problem at Tonbridge. He did not have the power to 'set the agenda' because he did not really run the school. The housemasters, not the Headmaster and certainly not the Heads of Department, were the powers in the land. Tonbridge was a baronial oligarchy, the Deputy Head was a senior housemaster (and highly influential Old Tonbridgian) and the school was decentralized through and through.

I was never at ease with the house structure of Tonbridge. It seemed to me to reinforce the totalitarianism of the peer group, so that happiness and mutual stimulus rested unduly on the accident wherein a relatively small number of boys happened to be thrown together intensively for five years. At that time Tonbridge could be far more selective than now in terms of the prior academic attainment of its boarding applicants. Even so, many of the marks gained derived more from systematic cramming than from any spark in the student or his teachers. Unconscious of the irony that much the same charge could be levied against myself, I felt that the house system served to blunt the impact of the challenging teacher on his pupils and I resented this. Years afterwards one of those pupils, himself a product of the most conservative of all houses, told me: 'At the time you taught me I disagreed with virtually every opinion that you expressed. Now I am grateful to you for making me think.' He is a teacher. As such he is perhaps in the minority.

I particularly resented the impact of inter-house competition on rugby. I had reverted to Under 15 coaching and had three years of moderate success, but I thought that the Tonbridge boys were very soft – as they inevitably were in comparison with their Brecon counterparts – and that time spent on house matches could better have been spent on the acquisition of Sevens skills. After three years, pleading the desire to spend more time on scholarship, I retired as a rugby coach. I am sure that I was not missed.

The scholarship was directed at Edward Stafford, Third Duke of Buckingham. Through the London Library I read every secondary work about the Yorkist and Early Tudor aristocracy. I devoured doctoral theses, met two of their authors, spent hours in the County archives in Stafford and elsewhere and took Margery to visit countless churches and castles associated with the Stafford family. Out of it all came a biography which probably had its merits but which suffered from the usual Tobin problem of being neither fish nor fowl – neither genuinely original in its scholarship nor sufficiently entertaining to a non-specialist public. I have no regrets. I learned as much about History and the writing of History as I had done in all my formal education – and I was able to convey increasingly to my pupils something of the passion engendered, above all a deep loathing for that vile tyrant, Henry VIII.

To me there was a parallel between the fate of good men in Tudor times and the equally agonizing dilemmas of men of integrity confronted with the awfulness of Hitler or Stalin. Thomas Cranmer, in particular, fascinated me, caught as he was between spiritual idealism and the brutal fact that his Reformation depended on the whims of his Monarch for its progress or arrest. How did a man, *could* a man, like Cranmer cope when God's anointed was the woman whom he had bastardized twenty years before? I made Cranmer the subject of my first Saturday chapel address, from a lonely lectern, alongside the Headmaster, looking down the parallel rows of boys and staff towards the distant altar. I was nervous, but I did not expect my knees literally to knock. I found myself worrying lest the sound of knocking knees should be carried by the microphone to cynical boys and amused colleagues. Thereafter, I positively enjoyed the experience of having a whole school as my audience.

Lucy, our Kentish baby, was by now a thriving toddler. Matthew had made a happy start in an excellent Catholic primary school, with Emma following him, despite a premature end to her pre-school visit when she bit the teacher's hand. Perhaps we would settle down after all. We may not have had much money, certainly not enough to afford holidays abroad, but we loved our weeks in Dorset with Evelyn and John, particularly the sleepy summer days in garden or on beach. The Chevette proved adequate for our purposes – although I did try once to enlarge its capacity through a roof rack recommended by *Which*. I proudly installed this before one summer journey to Dorset, and it did indeed reach that county, but as we sped towards Corfe Mullen it shot off the top of the car, mercifully clear of any other vehicle. Emma told Andrew Reekes, 'Silly Daddy forgot to fix the woof wack pwoperly.'

Once again, a Reading Party intervened, with consequences far more profound than a jaunt to the Middle East.

This time, it was in the Lake District. It was as damply cold as only the Lake District in April can be. As we teachers huddled for warmth in the local pub, and Jonathan Smith rhapsodized about his year in Melbourne, John Inverarity sensed that this was the moment to strike. 'Say Patrick,' he asked, 'Do you know of any Tonbridge historians who would like to teach in Australia for a year?' Yes, I did!

Between then and departure there were occasional doubts, as well as a possible diversion when I applied for the post of Head of a Catholic girls' school in the South West. 'Mr Tobin,' Tony Sutton asked, 'Do you suffer fools gladly?' – and that, thank goodness, was the end of that chimera. On Boxing Day 1979 we took off for Edmonton, Canada, to stay a week with Margery's sister, before winging the long flight across the Pacific to Sydney, with Lucy travelling free and on Margery's knee throughout. 'Mummy,' Matthew anxiously asked, as we made our second stop at Nandi, 'Do you think we've come too far?'

It was to be, in so many ways, the turning point in our lives.

CHAPTER 10

Lucky Country

4 Pieces of Advice:
1. Keep telling them what a great country they live in.
2. Avoid controversy or watch your teeth.
3. Buy your round and drink your beer.
4. Don't expect too much reading to be done on summer weekends.'

Mike Bushby, David Walsh, Jonathan Smith

And the bush has friends to meet him, and their kindly voices greet him
In the murmur of the breezes and the river on its bars,
And he sees the vision splendid of the sunlit plains extended,
And at night the wondrous glory of the everlasting stars.'

(A.B. 'Banjo' Paterson, *Clancy of the Overflow*)

As I begin this last paragraph, outside a misty afternoon drizzle gently but inexorably soaks the City of London. Down there in the street I can see umbrellas commiserating with each other. In Sydney Harbour, twelve thousand miles away and ten hours from now, the yachts will be racing on the crushed diamond water under a sky the colour of powdered sapphires…Pulsing like a beacon through the days and nights, the birthplace of the fortunate sends out its invisible waves of recollection. It always has and it always will, until even the last of us come home.

(Clive James, *Unreliable Memoirs*)

WE FLEW TO Sydney not imagining that it would be a very interesting place. We looked forward to the beaches, feared the flies and could identify the Opera House and the Harbour Bridge.

Disinfected before landing, we emerged from Customs about midnight, seeking the Deputy Head of The King's School and finding him in the tall and languid figure in shorts and long socks. As we sped westwards, and cars sped faster on our inside, I commented on the appalling driving, whereupon Tony Hill showed us how it was done. Would we like to see the shops next morning? In that case we should meet him at 9 o'clock at the crossroads.

We just made that appointment – and there was an immediate 'Hullo, Sir,' in a very English accent. There before me was a boy whom I had been teaching about a week earlier. It beggared the imagination that the first face we should see in Australia by daylight should be someone from Tonbridge, 12,000 miles away.

117

He lived in Hong Kong and just happened to be staying with a friend in Sydney to share with him the long, hot summer holiday.

It was a Saturday and we had an immediate invitation, to a lunch party given in honour of the Smees. Michael and Birgitte were leaving next day for Adelaide, where Michael was to be Deputy Head of St Peter's. Through the alcoholic mist of that first barbecue I recall a bikini-clad Birgitte leading me along the path to Forrest House so that she could show me the crack in the wall into which she had seen a black red bellied snake slither. For the next eleven months I would stare nervously at that crack.

Two days later Peter Rainey took Matthew and me to the Sydney Cricket Ground to watch the last day of the (unofficial) Test between England and Australia. At my request we sat down on the Hill. Against the best efforts of Botham & Co. Australia were inching their way towards their target, but Brearley rang every change. 'C'm ON, Brearley, Get a move on, Brearley.' Patience began to wear thin. Soon the tones became more raucous and the language bluer. There were frequent references to 'Pommie Bastards'. 'Daddy,' said Matthew, 'What are Pommie Bastards?' 'Matthew,' I replied gravely, '*We* are Pommie Bastards.'

Otherwise I remember only the swimming pool, and the nesting peewit that bombed us, and the thunder and spectacular lightning that sent us running for cover about 5 each afternoon – more or less the last rain that we would see in Australia in 1980. Eventually the day of reckoning arrived, when I would have to teach History and become House Tutor to the boys of Forrest House.

The King's School Parramatta (TKS) was Australia's oldest school and Forrest its oldest house. For 150 years it had catered for the offspring of the landowners and sheep farmers of New South Wales and beyond. One of the boys, destined to leave prematurely, was seventh generation Forrest House. Jon Wickham, my exchangee, could not have been better suited to the role of housemaster. 'Black Jack' had the build of an Olympic oarsman, a countenance that took no prisoners and a wife of effortless charm and boundless warmth. We had met them when they arrived at Hildenborough with their two sons. They would be a hard act to impersonate, even if the buck would stop with the house tutor, Colin Carpenter, and not with us.

On the day before term began we had to provide hospitality to the parents of all the boys in the House as they arrived for Founders' Day. This was an education in itself. Each of the parents introduced themselves, engaged in the most friendly conversation about our arrival and ensured, through much repetition of our own names, that they would not forget 'Margery' and 'Patrick', as I would typically have done. They may not have been sophisticated but they certainly were civilized. We were impressed.

We soon found that their sons were tough and self-sufficient. The twelve year olds had been riding motor bikes for six years. In the holidays they would drive their father's 'ute' around their vast properties, mustering sheep or injecting sick cattle. Some boasted of pig-shooting from helicopters. You knew where you stood with them. They would greet Margery or me without that English downward look of the eyes, or that interesting distraction on the other side of the road. After initial reserve about the Poms in the boarding house, they became very friendly. They had acquired courtesy from their parents and, if less at ease in party conversation, were much better than their gauche English counterparts at standing up when women came into the room. And they would write letters of thanks. I treasure one letter written to us –

> Thankyou very much for the beaut supper you gave us last week, Tuesday. It was beaut, and I enjoyed talking to you and meeting you. I really enjoyed myself down there and I hope the rest of my form did too. Thankyou very much again for the beaut cake and drink.
>
> Yours sincerely,
> Bill Stacy

In September Bill was a week late returning to school. He had been bringing a bull back from New Zealand for his father. He was then sixteen.

With such a background some free spirits found the boarding discipline hard to take. 'H' lived in the Northern Territory. His father had recently sold a million acres but still retained the bulk of his property. Young 'H', a fifteen year old, would take parties of Aboriginal workers out for a week to mend fences. Both his elder brothers had been expelled from TKS and 'H' was always 'in strife'. Finally he was sent to me for chewing gum in a Latin class. 'H…,' I said, 'You must make up your mind. Either you stay here and don't chew gum in class or you go.' Two days later 'H' went, taking Tom Combes with him. They went bush for a week, living rough, before they surfaced. Tom came back, but 'H's father said that 'H' had made his decision and sent him to 'jackaroo' on a nearby property. Tom settled back. When the time came for us to leave he and his friends gave me a little present of their own. It was a little pouch. I expressed my gratitude. 'Tom's father shot it, Sir. It's a kangaroo.' More thanks. Then, 'Do you know what part of the kangaroo?' Recognition dawned. 'It's to keep your valuables in, Sir.'

During our year in Australia, Simon Denison, a day boy at Tonbridge, stayed a few days with us before acquiring 'GAP' experience as a jackaroo near Hay. I hardly liked to tell him that 'Banjo' Paterson had written of 'Hay, Hell and Booligal' and off he went. He returned some weeks later, as if from Belsen.

Even at TKS we encountered intolerance, prejudice and xenophobia. The school itself was linked to the Anglican archdiocese of Sydney, then as now remarkably narrow and exclusive in its version of Christianity. When Pope John Paul came to visit Sydney, the Archbishop refused to share a platform with him. I have no doubt that this Calvinist slant in part stemmed from, in part contributed to, a view of society that saw those outside the 'elect' – particularly Aboriginals – as less than fully human. Few boys at TKS had a good word to say for the 'Asians' flocking to Australia and they tended to be as dismissive of 'New Immigrants' from Italy and Greece. It did Sydneysiders no harm at all to read in the *Sydney Morning Herald* the opening paragraph of a review of a study of Italian immigrants who chose to return to Italy rather than remain in Australia.

> A country where the water and air are not pure or good, a country of silent, unfriendly people who shut themselves away within their own four walls, a country the streets of whose cities and towns are deserted at night, a country where the old are rejected and where the children put their aged parents into institutions, a country whose men are lazy, aggressive and xenophobic; yet a country of honest officials, where there is no privilege and there are equal rights for all.
>
> Recognize it? It is Australia, as recalled by Italian immigrants who have returned to Italy.

When it was announced to the boys of Forrest House that, for the first time in years, they would have a Malaysian coming to board, there was outright consternation. It was made pretty clear, not only that the boys would not like it, but that their parents would be asking questions. Finally, after Colin Carpenter and I had worked to talk them round, the boy did not arrive. He had failed to obtain a visa. I wondered whether there was a Forrest Old Boy in Immigration.

Attitudes to Britain were similarly intolerant. Indeed the boys could not understand why I was returning, apart from those who had themselves made the journey, and even they had been appalled by the weather.

Yet I genuinely liked Forrest House and was sorry to leave it. One of the very best things that we did during our year was to visit the properties of parents. The first was a three day stay with the Ashtons on their property at Millamolong, near Mandurama, eighty miles south-west of Bathurst. We peer now at the flickering cine film, watch Margery, Matthew, Emma and me astride our horses and we wonder, 'Did this really happen to us?' The vision splendid indeed!

Our next foray was to two properties owned by Forrest House parents in Northern New South Wales. The Andersons owned a cattle station, 'Quirindi'. Sue Anderson thought that a few instructions would not come amiss.

> When you get to WILLOW TREE (just before) turn left to Blackville on the Merriwa Road sign. Follow that sign but you want to go to Blackville – about 35 miles. Go through the little town of Blackville to a turn off to Yarram/ Coonabarabran. Travel 6 miles to turn off to Coonabarabran. Follow that sign for about 5 miles till you see a sign on your right to our place – Coomoo Coomoo Creek and left mailbox and ramp marked Daymar. GO OVER ramp and travel three and a half miles till you see our mailbox. Go slowly! Road rough…The trip from Willow Tree will be about one and a quarter hours.

My sharpest memory of Quirindi was of what we did *not* see. We stood looking into the hills and Sue Anderson tried to guide our eyes to the kangaroos which she picked out but which were invisible to us. We headed north to stay with the Dights, clinging tightly to Sue Anderson's guidance.

> Left at Daymar ramp, travel about 9 miles to turn off Tamarang Lane, Spring Ridge. Turn right to Tamarang Silo. Turn left half a mile, then turn right to Gunnedah Sign Post. Travel about six miles to turn off South Wandabah. Take this right turn and travel about 10 miles passing Hames Hill. You meet Gunnedah Road again at Red Bobs. Head for Gunnedah.

Mr Anderson still banked at Gunnedah, a fifty mile journey each way. He had old friends in the town, where his father was a retired doctor.

Yetman, up near the Queensland border, had been established by a pioneering Dight in 1840. The Dights still owned the property, with the Macintyre river flowing behind the old farmstead and from time to time flooding it, but when we arrived all was drought. Mr Dight had put in some crops. If he did not get rain in the next fortnight, he would plough them back into the soil. The rain did not come. But our film shows no strain, only an utterly relaxed country lad, as young Peter Dight patiently led our two town children round his paddock as they clung nervously to their ponies.

It was hardly surprising that education at TKS inclined to the functional rather than the academic but this was true of New South Wales schools as a whole. There was none of the English pursuit of elitism. Emma at five went out to Sydney able to read, only to embark on a year where reading was specifically ruled out – so that no-one could get too far ahead and children could learn to socialize. It happened that the captain of my rugby team lived in Sevenoaks, so we commissioned him to return from his next two holidays weighed down with Ladybird Readers. That apart, Emma had a ball. It took her about a fortnight to catch up when she returned to England.

At the other end of education similar attitudes prevailed. The only public examination sat by boys and girls in New South Wales, taken at the very end of their school careers, was the Higher School Certificate (HSC), a complicated mixture of 3-unit, 2-unit and 1-unit subjects. This forced students into a wider range of subjects than in England but it fostered also a mark-counting utilitarianism that effectively excluded any depth, originality or reflection. Success in History could be achieved through reduction to essentials, rote learning and the parrot repetition of model answers, famous quotations and pundits' verdicts. Looking back I see the New South Wales curriculum as Scottish shallowness without any of the compensatory rigour. Some 'educationalists' today urge the abolition of examinations and a 'market-driven' broadening of the curriculum. I think of TKS on a hot summer's day and am sceptical.

Such attitudes filtered back into the lower school. It was up to the individual teacher to contend with the sluggish tide of indifference. I had wondered beforehand whether I might be challenged disciplinarily. I need not have worried. The hotter the weather, the more the boys wanted to be left alone. If I remember Jamie Rosenberg it was because he was different from his peers. I think that he found the over-enthusiastic Pom slightly ridiculous and realized that much fun could be derived from judicious baiting.

Even at TKS, where country boarders predominated and the day boys failed to leaven the dough, there were many highly intelligent boys, some of whom worked very hard. After House Prayers one evening, when I had said something about the courage of Germans like Count von Moltke who had actively resisted Hitler, young Andrew Ashton left me with a great one-liner, 'The Moltkes are family friends.'

I have no doubt whatever that the alumni of a school like Sydney Grammar School would vigorously dispute the truth of my judgements, but they too were shaped and to some extent limited by the system and by the underlying 'culture'. For Australian schools, like the Australian economy, felt sheltered from the competition intrinsic to Britain and Europe. I was preaching to the converted when I described to HSC Economists the havoc being wreaked on the structures of British society in 1980 by the follies of monetarism as practised by Margaret Thatcher. (The lecture has a resonance, twenty years later, as we count the cost of Mrs T!) The truth was that Australian society was already paying a price for its relatively poor education. Unemployment among school leavers was higher than in Britain, yet the country had to import skilled workers and technicians from abroad, even Asia.

The spirit of competition pulsed through sport, not the classroom. Thus the TKS rowing eight practised every day, plus a breakfast run, plus weight-training and a run at lunch, plus an evening run. Beds were made for them by junior boys – shades of 'fagging' – and it was regarded as unreasonable to expect them to remain awake in your classes, let alone do any work. The Headmaster, the Reverend Stan Currle, urged the school to learn the chants to be shouted as the TKS boys ran on to the field. Matches against other schools were amazing occasions, with each age group running up to seven teams. As the day progressed the less able teams massed to cheer on their betters until, at the end of the day, about 800 boys from each school lined up on opposite sides of the field to form a tunnel through which their first fifteen exploded on to the field. No wonder the rugby was hard. My TKS Under 16 'C' fifteen would have seen off most Under 16 'A' sides in England.

The same, sadly, could be said of cricket. Our final term was illuminated by a visit by the touring cricketers of Tonbridge School. If Tonbridge was soft in rugby it was pre-eminent in English cricket. This eleven contained a Cowdrey and all were accomplished cricketers. Yet they lost every game in Sydney before they came out to Parramatta – and then they lost to TKS who had failed to win a single game all season. They weren't outbatted or outbowled, they were simply outfielded.

That said, cricket in Australia would have suited me. The light was wonderful and the ball came on to the bat. I even found that bowling leg breaks became suddenly easy and rewarding. My great moment came just before I left when I opened for the Staff against the school first eleven. My partner was Peter Philpott, just recovering from a triple bypass operation. He was out first, with the score at 51, of which he had scored 49, there had been one sundry and Tobin had scored one. By now, the locals were doubtless mindful of Geoffrey Boycott but, no longer overawed by the spectacle at the other end, I speeded up, swept a six beyond the ropes of the Wight Oval and left feeling that I had not disgraced the reputation of English cricket.

I cannot remember whether there was a drink after the game. If so, the boys would certainly not have been allowed to participate. When the Tonbridge party came to TKS and we threw a party for both cricket teams in 'our' house, it was made absolutely clear that alcohol was forbidden. This edict was pure 'wowser', a black and white version of morality that effectively disclaimed any responsibility for what happened the moment the boys entered 'Uni' – and embarked on an orgy of alcoholic excess against which TKS had supplied no effective inoculation.

Australians have their own peculiar attitude to authority. They mock it and criticize it, in private, but they rarely engage in frontal questioning or opposition. Jon Wickham loved to refer to Australia's 'cultural cringe'. Thus it was that the attitude of the TKS teachers to the governors resembled the repressed resentment of a people to an occupying power. At the very moment when we were about to leave for the airport, the school's archivist came round with a package in his hand. It was the school history that he had painstakingly written – and which had been formally proscribed by the Governors, on the grounds that its central thesis was that the ills that had dogged the school through its history could be ascribed to a single cause, the unhealthy dominance of the Old Boys. For years afterwards, teachers from TKS would beat a track to our door in England so that they could have sight of the forbidden volume. It was Kafkaesque!

At the beginning of the year I had, in purely historical terms, anticipated a fallow year, teaching World History by choice and Australian History on sufferance. It was not like that at all. The shelves of Jon Wickham's study were filled with marvellously interesting tomes about the making of Australia. Freed from the cares of Tonbridge, I immersed myself in them.

And there was Parramatta itself. TKS had recently moved out of Parramatta, up to Pennant Hills and the Gowan Brae Estate. It took its old chapel with it but was otherwise an utterly modern and somewhat soulless campus. The town of

Parramatta remained behind, sprawling alongside the Parramatta river that flowed turgidly for ten miles or so down to the Harbour Bridge and the ocean. By now it was at the centre of the larger sprawl that was taking Sydney to the foothills of the Blue Mountains. On the one hand, Parramatta was a brash, thrusting suburb, a mixture of the sleazy ugliness of downtown America with a 'Neighbours' world of neatly kept houses and futuristic shopping malls. On the other, it had been the first real settlement and cradle city of Australia – with its first farm, its first churches and Old Government House, where Governor Bligh (Bligh of the 'Bounty') had been arrested by the 'Rum Corps' as he hid under his bed. Each Sunday we went to Mass in St Patrick's, Australia's oldest Catholic church, and we would sometimes gaze at the tombstones around the church, with their stark testimony to Irish suffering and enforced exile.

I became especially interested in one of the founding fathers of wowserism, the Anglican clergyman, the Reverend Samuel Marsden. He had come out to Australia with the Second Fleet in the 1790s to be the colony's second chaplain and, full of his mission to save souls, he had established St John's church in Parramatta. He soon realized that saving souls in New South Wales was beyond human endeavour, so he made a fortune instead from their bodily labour, as he pioneered his flocks of merino sheep. He retained enough of his Evangelical conviction to take the message of Christianity to the Maoris of New Zealand, where his name is revered. In New South Wales, by contrast, he is an object of opprobrium, the flogging parson who, as magistrate, ripped the flesh off Irish convicts' backs, a hypocrite who was not above the perversion of justice for his own ends. Governor Macquarie, in so many ways the true idealist of those early days, condemned Marsden for his rancour. Marsden became the 'great survivor', outliving all others of the founding generation and dying in 1838. At TKS I taught many of his descendants.

Manning Clark, then the doyen of Australia's historians and the author of a marvellous account of its development, was Marsden's great-great grandson. When he was a five year old, his aged grandmother talked to him about the Reverend Marsden. She had recalled him vividly. The Reverend Marsden, she said, was not a *cruel* man, he was a severe man. That was how immediate and how interesting Australian history was to the visiting Pom in 1980. I was led into writing an essay on Marsden and on the Established Church's attitude to the Aborigines. I gave a lecture on 'Erastianism', the subordination of religion to political expediency, linking Marsden in Australia to Cranmer in England and contrasting each with Bonhoeffer and the 'Confessing' Protestants of Nazi Germany. There was time to read and I was stimulated to think.*

We used our holidays to see as much as possible of Australia. In the autumn

---

*I could not have imagined then that the Twentieth Century would end with the appointment of a former Archbishop of Sydney as Governor General of Australia, nor that the Twenty-First would begin with his resignation following allegations as lurid as any levied against Marsden.

On top of the world – Pigeon House Mountain, New South Wales, 1980.

we spent three nights camping in the Blue Mountains, with further nights at Canberra and Kiama. Margery and I took off with Lucy for a couple of nights in Melbourne, which seemed grey and Manchester-like in comparison with Sydney. We had an idyllic week in Ian and Natalie McLeod's seaside cottage in Broken Bay. And in August, when the younger forms went on camp, I accompanied Colin Carpenter for a week at Yadboro, south of Nowra and not far from the Snowy Mountains. He had warned me to take two sleeping bags and as much warm clothing as possible. Even so I have never been so cold as I was then, unable to cope with the massive drop in temperature from the mid-day sunshine to the night frost. We climbed the Pigeon House mountain, so named by Captain Cook, and I keep a photograph in my study as a proud reminder of my toughest climb, if not of my getting lost on the way down. 'Carps' tracked me by my footprints, only to admit defeat when these vanished on the road. True to Tobin luck, I had hitched a lift back to camp.

Our biggest venture, at the end of August and beginning of September, was a 3,000 mile journey to Queensland. After Quirindi and Yetman we stopped in on-site caravans in caravan parks, reaching Shute Harbour after six days on the road. There we spent a week, with boat trips to the islands of the Whitsunday Passage and to the coral and marine life of the inner Barrier Reef. We inspected sugar processing concerns and pineapple plantations, then returned to Sydney via the coastal route.

Sydney itself was wonderful. In terms of travel time we were no nearer to the metropolis than Tonbridge was to London but the impetus of our 'holiday year', coupled with an abundance of baby sitters, propelled us time and again into the great city or on to its beaches or out to the 'Heads' or into its national parks. It was a great help to us that we enjoyed the friendship of a number of English 'émigrés'. Jim Armstrong was now in Sydney and was the same gentle, kind and charming friend of twelve years earlier. Margery's great school friend, Dene Newman, was living in great style with her banker husband and two children because Roy's Canadian bank had posted him to Sydney. And a Tonbridge connection led to a warm friendship with Daphne and Alan Mayes, who had been similarly posted to Sydney, in their case from New Zealand.

Michael and Phillida Preston became great friends. Michael himself came from Sydney. I had first come across him in the year before we went to Sydney, when he was 'on exchange' from Marlborough to TKS. One of his Marlborough students, who lived near Tonbridge and who had left school, now wished to have a go at entering Oxford for History. Michael had suggested that I give him private tuition. (An extraordinary consequence of this was that we were invited out to dinner by the grateful parents and there met Michael's exchange partner, Jonathan Persse, shortly to be my own Head of Department at TKS.) By the time we reached Sydney Michael was Head of History at his old school, Cranbrook. He helped to organize the Tonbridge cricket team's itinerary in Sydney and that was how we met him. Michael and Phillida's sojourn in Australia did not last long, Michael returning to Marlborough and a house-mastership. In their different ways, Michael Preston, the ebullient scholar/sportsman, and Jonathan Persse, exquisitely mannered and eclectic, represented the class of Australian that was more English than the English. As such they were a dying breed in Australia and in Australian schools.

The somewhat ironic consequence of all these friendships and contacts was that we had a far richer cultural life in allegedly philistine Sydney than we ever had in London, with concerts, operas and plays in the Opera House, Town Hall and University, school parties to the Nimrod Theatre and exhibitions in the New South Wales Art Gallery. 'Carps' pointed us in the direction of the best Australian wines and most 'with it' restaurants in Paddington – it was a revelation to see young Australians as fully and justly proud of their wines as the most patriotic Frenchman – and, of course, there were cricket and rugby Tests at the Sydney Cricket Ground. I was there when the Ella brothers began the revolution that was to oust New Zealand from their hitherto unquestioned supremacy in antipodean and world rugby union. My one Aussie rules match was a nightmare of flying elbows and giant athletes, in the whole of which I did not gather a single ball.

At school we received wonderful hospitality from all the housemasters and many other members of the Common Room, especially those with children the age of Matthew, Emma and Lucy. If I recall with particular force a dinner at the house of Keith Asboe, the bachelor Head of Music, it is because we were sitting outside his house in 114 degrees, while, at next door's dinner party, the hostess shimmered back and forth in her bikini in the barely endurable heat. We returned to find all the boarders up and far from sleep, the indoor temperature at midnight being 95 degrees. Then the 'southerly buster' arrived and in two hours the temperature dropped twenty degrees.

Margery loved the climate, more than I did. It reminded her of childhood years in Bulawayo and Cape Town. Could we have stayed in Australia? Tony Hill asked if I was interested and I said 'No', pleading our respective and aging families back home. This was a valid enough reason but there were others. I noted that the young man from England, who had emigrated to Australia and who had started teaching Maths at TKS at the same time as we arrived, looked daily more miserable. An exchangee knows that he should enjoy the good things to the full and he knows also that every problem or negativity is a reason to celebrate going home at the end of the year. The emigrant cannot afford to dwell on the bad or not so good.

'Daddy,' Matthew asked when we touched down at Heathrow on the greyest of November days, 'Has there been a bush fire?' Everything in England seemed to be so drab, so small, so crowded, so colourless. The people seemed dull and dour. It was only too easy to forget that, in the TKS community, we did not encounter a representative sample of Australia, and that there were many aspects of Australian life that would have chafed and riled had we been seriously thinking of putting down roots and raising our family as young Australians. Little did we know that Australia was, in many of these facets, simply a decade or two in advance of where Britain would be.

There were also aspects of Australian life that we found very attractive. 'Class differences' were less obtrusive and less pronounced. What Ellen W, a poor immigrant from England, had written in 1846, remained broadly true.

> Oh, what a difference there is between this country and Home. I know I would not go back again – I know what England is. Old England is a fine place for the rich but the Lord help the poor.

Compared to starchy Kent we could not fail to be attracted by the general friendliness and by the absence of reserve or affectation that we encountered at TKS. The children led a more active and healthy existence, with the outdoor life making for easier friendships, even if we found their directness of utterance somewhat hard to take. In our imaginations, as in our cine film, we see Matthew and Emma dancing at Lane Cove, Emma and her friends Jacqui, Karen and Larissa, bobbing home from Burnside in a sunlight as magical as that in *Picnic at Hanging Rock*, Lucy rushing around in excitement as she chases the peacocks in the Koala Park and Peter 'Spanner' Spencer sitting at an endless barbecue with all our newfound friends. We took away with us the feeling that Australia was fully confident of 'making out', even if it was not at all sure of its identity or of where it was going. It was still the 'Lucky Country'.

Batteries fully recharged, we were convinced of the virtue of that great Australian institution, (paid) Long Service Leave. Back in England our family, friends and colleagues still nurtured the convenient English prejudice that it is rather irresponsible and pointless to suspend your career to cross the world and bask in the sun. Thank God, so many of our Australian friends would conform to Australian wisdom, pursue their own exchange years in Britain – and come to remind us of our good fortune in saying 'Yes' to such a chimerical proposition.

I returned, bronzed, slimmer, fitter in mind and body, to a once-in-a-lifetime opportunity job that might never have come my way had I not been rejuvenated in Parramatta – the headship of Prior Park College.

CHAPTER 11

A Sense of Mission

Whatever education I had in English landscape, in architecture, in corncrakes and nightjars and fields of cowslip and deep grass, in woods full of wild garlic, in the underworld of caves and abandoned quarries, in river swimming and in solitary reading and in wandering about at night, I got in that artificial paradise running gently to seed.

(Peter Levi, *The Flutes of Autumn*)

IT WAS MY AUNT KOO who saw the advertisement in *The Times* and sent it to me in Parramatta, with a postscript, 'By the time you receive this it will probably be too late to apply.' Mail normally took a week, either way. If I posted an application that day it would probably arrive on the closing date. As it did, after I had hammered out application letter and curriculum vitae on the Common Room typewriter. Next day we headed for Queensland.

Prior Park College was seeking a lay headmaster, the first Catholic boarding school run by a religious order to do so. The advertisement did not say that the Congregation of Christian Brothers had at first announced the closure of the school, granting a stay of execution only in response to the vigorous campaign of a group of Old Boys, including three Catholic bishops. To me it seemed like the answer to a prayer. I had left St Benedict's in part because the laity had been denied the influence implicit in the Second Vatican Council. I had admired the order and efficiency of Christ College and, especially, Tonbridge, but knew that I could never be the Head of an Anglican school. And although I had been neither a boarder nor a housemaster, I had spent the last ten years in three boarding schools, including five as a house tutor.

So I had no hesitation in applying and when we returned from our Queensland holiday I looked eagerly for a letter from Bath. And there it was, from the Clerk to the Action Committee, Mr John Bogie, summoning me to interview.

My three male Good cousins had attended Prior Park College, but it was as John Bogie's friend that I had made my one visit in 1964, making up the numbers of the Old Boys' Tennis VI against the School. John and I had sustained Christmas card contact since then but I was unaware that he had fallen out with the Christian Brothers at St Brendan's College, Bristol, and that he had left teaching and gone into the construction business. Hence he was free to intervene when the Brothers announced Prior Park's closure and to become the driving force behind its salvation. Prior Park was remarkably fortunate to enlist so bold a buccaneer in its hour of need. As for me, it was hard not to hear the whispering of providence.

There were two rounds of interviews but, in view of my need to organize flights at relatively short notice, the Action Group selected me for the final round and asked me to attend interviews on consecutive days. 'Christ, you must be in with a shout,' exclaimed Carps, 'Unless you vomit on the carpet.'

On the long journey home from Sydney I had ample time to write out every conceivable question and mull over my answers to them.

> *What do you see as the role of the Catholic school in today's world?* To bring home to every boy that the Church teaches that God loves him infinitely, so that what he does and what others do MATTERS. To help a boy's grasp of cradle truths to develop along with other facets of his personality. To train Catholics to play their full part in the world. My belief in Catholic education has increased in the years that I have been out of it. I have missed in non-Catholic schools that feeling of shared commitment which I experienced at St Benedict's. I am interested that in Australia non-Catholics, confronted by the choice between the Kingdom of God and the Kingdom of Nothingness, are increasingly sending their children to Catholic schools.

And so on.

Such ideas were very much my own, to the extent that they have hardly changed twenty years later. There was, however, someone giving shape to my thoughts on headship as such, Dr James Darling, the renowned Headmaster of Geelong Grammar School. I had found his autobiography in Jon Wickham's study. By an extraordinary coincidence Darling had been born in a Victorian house in Tonbridge that now belonged to Tonbridge School. His writings were full of pearls of wisdom. The boys themselves were the only valid advertisement for a school. At Geelong boys could, of course, 'drift' – but they could not drift with a clear conscience. At the beginning of every term he always tried to have something new for the boys to find when they came back. This was not only a morale boost; because they wrote to tell their parents it was also a very good advertisement for the school. And – most obscurely and, as I was to find, most wisely – the Headmaster must always be certain of the purity of his own motives.

This was an 'Around the World in Seven Days' trip. I travelled directly from Sydney to London but for my return, conscious that the Prior Park governors would have to meet the bill, I booked a very cheap flight from Los Angeles to Sydney. When I reached London I would have to buy a 'pondhopper' ticket to Los Angeles. Fog threw these plans into disarray. By the time I reached Heathrow I had been on a six hour diversion to Scotland. I rushed frantically to a travel agent to purchase my ticket to Los Angeles, then turned up exhausted at Hildenborough to spend the night in my house as a guest of the Wickhams. At

3 a.m. I was woken by the unmistakable sound of the failed pump of our dishwasher!

The Tonbridge History department seemed to be thriving in my absence, despite the subsequent departure of Andrew Reekes to run his own department elsewhere. David Walsh had become 'caretaker manager', while Andrew's shoes were now filled by my ex-pupil, Joe Davies, who had won his Blue at Cambridge and established an outstanding reputation for himself at St John's College.

A letter from Christopher Everett awaited me, inviting me to see him before my interview. He was hugely reassuring. 'Don't worry. If the school closes they always need the Headmaster to stay on for a few years afterwards to clear up the mess.'

John Bogie met me at Bath Spa Station and drove me into the school grounds by the lower entrance so that my first impression would be of that majestic sweep of Palladian architecture and of the ravishing view of the valley and its bridge. We then walked around the school and he described impressively the flats that were already being fashioned for the first lay housemasters and house tutors. I suspect that I did not need to be converted but it was impossible not to be fired with the excitement of launching such a brave new world. I remember visiting the local Catholic church, praying that God's will be done – and reading a pamphlet that would serve me well in my second interview.

The first interview went well, but jet lag set in a with a vengeance next day. I found difficulty in supplying intelligent answers to questions that I had already answered on the previous day, the more so as three of the interviewers had been on the earlier panel. The Chairman of Trustees, Bishop Cormac Murphy O'Connor, was friendly, courteous and positive, as was the external assessor, Michael McCrum. At the end of it all John Bogie hinted that he would try to let me know the outcome before I flew home. I wondered which would be the greater ordeal – thirty hours in ignorance or thirty hours in the knowledge that my round the world trip had been in vain. As it was the news was good, I phoned Margery and then winged my way to Los Angeles – the only night I have ever spent in the USA – and across the Pacific in a beatific daze. I had fulfilled Paul Olsen's promise to my mother, and with a month to spare.

Back in Sydney Margery had had to explain my absence to the children. 'Mummy,' Matthew asked, 'Do you think Daddy is *ready* to be a headmaster?' 'Aaw, it'll be awl ryte,' Emma rasped, 'Ee won't get the jawb!' When Margery told the children that I had indeed been appointed Emma became a little confused. While I had been in England there had been a General Election in Australia, leading to the re-election of Malcolm Fraser's government. Emma therefore concluded that her father was the new Prime Minister – and was mortified when she discovered that this was not the case. Thereafter she referred to my headship as 'Daddy's little job'. Some of my TKS colleagues were equally unwilling to be impressed. I inadvertently overheard a Common Room conversation – 'What do you think of Patrick's job?' 'I think it's a pretty rum school.'

Prior Park's history was indeed as idiosyncratic as that of any HMC school. Peter Augustine Baines, a monk of Ampleforth and an 'ideas man' of boundless vision, had conceived the idea of a Benedictine return to Bath nine years before his consecration as Vicar Apostolic of the Western District in 1823. He had first tried to persuade the monks of Downside to move nearer to Bath. Thwarted in this, and with much encouragement from the prior of his own monastery, he suggested an exchange whereby the Downside community moved to Yorkshire and the Ampleforth monks joined him in his missionary work in the South West. There then came on to the market the magnificent house of Prior Park built by John Wood for Ralph Allen a hundred years earlier. Baines would have found the sumptuous Palladian mansion irresistibly redolent of Rome, so he purchased it, seduced three monks and twenty-six novices and students from Ampleforth to Bath, and assured himself of enduring infamy in Ampleforth's collective memory. 'That scoundrel, Baines,' was the curt comment of Cardinal Hume on the only occasion I met him.

Baines established Prior Park College in 1830 as school and seminary. From the outset it was fraught with problems, human and financial. There was a disastrous fire in 1836, the Fathers of Charity imported from Italy left after about seven years and Baines died a broken man in 1843. His successor, Bishop Baggs, survived only three years. Bishop Ullathorne, himself a Downside monk, loathed Prior Park, this pagan palace where the Anglican Bishop Warburton's cross was the only exterior sign of Christian identity, while inside there was not one statue of a saint, not even the Virgin Mary. Ullathorne quoting with relish the comment of Dr Gentili that 'the devil was in the place', dismissed it as 'a bottomless pit, receiving everything, giving back nothing.' He moved his headquarters from Bath to Clifton, so that Prior Park's future became even more questionable. When Ullathorne's successor, Bishop Burgess, went early to his maker in 1854, it was said that Prior Park had killed three bishops. The school was closed in 1856 by Bishop Errington and rapidly became a wilderness. Some Downside monks, visiting the wasteland of Bishop Baines' dreams, were startled to find in a classroom two coffins, containing the unburied bodies of Bishop Baines and his nephew. Out of Christian charity, the corpses were taken to Downside for burial.

Eleven years later, Baines' dream was rekindled. Bishop Clifford, himself educated at Prior Park, saw fit to re-purchase it for the diocese of Clifton, transferring the Catholic Clifton Grammar School to Bath. In doing so he braved the displeasure of his father, Lord Clifford, who warned him that Prior Park would be a 'white elephant'. In fact it flourished under the gifted leadership of Monsignor Williams and for a quarter of a century there was hope.

The magnificent chapel was opened in 1882 and the corridor next to it became the burial place of Bishop Errington, Monsignor Williams and, in time, of Bishop Clifford himself. But the health of the College and of Bishop Clifford declined together. Clifford's successor wanted only to relieve himself of the white elephant and in 1895 he devolved the running of the school to the Irish Christian Brothers, on a seven year lease.

The Brothers proved so successful that in 1902 a new Bishop was persuaded to terminate the Brothers' lease and bring Prior Park back under diocesan control. This calamitous decision rapidly led to the second closure of Prior Park College. It had become a borstal by 1924, when a boy who had escaped from his dormitory was found in chains in Bath. The unfavourable publicity induced the Bishop to eat humble pie and hand to the Christian Brothers the freehold of Prior Park, on condition that they reopen the school.

Under the Christian Brothers it had become Irish to the core – it was said that it even kept Irish time – and there was a puritan austerity about it, flavoured, as visiting rugby coaches found to their delight, with much whisky. In many ways it resembled a seminary rather than an aspiring public school.

Many parents who had themselves been schooled by the Brothers specifically liked this lack of affectation, although it is fair to speculate that as many had been repelled by their traditionally caustic discipline. The paradox was that Christian Brother Prior Park was more than usually successful in producing its minority of eccentric notables – poets and professors, Peter Levi was both, theatre directors and bishops. Cameron Mackintosh, later to be very generous in his funding of the Prior Park theatre, owed a great deal to the genius of Hedley Goodall, a visiting impresario to whom the Brothers accorded dictatorial licence in his annual school productions and under whom Prior Park acquired a notable theatrical reputation.

During our final weeks in Sydney I sought and found some inspiration in the history of New South Wales Catholicism. If I did not make Ned Kelly one of my heroes, I did note that two of its greatest apostles had emanated from Downside. The Spanish Benedictine monk, Rosando Salvado, learned his English there before he embarked on his heroic mission to the Aborigines, while Ullathorne rendered devoted service to the Catholic convicts of New South Wales before he was shipped home, from the flogging triangles and convict huts of Sydney to the Palladian grandeur of Prior Park. More to the point, I took myself off to St Ignatius' College at Riverview in Sydney to see how the Jesuits tried to give structure and meaning to their educational mission through the programmes that they called 'Conscientization'.

We had intended to cross Australia on the way home and had booked seats on the 'Indian Pacific' train to Perth, via Adelaide. Instead we rushed home so that I could attend Prior Park's Sesquicentennial dinner. John Bogie had arranged a challenging programme for me, a reading at Mass, a place in the Old Boys' rugby team against the school and the final and seventh berth as after dinner speaker. I doubt whether I distinguished myself in any of these. It was many years since I had last played rugby, and it showed. At Mass, when I moved forward to deliver my reading, I found no clue in the Lectionary as to what it should be and had to stand mute for an unconscionable time before someone came forward to rescue me. And at the Dinner, everyone had had enough by the time I stood up to speak – notably one female partner of an Old Boy who, when I was announced, shrieked, 'Oh God, not another one,' before she was escorted from the room.

The dinner had a more unfortunate and near catastrophic aspect. The Chairman of Governors, Fergus Lyons, himself an Old Boy, sought humour in some of his recollections of some of the Christian Brothers who had taught him. This so enraged the Provincial, Brother Coffey that, for a while, it was in doubt whether the Order would proceed with the grant of £200,000 to its fledgling successor. As it was, Brother Coffey insisted thereafter on dealing with the new Governors through me, rather than through my Chairman. It was an inauspicious start.

I had two terms still to teach at Tonbridge. I remember little of this brief phase, other than that one of my Sixth Form historians, Charles Hoare, told me innocently one day that he thought that I had 'improved' in consequence of my year in Australia. I have no doubt whatever that he was right. I emerged as the equal of Jonathan Smith in my advocacy of all things Australian – and I waxed boring to the Winebibbers on the subject of Samuel Marsden and Erastianism.

I took as a text a throwaway remark in the Common Room by Robert Austin, that gentlest and most civilized of housemasters, to the effect that the great thing about Chapel was that it brought the whole school together. I chose to see in this the parochial recapitulation of Napoleon's classic summary of Erastianism – 'I see in religion not the mystery of the Incarnation but the mystery of Order in society.' I drew on my Australian insights, particularly the reflex of the Protestant establishment, confronted in the second half of the nineteenth century by the ever increasing influence of the Catholic Church, to prevent public funding for Catholic schools by insisting that all State education should be secular. Thereby they had effectively destroyed the educational roots of Protestantism in Australia. Meanwhile, the Catholic bishops and priests had mobilised their congregations into building their own schools, out of minimal resources, with the consequence that every Catholic school in Australia was an Independent school. By the middle of the twentieth century, as Donald Horne recounted in *The Lucky Country*, the result of this was that Australia had become, in terms of religious practice and commitment, two very different nations.

The non-Catholic churches are now stripped of all except the most vague doctrines...Protestantism has been drained of almost all serious intellectual and moral content. Seriousness might keep people away from the Church...What is unAustralian about the Catholic Church is that it still instils a belief in the Church's universal teaching. Catholics are provided with a much more complex set of attitudes to life than other Australians. They are expected to learn these and make it part of their lives.

At Tonbridge the cycle of chapel worship seemed to induce the stupefied passivity of the London commuter enduring his train journey to work. There was a yawning contrast between the commitment and evident integrity of the Chaplain and the apathy of pupils for whom Tonbridge was essentially the route to academic success and worldly status. In my final chapel address at Tonbridge I tried to put this message to the boys.

> Tonbridge chapel should mean an opening to questions and to mystery, not a cool place to get married in. Nor should a regard for standards produce the cool brush-off for which English public schoolboys are notorious, the haughty disdain which makes you feel pleasantly superior but which gets in the way of so many relationships, so much love.

I wanted Prior Park Catholicism to be a confident, lay affirmation of the Catholic *family*. It should be demanding, outward-looking, speaking of pilgrimage towards God. Yet, if pressed, I would have had to admit that I suspected that the Catholic Church in England was going the way of its Anglican brethren. No longer did young Catholics perceive that they owed a loyalty to the blood of their martyrs. The intensity of the ghetto was giving way to the enjoyment of social acceptability. The Catholic laity, none more evidently than myself, had generally failed to listen to the call of the Spirit to transform the world around us. The Church had shaken off its deference to the clergy but the responsible laity had not thrust forward to fill the vacuum. The Catholic teacher tended to be less focused on academic success than his Anglican counterpart. It did not follow that (s)he was necessarily more spiritual or apostolic.

I thought that it was tragic that modern man should be so oblivious of the lessons of the Twentieth Century, when bloodshed and misery hitherto unimaginable in their scale were inflicted on millions by avowedly godless regimes. For some years I had been teaching Nazi Germany as the Advanced Level History Special Subject. I was struck by the fact that, while most Germans either supported Hitler or were acquiescent, a few had the vision and courage to know that they owed a higher loyalty. Some of these were Communists. More were Christians. That was why I had been talking about Count Moltke to Andrew Ashton and his friends in Forrest House. Moltke once said that, before the War, he had held that Christianity should not be taught in schools. Now he knew that this was wrong, quite wrong.

I wanted Prior Park to be *different*, not only from the typical Anglican 'public school', but even from the moneyed bastions of 'upper class' Catholicism, the

Ampleforths and Stonyhursts, with which, after all, my struggling school would have to compete. At my interview I had spoken of my 'vision' for the school. It was, in truth, a half-baked vision, cerebral rather than truly personal, lacking as it did a firm basis in active personal commitment, but it was sincere as far as it went and it explains some of my more extraordinary decisions and actions in my first years of headship.

Such was the 'philosophy' that I brought to headship. Looking back I blush at my stew of superficiality and prejudice. The Tonbridge Common Room was characterized by the devotedly Evangelical commitment of many of its members, men whose sincerity and integrity far eclipsed mine. My critique rested on a bare modicum of religious practice and on a particular view of History. I was to find that it is very easy to criticize others for their failure and notably difficult to succeed in creating anything truly substantial when given the chance to do so. I would leave Prior Park knowing not so much that I had largely failed as that I had barely begun to scratch at the task.

Which was why I was so pleased and surprised twenty years later by something Jack Ind said to me. He had taught at Prior Park for two spells after his retirement as a headmaster and he had loved it as much as Prior Park had loved him. 'Prior Park is a wonderful school, Patrick, and I tell you this. It succeeds where Tonbridge fails – in giving religion a central place. I hear that you had something to do with that.' If so, I can only murmur, 'Ex opere operato'.

During my last two terms at Tonbridge I had more mundane tasks on my mind. The Christian Brothers were pulling out totally from the school, although they would go on occupying 'The Priory', an elegant house in the grounds, as the Provincialate for the Order in England. This meant that I had to appoint one third of the teaching staff between January and June 1982, not to mention a Bursar and the Housemasters of the senior and junior boarding houses, respectively St Paul's and St Peter's. Scarcely a week passed without its train journey from Tonbridge to Bath. Few headmasters, in modern times at least, can have been free to write on such a blank sheet.

I made my appointments after I had composed a new timetable for the school. In the old Prior Park the Brothers had run the boarding side and the lay teaching staff tended to go home as soon as classes ended. So pronounced was this division, indeed, that the lay staff were known as the 'visiting' Common Room. I was determine to make it clear from the start that the new Prior Park would be seen from the start to be engaging the boys after school and at weekends. My predecessor, Brother Miller, was generously supportive of my radical changes.

I was lucky to secure some very good teachers. Three of these were talented young women, Ginette Ayres (to teach Physics), Anna Greenwood (English) and Helen Carpenter (Head of Modern Languages). A key appointment was that of Director of Music. Andrew Mock would achieve a great deal during the next eight years. Into the Biology department came Richard Wells, then working with The Wildfowl Trust at Slimbridge, who came into teaching at Prior Park without any formal training or qualification other than his degree and doctorate. He thought that he would give it a couple of years. He is at Prior Park still, as Head of Science and ex-housemaster. Gerald Davies also remains, after a brief period as headmaster elsewhere. In him I found a Catholic Mathematician, Deputy Housemaster of St Paul's, School Timetabler and First Fifteen coach.

Perhaps the most significant challenge was the appointment of the two Housemasters. None of the existing staff had been involved with the boarding houses. I selected one of them, John Moran, as Housemaster of St Peter's and he proved to be as rocklike in faith and support as his house's patron saint. For St Paul's, by contrast, I did not select the inside candidate but gambled on the class and charisma of an outsider.

Dr Peter Walshe, Professor of International Relations at Notre Dame University, Indiana, happened to be in England at the time we advertised and he came over to meet John Bogie. Here was a man who seemed to fit my vision of the Catholic Independent school for the 1980s. In terms of Church politics he was on the Radical Left, the fierce critic, for instance, of United States policy towards El Salvador or Guatemala. Having played for South African Schools in Cricket he had won Blues at Oxford University in Cricket and Hockey. And he had been educated at Milton School, Bulawayo, where Margery's father had taught before the war. Serendipity ruled.

As it did in the even more problematic appointment of School Chaplain. This was a crucial post if we were to persuade parents that the withdrawal of the Brothers did not spell the end of the School's authentically Catholic character. No advertisements and none of our three bishops availed to fill this vacancy. It was then that we took Matthew for his First Communion class in the Catholic church in Tonbridge, where the visiting speaker was a gentle priest from Sussex with a quaint sense of humour and a Father Christmas beard. He had been a prison chaplain and was, we were told, not responsible for a parish because of problems with his heart. Father Paul Edwards seemed to me to have much to recommend him – and he was in Bishop Cormac's diocese of Arundel and Brighton! The Bishop was at first surprised, then impressed, by my suggestion. Father Paul would be one of our number in September 1981.

We needed an Infirmary Sister too. The two House Matrons had left with the Brothers and we intended to replace them with one School Matron, who would have her base in the main mansion. Eileen McPeake, then Matron at Berkhamsted, approached the school as a prospective parent, rather than as a potential Matron. In the event her son went to Stonyhurst, but Eileen has been, from January 1982 until the time of writing, central to the success of the lay enterprise at Prior Park.

John Bogie, meanwhile, had been appointed Headmaster of Cricklade, Prior Park's Preparatory School near Swindon, a mere 37 miles from Bath! He too was busily assembling his lay team. During these two terms, however, he also continued to play an indispensable role in preparing for the new order at Prior Park, disbursing £481,000 on the physical adaptations without which we could not have started in September and personally directing this work. John found his Clerk of Works in George Jenkins, an NCO in Clive Bogie's regiment in Germany. He had also recruited an exceptionally quick, talented and personable PA in Susie Holmes and I was fortunate indeed when she agreed to remain at Prior Park as my Secretary. Brother Miller's Secretary, Jane Floyd, now undertook the Clothes Shop, no small task as the whole school had to be provided with a new school uniform. In place of grey suits the boys would now wear herringbone jackets or blue sports jackets, creating a much less 'institutional' feel to the place. All of these would see me out of Prior Park and most would be there fourteen years later.

I have left until last perhaps the most crucial of all the appointments made by John Bogie and me, the Bursar whom we would share throughout my time in Bath. In John Leay, a young accountant without any previous experience in schools, we found the ideal Bursar, quick and creative with figures – and not averse to driving school buses or dirtying his arm down drains. Later he would prove as adept in shaping salary scales and in cultivating our bankers. On my advice, the Governors agreed that the Bursar should answer to the Headmaster and that he should not be Clerk to the Governors. Nothing in the next two decades has weakened my belief in the wisdom of this course. Many schools have paid a high price for sticking to outworn formulae in this regard.

At a special Open Day on 7 March 1981, as much to reassure existing parents as to recruit new pupils, I was able to report on most of these appointments. I ended by speaking of 'an unique opportunity' –

> to build an Independent Catholic school, in tune with the spirit of the Church today, on the basis of the dedication and commitment left by the Christian Brothers. That is the mission for Prior Park which distinguishes it from all other Catholic schools in The Headmasters' Conference. I can assure you that to be at Prior Park in the next decade will be an exciting and stimulating experience.

There was a delicious postscript to my list of new appointments. We had been in Bath several days when I was phoned by Pauline King. She knew an excellent young man, a Catholic and Oxford Cricket Blue, who had taught Classics at Marlborough before attempting to become a county cricketer with Worcestershire. He was looking for a post for a term before going out to New Zealand. I am sorry, I replied, but we are full. An hour later, Michael Preston rang. Was I interested in an excellent young man, a Catholic Cricket Blue and wicket keeper for Worcestershire, who had been a colleague of his at

Marlborough. Tuned as I was to Serendipity, I gave a different answer this time. I had no paid job to offer, but would the young man like to do some teaching and rugby coaching and house tutoring for 'pocket money' for a term? Paul Fisher duly moved into the new flat on the first floor of St Paul's. A month or two later he came over to our house. 'Patrick,' he said, 'I thought you ought to know. Helen and I have become engaged.' 'Helen who?' I asked. Paul was clearly gobsmacked. I was the only person at Prior Park not to know that his Helen was my new Head of Modern Languages. Paul would not be going to New Zealand, after all. Instead he stayed to become Housemaster of St Paul's and, in time, the headmaster of two HMC schools.

It was all a wonderful opportunity and a heady and seductive experience. I fear that I was insufficiently grateful and appreciative towards two headmasters, Christopher Everett, who never once objected to my repeated absences from Tonbridge School, and Brother Gregory Miller, the last Christian Brother President of the College. (I was somewhat sad when the new Governors decided that 'Headmaster' was preferable to 'President'!) It cannot have been easy for Brother Miller to behold this brash young man reconstructing the school that he loved. No one could have been more patient or more generously supportive. In Nick Gompels and Paul Wolstencroft, Head Boy and Deputy respectively, he bequeathed me a thoroughly dignified and decent leadership duo.

On the day before the boys returned to their much changed school Bishop Cormac presided over a 'Colloquium' of the Prior Park Common Room, during which he commended an increasingly neglected virtue, 'Stickability'.

The 'Old Guard' seemed tentative. Traumatized by the announcement that their school was about to close, hardly daring to believe that it might yet be saved, they were now being asked to put their trust in someone who was doing his best to make the school different from what it had ever been before and to welcome an unprecedented number of newcomers into their hitherto small and tightly knit body. Sidney Ash, the Deputy Head and veteran of 35 years at Prior Park, was wonderful in his handling of the challenge. To me he was the unfailingly tactful spokesman of the concerns of his long-time friends and associates. To them he provided unswerving leadership in the 'right' direction. There must have been many times in the next two years when he must have wondered whether the tension between these two roles was actually bearable.

The clouds were already visible. The A/L and O/L examination results were not merely worse by far than Tonbridge's; they were dreadful. More serious even than this was the shortage of pupils. The new Governors had approved the proposal of John Bogie and myself that the Cricklade boys, who had hitherto come to Bath at twelve, should stay a further year at the Preparatory School and sit the Common Entrance examination as their route to admission into Prior Park. John and I argued that the long-term interests of Prior Park College

September 30th 1981, Sophie's entry into the Tobin family.

depended on the viability of Cricklade. On the other hand, this strategy carried with it the concomitant risk that Common Entrance would enable parents to use Cricklade as a springboard into other HMC schools. We were prepared to take that risk. It was, therefore, an extremely nasty shock to arrive in August and discover that, in place of the 260 pupils promised for the Senior School, there would be only 232. In effect, we were without the fees that paid two teachers. Every small boarding school tends to be dragged down by its fixed costs, so that even the smallest surplus becomes a struggle. Prior Park, with its palatial overheads, faced early extinction. Our 'brave' decision to turn away 12+ boarders now seemed foolhardy. Time perhaps would prove us right. In September 1981 time was not on our side!

Meanwhile, two boys gave us an early indication of the human storms that lay ahead. 'M' and 'S' knocked on the door of the new Headmaster's house, 'Kent House', and asked to speak to me. Margery invited them in and we sat them down. They told me that they had heard that I was trying to turn Prior Park into Eton. They informed Margery that it was inconceivable that a married man could successfully run Prior Park. It was clear that these views were not their own views so much as prejudices sown and fostered by some of the outgoing Brothers and House staff. We had been warned.

It was a rude reminder that life in 'Kent House' would not be the rural idyll suggested by those last days of holiday. Kent House was the little cottage that had been expanded and embellished into the new headmaster's residence through the financial support of a millionaire Old Boy, Michael Kent. Behind it reared woods in which the children would spend happy hours. For Matthew, Emma and Lucy, Kent House is a blessed memory. For Sophie it was something more, her home for the first eight years of her life.

Our Australian odyssey had yielded this last and greatest benefit, the urge to increase our family. When I told David Walsh, as we walked down Tonbridge High Street, that Margery was expecting a baby in September, he replied, 'You must be mad.' Sophie was born on 30 September, just a fortnight after I became Headmaster. I gave the school a half-holiday, on the grounds that this was a unique occurrence in the school's history, and Sophie was baptized in the lovely chapel during a Sunday Mass.

This was honeymoon indeed! How long would it last? Its ending was earlier and more brutal than we could have imagined or feared.

CHAPTER 12

Honeymoon, what honeymoon?

To a greater extent than with other masters, a headmaster's work must be a Christian vocation. He must never forget his responsibility for every human soul, man and boy, over whom he exercises for a short or long time so great an influence. To do it adequately he should be saint as well as scholar. In addition he needs more pedestrian qualities, those of the orator, even the actor, the organizer, the financier, the architect, the lawyer and sometimes even the detective. Heaven help us! It isn't surprising that we weren't very good at it.

Sir James Darling, 1965

ON THE VERY FIRST evening of the new order, Gerald Davies telephoned and asked me to come across to St Paul's. He showed me round a selection of sixth form rooms, most of which were already in a disgraceful state. What was to be done?

In retrospect an easy answer suggests itself. We should have 'cracked down' immediately, banned all smoking in rooms on grounds of safety, introduced a regime of stringent room checks and dealt decisively with any and all who refused to toe the line. Perhaps that is what Gerald favoured. It was clear that he was truly shocked by what he had found. But there was something else. He was dissociating himself immediately from the liberal, anti-authoritarian, 'hearts-and-minds' philosophy of Peter Walshe – and I had chosen Peter, not Gerald, to be the housemaster of the senior boarding house. Battle lines were being drawn, within the Common Room as much as between staff and boys.

I was in the middle. My instincts were authoritarian. On the other hand, with the school balanced on a tightrope and with every nerve end telling me that I had never been in a school or a situation like this, my brain was telling me to play for time, co-exist with attitudes and boys foreign to me and yet try to build the new school out of the old.

On my side was the very real affection of the senior boys for the school that they had so nearly lost. The First Fifteen, led by the future Scottish international, Damian Cronin, happened to be remarkably strong. They responded well to the coaching of Gerald Davies and Paul Fisher and they won most of their school matches. There was something deeper too. As the new regime mounted Open Day after Open Day to proclaim its survival and intentions and to show off the sumptuous Prior Park landscape, the boys picked up the theme. At the end of the first term they organized a 'Palladian Ball' with some swagger and panache.

Against me was the shared perception of these senior boys that I was trying to make Prior Park a *different* school. They were torn between a desire that they and their school should flourish and an utterly human instinct to look backwards towards the world and the Brothers they had known. I was told later that one of those who had greatest difficulty in managing the transition had a telephone conversation every evening with his former housemaster in Liverpool. Later events suggested that the 'counselling' was anything but helpful.

Each Sunday two sixth formers would come over to Kent House to have Sunday lunch with the Tobins and each Sunday we would get the same message. Prior Park was a 'happy' school. Why did we want to change it? My Head Boy, sensing the malaise, advised me to appoint as a prefect a boy who had not previously commended himself to Sidney Ash. I decided to accept this advice. At the next school assembly I formally announced the new appointment. The young man came up casually, shook my hand, took the tie, turned – and waved to his friends at the back.

Even so the illusion of honeymoon was briefly sustained. Peter Walshe gave a series of inspiring talks to the Sixth Form about South Africa. Peter Sibley, veteran teacher at nearby Monkton Combe, told me that there was now a real 'buzz' about the school. Then, at supper after the Second Fifteen had achieved their first victory of the term, two of its more popular members jumped up and down on the thick dining table so hard that it split. Their suspension was taken as a declaration of war.

These circumstances blighted Prior Park's first ever Guy Fawkes celebration. This was an arguably tactless initiative by the first lay headmaster of a robustly Catholic school, but the slopes below the Mansion had seemed the perfect setting for a fireworks party and this would be the first of many. We did not burn a Guy but we lit a good fire. Through its kaleidoscope of spurting flame and dark shadow, shapes scuttled with conspiratorial menace. We heard that a prefect had cast his tie into the blaze.

It transpired that this report was true. Peter Walshe recommended that we treat the incident as a case of undue emotional stress and that the resigning prefect should be sent home to collect himself. If we hoped that this would be the end of the affair we were disabused at the hymn practice on the following Saturday morning. The boys sullenly remained silent. I went up to the front and told them that there would be no leave that afternoon until we had had an adequate hymn practice. This time they sang. I think that it was after this traumatic experience that I was walking back to Kent House and had just passed the Mansion when a middle-aged man stopped me. I did not recognize him and I never saw him again but it was for me a momentous encounter. He said simply that I was doing a great job and that there were very many people out there who were solidly behind me. Then he walked on and away. It was like an apparition. Peter Walshe, meanwhile, addressing St Paul's in the school chapel with the authority and eloquence of a paternalistic prophet, movingly compared our troubles to the pains of childbirth.

Another week passed and another Saturday arrived, this time a normal Saturday with a First Fifteen match. Gerald Davies picked a side without the absent ex-prefect. We were having our family lunch when Gerald telephoned with the news that the young man had turned up, that he had insisted on his right to play and that Gerald had sent him over to me to present his case. I stood my ground and told him that the side that had been announced would play. He yelled that I was the 'biggest all time bastard' and stormed out, leaving behind him my shaken children. So much for the 'family school'!

In these circumstances my first Old Boys' Reunion was bound to be a challenge. The more elderly members of the Prior Park Association were positive and supportive. It was left to a more recent leaver to articulate the feelings of many. Taking me into a corner after tea, he told me that he was sick of hearing about all the improvements that we were claiming. He himself had been very proud of his old school and I had no right to challenge that. I imagine that I replied by agreeing with him and by telling him that my only wish was to secure a future for his school. The fact that I remember that brief exchange is proof that his message sank home.

By the end of term the worst seemed behind us. A blanket of snow threatened to obliterate the Palladian Ball, as the two girls' schools that had agreed to supply partners for our boys cancelled at the last minute, but frantic local research supplied a sufficient number of replacements and the Ball's success eclipsed the expulsion of an arrogantly recalcitrant young man whom Peter Walshe discovered in bed with a girl. On the final evening of term, the school assembled in chapel for a truly lovely Carol Service, Mrs Fox told me that I must be very proud and I got into bed full of sentiments of peace and goodwill. A moment later the phone rang. It was Peter Walshe. During the service the house safe had been burgled and all the boys' money (£130) had been taken. What should we do? I told him that he should call the police and I was on my way over.

As I strode across to St Paul's my only sensible thoughts were of needles in haystacks. Marching into the House and trying to seem composed, I passed 'M', one of the two boys who had visited Margery and me on the day before term. 'Were you in chapel?' I barked, not waiting for an answer as I had no reason for asking the question. Peter, Gerald and I gathered in his study and waited for the police to arrive. A minute or so later there was a knock at the door. 'M' and two others were outside. He had rushed from his encounter with me to tell his friends that I knew. They handed over the money and stood by as we requested the attendance of their parents next morning. The police arrived and told us that there was nothing for them to do. 'You seem to have solved it already.' Peter, Gerald and I unwound over a long whisky. A mighty Providence seemed to have delivered us.

Prior Park always looks wonderful, but in the snow...!

Perhaps it was that sentiment that impelled me to give the three boys their last chances, perhaps I was swayed also by thoughts of the School finances, but it was clear by then that they had danced to another's tune. The young man who had cast his prefect's tie into the fire had been seen in the House. This was his blow against the new regime. I brought to an end his status as a pupil of the School, but we assumed his involvement later that year when we awoke to find that the tyres of our new estate car had been slashed and that acid had been poured on to its bonnet. A few years later he would die tragically in an accident at home. I grieved then and I grieve now for him and his family.

As usual we spent Christmas in Chideock, but this time in our own home rather than with Margery's parents. For the price of our main road house in Hildenborough, we had acquired a relatively new house that looked up to the hills – and to the cross that commemorated the Elizabethan Catholic martyrs of Chideock. 'Willow House' would be our haven and sanctuary for nearly twenty years.

We returned to find Combe Down submerged under snow and the St Paul's boiler defunct. While the children tobogganed ecstatically down the valley, I telephoned all boarders and told them not to come in for three days.* When they arrived they learned that they had had their half term. That was probably

---

*In these days of transparency I see, to my shame, that I explained the late start of term as being driven by consideration for our pupils in view of the appalling state of the roads!

the worst of the challenges left to us in that extraordinary first year. Eileen McPeake, taking up her post as School Matron after serving her term's notice at Berkhamsted, immediately imparted order and discipline to her sanatorium in the Mansion. We who were less experienced in running a boarding school took heart from our survival. Peter Walshe's sharp eye discerned the identity of a dormitory thief from his distant silhouette. I managed to break down the obfuscations of another through patient juxtaposition of his evidence with the conflicting witness of others – 'You've really got me in the shit house,' was his grudging tribute. He had been 'M's companion both in the burglary of the house safe and in that pre-term conversation with us in Kent House. Like 'M' he saw out his time in Prior Park and I was delighted, for him and for his mother, when he returned a few years later to be married in the Chapel.

Even Peter Walshe could not disguise his exasperation. He had joined Prior Park as a teacher, not as a policeman. By now, however, it was St Peter's, the junior house, that was becoming the hotbed of dissent. Not for John Moran the equivocations and compromises of St Paul's. With admirable and stoic determination he established his rules for a group of boys of whom their previous housemaster had despaired. They included the last to come across from Cricklade at twelve. In the year before I arrived they had been at the receiving end of the sort of customary discipline whereby senior boys made them take runs barefoot in the valley through fields of nettles. I would have much to do with them in the years ahead.

As a means towards introducing Bath to the charms of the new lay order in Prior Park, Denis Gilmer, Deputy Chairman of Governors, organized a 'Round Table' drinks party in the Mansion. The temptation was too strong for the latter-day Stalky & Co of St Peter's. They climbed in through the windows of the Mansion to remove the bottles of gin. 'They were like rats,' hissed a grim-faced John Moran, but they had miscalculated their house prefect, the elder brother of one of the more influential in the pack, and he 'shopped' them. Not long afterwards, I was tipped off that a group of boys were planning a 'mass breakout' from St Peter's. I headed for the dormitory, got the group together and told them that this would be a prank too far. Ten minutes later they were off! This time another senior poacher, the third of those I had suspended after the house safe burglary, guided me deep into the quarries under Combe Down and there, on an extraordinarily unforgiving monsoon of an afternoon, we found the group huddling. These were signs that the tide was turning.

The Governors had been unswerving in their support and resolve. But they shared my concern about the grim financial outlook. The Thatcher government had wreaked havoc in the national economy and there were no fairy godmothers in sight. Michael Kent came to the school one Saturday morning. All he gave to us was some pithy advice: 'Never plan for failure'. I have never forgotten it.

It seemed impossible that Prior Park could recruit a sufficient number of boy boarders, Catholic or otherwise, to remain afloat. The only ray of sunshine derived from our success in recruiting day pupils from Bath and Bristol. Of these a majority were non-Catholic, their parents and probably their head-masters finding the lay regime more attractive than the Brothers, but few came with great academic credentials for there were other schools in Bath with good reputations of provision for the brighter pupil. Time was not on our side. It would take years to transform our mediocre examination results. We needed a more immediate academic transfusion and I urged the Governors to open Prior Park to Sixth Form day girls.

The argument was vigorous and the outcome uncertain. Some Governors felt that Prior Park was too unsettled for immediate coeducation. If the experiment failed because the School was not ready, we would repent at leisure. Adrian Snow, Headmaster of the Oratory School and a great help in planning the transition to lay administration, pronounced bluntly that we would not recruit enough girls to pay for the £6,000 needed to convert some toilets in St Peter's to female usage. I was certain that prudence was a luxury that Prior Park could not afford at this juncture. Somehow Fergus Lyons managed to swing his team into line and we announced that Prior Park would admit its first Sixth Form Day Girls in September 1982.

I achieved another coup that was to be of lasting significance. I thought that all would benefit from a scheme whereby boys, on joining the School, qualified for 'life membership' of the Prior Park Association through the payment of ten termly 'subscriptions' of £5. Parents could opt out, but very few did, and the consequence was that the School's cash flow was boosted and the Prior Park Association progressively rejuvenated. What was more, the Association ploughed money back into the School through its subsidy of the school magazine to which recent leavers were entitled.

Anna Greenwood successfully produced our first school play. Andrew Mock entered our choir for the 'Wells Eight Hundred' Festival and, incredibly, they won their section. Alan Hall's Hockey Eleven achieved the success that would characterise all his teams during my time in Bath. Against the backcloth of the Falklands War Sir William Rees Mogg presented prizes at our first Prize Day and it was blessed by glorious sunshine. Next day I took Matthew and a number of pupils to Coventry airfield and the Mass said by Pope John Paul II. Bishop Mervyn Alexander came to preside at lay Prior Park's first Confirmation service and unwittingly provided Margery with one of the most memorable moments of the year. He arrived a few minutes earlier than expected and rang on the door of Kent House. Margery, breast feeding Sophie at the time, peered out of the bedroom window to see a bishop waiting in patient and purple splendour below. Hurrying down and ushering the bishop into an armchair, she noticed with horror a mouse scurrying up the curtain.

Nor was I spared embarrassment in my relations with my local bishop.

Shortly after the Pope's visit, I was invited to share my impressions with an ecumenical group in Glastonbury. Arriving hideously underprepared, I was horrified to find that my audience contained Bishop Mervyn and an array of other Catholic 'heavyweights'. I fear that the episode did nothing for my specifically Catholic credentials.

Those days of wild garlic and early summer in our artificial paradise were heady times indeed. The Bath Festival Fringe held a magnificent fireworks supper on the Mansion steps. Our first year ended with the first Prior Park fete, organized by the new Society of Parents and Friends and attended by over 700 people. For me the highlight of this Summer Term was a conceit of my own historical devising, the celebration of the centenary of the opening of the Prior Park Chapel of Our Lady of the Snows on 5 July 1882. Our three Prior Park bishops – Alexander of Clifton, Murphy O'Connor of Arundel and Brighton and Ward of Menevia – concelebrated High Mass, following a procession of which Bishop Baines would have been proud. Television came to record these happenings and, sitting down nervously that evening with Brother Miller to watch the local news, I was gratified that the report included my own very upbeat remarks. My voice then faded away and the commentary continued: 'Mr Tobin went on to say that this sort of occasion would have been inconceivable under the Christian Brothers.' My indignation was so immediate and un-restrained that my amiable predecessor expressed total confidence that I could never have said such a thing.

Beneath the confident exterior presented to parents and the public, however, there were damaging fissures in the new order. Tales and rumours emanating from St Paul's inevitably rekindled apprehension among those colleagues who had worked under the Christian Brothers, but it would be wrong to analyse tensions in terms of a division between the old guard and the new. No-one was more committed to the success of lay administration than Sidney Ash or John Moran, and most of the 'old' Common Room showed great generosity in their support of the much widened programme of extra-curricular activities. Rather, the Common Room was becoming splintered. Some saw Peter Walshe as their inspiration and guru. Others were worried by his radicalism and feared that St Paul's was coming apart at the seams. Others again, taking neither side, wondered simply whether the 1981 experiment would succeed or founder. The extraordinary thing, in retrospect, was that no-one jumped ship.

Peter and Ann Walshe, conscious of their sacrifice in giving up his Chair and their relatively comfortable and affluent life in the University of Notre Dame, were not prepared to humour their critics by tempering their radicalism. In their first days at the school, they invited me over to their flat to meet their friend, Ian Linden, a man more doctrinaire than most in his belief that the Catholic Church should have no truck with Independent schools. As Head of Religious Education, Peter expounded a 'preferential option for the poor'. Many boys and

The centennial Mass in the Prior Park chapel – Bishop Alexander with Bishop Murphy-O'Connor and Bishop Ward.

colleagues will have been enlightened by his clear and prophetic analysis of the needs of Africa and its challenge to affluent Catholics. Towards what he coolly dismissed as 'cultic Catholicism' Peter was, literally, not prepared to bend the knee. Yet this was the culture of Father Paul and of most of his Catholic colleagues. Ann volubly denounced the male priesthood and the iniquitous conservatism of the Polish Pope. I was back on my St Benedict's fence, happy to be associated with the liberal camp but temperamentally with Father Paul and the conservatives. Even the happy social events tended to come unstuck. After we had all enjoyed the hospitality of the McMahons, the personification of the warmth and camaraderie of Christian Brother Prior Park, Ann Walshe switched on their television and summoned us all to watch. 'Look,' she exclaimed excitedly, 'It's Tony Benn. I think he's MARVELLOUS.' Today, of course, we all do. Then, in 1982, he was for all of us who felt imperilled in our Independent schools, the wolf circling the fold.

I did my best to bring my colleagues back into a single camp. One summer day, immediately after lunch, I summoned the whole Common Room to assemble. Like Oliver Cromwell I besought them to pull together for the greater good. As they dispersed, a senior member of staff asked me for a private word. He was considering the purchase of a larger house, with a higher mortgage, but he needed to be certain that he would continue to have a job. What was my real opinion? I assured him solemnly that Prior Park would survive. What I really meant was that I would fight to the death to ensure that this would be the case. Some while later Sidney Ash took me aside and referred to this lunchtime meeting. 'Don't do that again,' he said quietly. 'The last time we were called together in that fashion and at that time was when we were told that the School was closing.'

The trouble was that by now I shared the misgivings of the Common Room critics. Discipline in the senior house remained lax. Most of the senior boys seemed incorrigibly idle and complacent. After 'Mocks' I took 'A', the lately appointed prefect, on a walk around the cricket pitch in an attempt to din some sense into him. He was as casual now as when he had collected his tie. There was no cause for worry – he'd be fine. In the event he achieved three 'F's that summer. Grimly I thought of Tonbridge. I recalled Jack Ind's insistence that silence during homework had to mean silence. I did not have the impression that such standards were seen as remotely practicable in St Paul's. The smoking, the posters and the loud music unnerved me. How could I go on selling the future Prior Park to parents when the present Prior Park was stuck in its rut? How could I even persuade parents (like those of 'A') with younger sons at Prior Park that these should remain into the Sixth Form?

At the end of that first year I wrote Peter Walshe a letter. Like all written reproach, however honeyed and qualified, its effect was purely negative. Its only and immediate effect was that Peter decided that he would return to Notre Dame in the summer of 1983. In addition he informed me that his involvement with a Franciscan Third World programme during the next academic year would curtail his commitment to Prior Park. He would serve a further year as House-master but on half a timetable. I could have turned him down, given him a stark choice and, if he stood firm, replaced him by Gerald Davies. I felt that the lay Prior Park could not afford to lose its biggest figure before anything had taken root. 'Doc' Walshe's compassion, quiet authority and wry humour had made him genuinely popular in the house and he had facilitated the steady and significant improvement in its morale. I judged it essential to sustain a sense of continuity and cohesion, however illusory such appearances might be.

We also needed money. Towards the end of our summer holiday John Bogie and I flew out to Hong Kong in support of our still extant Appeal. The trip barely paid for our flight but I returned with some signed registration forms. There was one hilarious moment. We had signed up for a day visit to China and were waiting in the hotel lobby when a driver entered with a sign, 'China Light'. 'China?' I asked, he nodded and we climbed into the minibus. Up and down hill we went before coming to the shore and an immense building site. It was the new China Light and Power factory, shortly to be opened by Margaret Thatcher. We returned indignant to the hotel and were fobbed off with a hydrofoil trip to Macau.

September 1982 found me older, wiser and more realistic than in 1981. Even so, I was clearly feeling energetic, as I undertook to become a rugby coach again and train the Under 15 XV. I also inveigled Margery into teaching some French at Advanced and Ordinary Level. The optimism and excitement surfaced in my letter to parents.

> Our second year of lay management at Prior Park has opened in brilliant weather and in a spirit of great buoyancy and optimism. In part this derives from a confidence that we – oldstagers and newcomers alike – could not feel at this stage last year. Then faith and hope were the two qualities most required. Now we are supported by the evidence of a year of steady growth and by the fact that numbers at Prior Park have risen very dramatically. We now have in the School a total of 256 pupils, of whom 197 boarders, 53 are day boys and 6 are day girls.

I used the 'buoyancy' described in my letter to justify heavy fee increases in both January and April 1983. For the Governors and I were well aware that the success was illusory. Our numbers had been inflated by a once-for-all transfusion of pupils from Redrice, a Hampshire Catholic boarding school which had, unlike Prior Park, been run by the laity from its inception. Prior Park's survival presumably removed its own last hope of survival and I paid a melancholy visit to its founders to negotiate the transfer of some of its pupils and one of its teachers. This was Stewart Woodward, who was to make an invaluable contribution to Prior Park during the next four years. I was acutely aware that most of the Redrice pupils had only their Sixth Form ahead of them. The same was true of many of the Cantonese-speaking pupils whom I had recruited in Hong Kong.

John Bogie, whose first Common Entrance group had just transferred to Bath, was involved in a similar race against time at Cricklade. He now persuaded the Governors to authorize complete coeducation in Prior Park's Preparatory School, with effect from September 1983. The pursuit of survival was clearly driving us in the same direction, yet the logistical and financial obstacles seemed overwhelming.

Meanwhile, my second Head Boy, James Dixon, had already done me great service. On his return to school at the beginning of term he told me that he had brought the Upper Sixth together and given them a simple choice – cooperate with the Headmaster and have a good final year or fight him and waste it. Within a week his actions had proved as good as his words. He brought me information that one of the younger boarders had returned with cannabis from the Middle East. Even though he had taken immediate action, it had not been quick enough to prevent five other boys from being involved. I expelled the supplier and suspended the others. Together we had put down a crucially important marker for the future.

Just after Christmas my pastoral responsibilities assumed a more poignant dimension. One of the most equable and friendly members of my first Upper Sixth at Prior Park had been a burly, open-faced young man from Hong Kong, Alvin Lo. Universally popular within the Sixth Form, Alvin had had no problem in being equally open and positive towards his new headmaster. That did not save him from the academic fate of most of his peers. His parents wanted him to return to Hong Kong but he prevailed on them to give him another chance at a 'crammer'. Alvin never drank alcohol. For that reason his friends would often ask him to drive them to and from their parties. Returning on a dark and icy road, his car spun out of control and Alvin was killed instantly. None of his passengers was even harmed. Alvin belonged to no religious denomination, but it seemed the right and natural thing for Father Paul to conduct his funeral service in the Prior Park Chapel. Nothing in my career as a schoolmaster had prepared me for the sadness of welcoming his grieving parents to a school that they would never otherwise have visited and into a culture wholly alien from theirs, or for the challenge of trying to console them for the loss of a son in whose future they had invested so much love and faith. Their dignity and forbearance were amazing.

Towards the end of the term Sidney Ash came to tell me that he would retire at the end of the year. He was already 63 and his continued work for his beloved Prior Park had been as courageous as it had been indispensable. With his full support I advertised the post outside the School, while welcoming applications within the Common Room. There were 80 applications and we interviewed 14. Many of these were clearly startled by the interior state of St Paul's and offended by its culture of smoking and general lassitude. The mood of the most detached of my visitors – he soon became a leading light among the Heads of Catholic maintained schools – was not enhanced when he left the Mansion to find that a tyre was flat. For me, there was only one strong candidate and he, thank God, emerged at the head of the field. In Wilfred Hammond I gained a Deputy Head beyond price.

Little by little we were coaxing the old fabric of Prior Park into forms and appearance acceptable to potential parents of the 1980s. Sir James Darling had taught me the importance of giving the boys something to surprise them on their return each term, so I was gratified when a boy misunderstood my question, 'Do you find each year (i.e. year group) different from the next?' and he replied, 'Oh yes, we always look on the notice board at the beginning of each term to see what changes you have made.'

Before Easter Stewart Woodward and Andrew Mock collaborated to marvellous effect in their production of *Oliver*. Nowadays splendid musicals are ten a penny in good schools. In 1983 such a triumph seemed like manna in the desert. Anna Greenwood assembled material from our first two years and published the first school magazine of the lay order, the previous editor having called it a day. For Ascension Day I ordained that the whole School should disperse on 'outings' and this endured as a tradition until English schools generally became submerged under coursework and utilitarianism.

The Walshes confirmed that they would definitely return to Indiana and I decided to break up the St Paul's conglomerate and to divide it into two houses, 'Allen', after Prior Park's builder, and 'Roche', after the distinguished Christian Brother Headmaster and historian of the School. Gerald Davies would run Roche and Stewart Woodward Allen, and I expected each to have a far tighter grip on their charges than had been practicable in the larger house. On the other hand, experience had hammered home to me the wisdom of Brother Miller's advice to me on the eve of his departure: 'Patrick, never let your housemasters become barons.' From September 1983 I would intervene personally to ensure that the culture of St Paul's changed for good.

When the Advanced Level results came through this determination hardened. The Secretary of HMC asked me, politely but coldly, for my response to results which, if continued, would put at risk the future HMC membership of Prior Park College. In a little handwritten postscript he added, 'I see that the previous year's results were even worse.'

It was a grim summer holiday in Dorset that year. I pored over my tables predicting future numbers and my conclusions were bleak. Nothing suggested that we could recruit new boarders and new day boys at a rate that would replenish the loss of our current boarders. The only hope was full coeducation.*

---

*I was right to be concerned. The next twenty years would not be kind to Catholic boarding schools, with no fewer than four Benedictine schools – Belmont, Buckfast, Douai and Fort Augustus – expiring. In this light, Prior Park's survival may be seen as a vindication of lay Catholic management.

CHAPTER 13

Questions and Answers

Imagine then the scene on 29 May 1834 – Bishop Baines attired in pontifical robes, surrounded by his attendant ministers and bearing the Blessed Sacrament in his hands, ascending to the magnificent portico between long files of surpliced worshippers and giving the ceremony of the Benediction for the first time to crowds of laity massed together on the lower flight. Such are the recollections of James Shepherd, who wrote his reminiscences in 1886 as one of the few men then alive to remember Bishop Baines and the opening of Prior Park. Monsignor Shepherd wrote that Baines must have felt himself privileged by the Almighty in being the means by which the beautiful worship of Catholicism was again to be manifested to a Nation which had for so long been deprived of its old historic faith. 29 May 1834 must indeed have been memorable. Mass in the Mansion Chapel was followed by no fewer than three Benedictions, as a procession of priests and students moved slowly around the grounds on what was the first of many Corpus Christi processions at Prior Park.

(Prize Day address, May 1984, celebrating the
150th anniversary of the building of the Mansion steps)

IT DID NOT take me long to realize that the attitude of the Catholic Church to Prior Park was at best ambivalent. No school had caused as much embarrassment and uncertainty to the Church. From the 'original sin' of its foundation to its phoenix-like escape in 1981, Prior Park College was seen more as a cuckoo in the nest than as a proud standard bearer for resurgent Catholicism. It was the more ironic in the 1980s that no other Catholic school could boast as many Old Boy bishops. The most local of these, Bishop Mervyn Alexander of Clifton, Prior Park's diocesan bishop, must have had mixed emotions concerning the prospect of his old school's survival. It had caused so much heartache to all of his predecessors. Why should the latest experiment prove any different or any more viable? It was the more creditable that Bishop Mervyn was unfailingly warm in his personal support of lay Prior Park. The attitude of those who administered educational policy in his diocese was notably less positive.

I was alerted to this before I took up my post. I had placed an advertisement in the Catholic press, to the effect that Prior Park offered the only Catholic Sixth Form education in Bath. This seemed to me an unexceptionable statement. There was no maintained provision for Catholics beyond the age of 16, as all were expected to attend the Sixth Form College of St Brendan's in Bristol. I was surprised, therefore, to receive a letter from the Abbot of

Downside. He observed that Downside saw itself as a Bath school, Bath being the nearest town to Stratton on the Fosse. As a Trustee of St Brendan's he went on to criticize the promotion of an Independent Catholic alternative to official diocesan policy. I replied politely that it was odd that an Abbot of Downside should question the right of an Independent Catholic school to promote itself. Privately, I wondered whether the Church found it natural that its more genteel and moneyed adherents should patronize Independent Benedictine boarding schools but expected other Catholics to toe the party line.

In the 'Priory', the Christian Brothers maintained a friendly and unobtrusive presence in the grounds of the school. Only once did they express concern. Brother Anthony thought that boys from St Paul's were semaphoring across the valley to St Peter's. He had found sticks laid out in a suspicious pattern outside Kent House and into the woods. Perhaps there was a drugs ring? There was, thankfully, a more innocent explanation. The Tobin children had been pursuing fantasy in elaborate tracking games!

The Brothers had gone but those who worked for them stayed and served the new order as devotedly as the old – Reg Martin, the Assistant Bursar, Tom Fulman and Bill Bridges, the handymen, and Kathy Rowsell. It was not long before three of these were dead, Reg, Tom and Kathy. Looking back, I am struck by the extent to which these utterly unassuming members of the Prior Park community were greatly mourned by so many of the school's teachers and pupils and I wonder whether that would ever have been as true of any of the other schools in which I have worked.

Kathy Rowsell had served the Christian Brothers for decades at Prior Park – since she came from Ireland to Bath in her teens. She lived in the Mansion with the Brothers, who gave her home, upbringing and holidays. Pay was minimal, heating less and the tasks exhausting. Merely answering the single telephone and running messages demanded speed and stamina as Kathy ran up stairs and along corridors and arcades, her auburn hair streaming behind her. In time, she married Frank, raised her family and became a proud grandmother. Prior Park took on her imprint. Never has great building been more polished or cosseted by one small person – and Kathy trained Ellen and the others to the same standard.

People mattered far more to Kathy than stone or wood. She understood the pressures on boarding boys and they loved her for it. 'The boys are wonderful,' she would say, even as she lay dying. She hated the holidays when they went home.

To me she confided a faith and a love which were beyond repaying. She cleaned my study, brought me tea and coffee and fussed over me as she had done for countless Presidents before me. It was not the least extraordinary thing in this remarkable woman that, having given fifty years of her life to the Christian Brothers, she should give me her unqualified loyalty, friendship and commitment. Whenever something really bad occurred during those first years, she would bring in my coffee, place it on the table, turn to go, pause, and then say, with a conviction that brooked no disbelief, 'Everything will be all right, Sir. You'll see.' On my last visit to her, after weeks of cancer when she had visibly declined and her discomfort was often acute, she told me, as she told all the others, that she was so HAPPY. 'I love you,' were her last words to me.

Kathy died on the Feast of the Immaculate Conception 1983. On the following day a Mass was said for her in the Chapel. At her request there was no fuss and no publicity. The Chapel was full. Virtually every boarder was there, along with domestic staff, maintenance team and teachers. It was a powerful reminder of the holiness of the heart's affections. Amid the sadness of loss there was a profound sense that all was well.

Kathy's death and funeral fortified my faith that we could answer the central question, 'Did Prior Park have a continuing role to play as a Catholic school?' The great thing, the saving grace, about Prior Park was the truth known to Kathy Rowsell, that it had a very warm soul. The Sunday Mass was a wonderfully numinous experience, to the extent that the parents of non-Catholic day pupils were as likely to attend as the Catholics. The boys loved to participate as altar servers, the choir became ever more impressive, the chapel was austerely beautiful and Father Paul was quaint, quirky, bearded, reflective and avuncular Father Paul. He had a flat in the Mansion, shared with his Jack Russell 'Dona' and her intermittent puppies, and kept open house there for boys who liked dogs or wanted to use his computer or needed someone to talk to. Every weekday Father Paul would say Mass in the little Oratory on the first floor of the Mansion. I would as often as not be there and there would always be a good scattering of boys of all ages and types.

It was a community generous in its affections. In that sense Ullathorne was right to see it as a 'bottomless pit'. Once sucked in, its devotees never stinted their commitment. Thus did Andrew Mock and Stewart Woodward achieve miracles of improvisation and the most improbable of triumphs – and these in turn were notable also for the involvement of an extraordinarily high proportion of the teaching and non-teaching staff. Nobody better exemplified this spirit than John Weston. John had been coming in to Prior Park since 1956 to run its Radio Club. Now he was running four such societies! New staff immediately entered into the spirit. Michael Barnes, who succeeded Helen Fisher as Head of Modern Languages when she moved on into motherhood, was as avid an exponent of the joys of cross-country running as he was a promoter of French exchanges.

It was crucial that I, as Prior Park's chief salesman, should be *convinced* that this generous community deserved to survive. I would argue to every visiting parent that, precisely because Prior Park was such a small community, everyone knew everyone else – and everyone tended to get involved in what was going on. All of our first Sixth Form girls were in the casts for our Musicals. In a myriad of different ways the School developed talents previously unknown to the girls and boys who now evinced them. Whenever I sat down with potential parents in my study, this was always my strongest selling point.

I needed it. In our first year Margery and I went to a meeting of South West England Independent Heads at Sherborne. We each carried away with us a searing feeling of inferiority. Such knowledge made it much harder for me to 'sell' Prior Park to discerning parents and sceptical Prep School Heads. How could we increase our share of a finite and probably diminishing market when our boarding facilities were so dilapidated and when the most important determinant of parental preference, our academic standing, was so low in comparison with the other HMC schools in Bath and the South West?

For their tours of the school I would keep visitors to the 'golden mile' planned, Potemkin-style, by John Bogie and the Governors. They did not envisage a rat sunning himself so contentedly in a doorway that he refused to budge as we approached. ('Do you like mice?' I heard myself asking the parents. Incredibly they signed on.)

I think that I was quite good in the arts of persuasion. I also enjoyed the support of my Chairman and Bursar in adopting a relatively cavalier approach to the provision of financial inducement. My lack of orthodoxy in this regard owed much to the Economics that I had taught at St Benedict's. A school with the relatively high fixed costs of Prior Park could not afford to be fastidious in the funding of its awards and bursaries. The 'bottom line' was, simply, that the marginal revenue from each extra pupil should at least exceed the marginal cost. As classes and dormitories at Prior Park were never 'full' in those early years, the marginal cost of an extra pupil was minimal. Even a pupil who generated *no* revenue conferred the benefit that the School looked and felt larger. He might also contribute significantly to the image of Prior Park in other ways.

This was the case with 'M'. His Irish mother had several other children and she laid her cards on the table as soon as we met. She had no money whatsoever for fees, but 'M' was notably musical, she had read our advertisement for Music Scholarships in the Catholic press and when she realized that I had arranged to see her on the Feast of the Sacred Heart, she knew that it was God's will that 'M' should come to Prior Park. 'M' did well enough in the competition for our Music Scholarship to justify his selection. He would contribute much to the musical reputation of his new school. 'D's father, also the parent of many children, was equally forthright about his financial circumstances. He was an artist and he promised that, in time, he would recompense the School by undertaking the restoration of the large pictures that hung in the Mansion. I was gratified to hear later that he had been as good as his word. 'J', the headstrong only child of a hard pressed mother in North London, proved hopelessly out of his depth in the 11+ Scholarship examination. I found room for him nevertheless and he would leave Prior Park with Advanced Levels. Sometimes charitable trusts underpinned such benevolence. 'S' obtained a 'JET' Scholarship and in time became Head Boy.

Most winners of our generous academic and music scholarships were not in need of further support from bursaries, but they would not have come to Prior Park without them. Peter Donnelly and Dominic Cave, the first winners of 11+ Scholarships, gave hugely to the School during their time in Bath. They would be my final Head and Deputy Head of School. In each case a sibling followed them to Prior Park.

Personal connections and recommendations could tilt the balance towards Prior Park. Dominic and Anna Cave's father was Paul Olsen's doctor in Burnham on Sea. In the case of Gregory Lee, the 'agent' was the enthusiasm of Denis Tobin in the bar after he had umpired a cricket match. Years later, Tony Lee wrote a lovely letter.

> From being introduced to your father after a match between Roehampton and Old Wimbledonians, discussing with Paul Bruschi who worked with me and getting in touch with you seemed to take about 30 seconds. We have never doubted the wisdom of our decision.

Other schools had long waiting lists. At Prior Park there was no queue to jump and few formalities to delay decisions. In two cases the boy chose us, seemingly, without any reference to higher authority. Ricardo Manotoc from the Philippines was sent by his father to England with instructions to visit a number of schools and select the one that most attracted him. I vividly recall the two of us, strolling across the slope above the Mansion, the Headmaster being interviewed by his prospective pupil rather than the other way round. I evidently did enough to persuade Ricardo. In time Teddy followed him, through more conventional procedures.

'A', a Cantonese boy from Hong Kong, made all the arrangements himself, including his flight plans, and we panicked when he vanished after his plane arrived at Heathrow. Had we been grossly negligent of our duty of care? 'A' calmly arrived a day later – and was a model student for two years. Then he found a much cheaper school in Liverpool and threatened to play 'pied piper' and lead a mass exodus to the Mersey. It was time for ruthless action. 'P', an admirable young man from the New Territories, was the last of three Hong Kong brothers at Prior Park. I had met his parents in 1982. I now suspected that if I could persuade him to stay, his friends would do likewise. I also knew how crucially important 'face' was to the Chinese. I took 'P' aside. I told him that Prior Park had gained a great deal from 'P' and his elder brothers and that I wanted to convey to 'P's father my esteem by awarding 'P' a Sixth Form Scholarship – *but* that this must be *confidential*. 'P' stayed at Prior Park. 'A' left, but he went to Liverpool alone.

Although such confidentiality was necessary, else every other parent would have asked for Sixth Form Scholarships, it could backfire. There was one young man without whom Prior Park's sporting record would have been much the poorer. With the help of an 'all-rounder scholarship' I persuaded his parents to change their minds about withdrawing him from Prior Park and he duly fulfilled every sporting hope that I might have had of him. I was silly and wrong to expect more than sporting achievement. The boy himself might have found it easier to match my hopes for him if his peers had known that he was the recipient of an award. As it was, my manipulative diplomacy would ultimately receive its just desserts.

Such juggling preceded the imposition by HMC of strict rules concerning the award of scholarships and bursaries and I was fortunate in this regard. It did not take me long, however, to be reminded that clever salesmanship would not suffice to save a school. Between June and September 1983 there was a net loss of eight pupils. It was a further, brutal reminder that time was not on our side and that I must use Peter Walshe's departure as a spur to reform and renewal.

Stewart Woodward, who took over from Peter Walshe as head of RE, now injected his own marvellous and memorable fillip. With Andrew Mock and Father Paul he wrote *Reflections*, a Musical conveying St John's account of the Passion. Father Paul would be the aged evangelist, penning his gospel and recalling various scenes from Christ's life, who supplied the link between a series of scenes that pulsed with Stewart's lyrics and pounded with his (somewhat derivative) rock music.

Somehow it all came together and I drove the family down to Dorset for our Easter holidays in a mood of exaltation and sheer joy. On our arrival, our neighbour told us that his wife was ill and asked us to keep the children quiet. Five year old Lucy was not to be silenced. Higher and higher she swung on the swing and louder and louder she sang, 'I am the Resurrection, I am the Life.'

Meanwhile, I tried to harness History to the cause and instil in the boys and girls a sense of the colour and richness of their extraordinary inheritance. I looked beyond the Christian Brother era and found in Bishop Baines' career at Prior Park a seemingly endless sequence of sesquicentenaries. The 1984 Prize Day evoked an occasion worthy of our founder. Bishop Cormac Murphy O'Connor presented the prizes. He then celebrated on the Mansion steps a special Benediction, in honour and repetition of the events of 29 May 1834. In my own speech I recalled that remarkable occasion and I took the opportunity also to wax lyrical on an even earlier treasure, the 'victoriously perfect' Prior Park landscape, shaped by Ralph Allen and Alexander Pope, to which Peter Levi had so recently sung his far more eloquent hymn of praise in *The Flutes of Autumn*. In this autobiographical sketch, Peter Levi explained how its beauty had eclipsed the pains of bullying and of hockey in February and he thanked his father for the 'mysterious gift' which, more than any other influence, had nourished the poet within him.

> 'The joy I got from it has remained, while the misery disintegrated to rags and tatters. The worst it did was to leave me in spirit unteachable, almost intractable, difficult to handle…What I wanted to become I chose freely, and the sense of tranquil inner freedom has never deserted me in any crisis…Is that the private territory of God in the human soul, or am I right to associate it strongly with a landscape?'

Thus did I seek to promote the self-belief of an increasingly vibrant community. The academic realities kept on wrenching me back to earth. As Sidney Ash put it, shortly before his retirement, 'the centre of gravity' was low. As long as financial necessity and Prior Park's place in the market forced us to admit pupils whose academic standards and motivation were modest, we would be unable to transform the School's academic reputation and thereby attract a sufficient number of able pupils. I would confer little benefit on that headstrong young man from North London unless Prior Park gave him self-discipline, but I could only be confident of this – and only restrain him from dragging others down – when the general environment was more conducive to virtue.

The greatest risk to warm, friendly Prior Park was precisely that it was too quick to believe that being warm and friendly was all that was needed for it to be a good school – and that the professional pursuit and attainment of academic success were correspondingly soulless. Arrogantly, perhaps, I saw this tendency as endemic to Catholic education. Local Catholic schools seemed to be full of men and women who had been appointed because they were seen as 'good Catholics', rather than because they were the best people for the job. To me, 'friendly' too often meant bumbling and careless, and 'warm' too often meant unprofessional, while an anti-elitist and narcissistic affirmation of equality thinly disguised a lazy avoidance of the rigours of competition.

Furthermore, in a Post Vatican II reaction against the austerities and punitive excesses previously associated with schools run by the religious, Catholic education seemed to be embracing Rousseau – at the very time when sensible schools and concerned parents were eschewing his ontological optimism. By the end of the hairy 1970s, boys from Catholic schools came across as the most louche and laid back of their generation, while indulgent monks and brothers doubtless perceived in the spirit of the age the mysterious workings of the Holy Spirit. At our first Open Day for Prep Schools Heads, Simon Arbuthnott, who had once packed down behind me in the Christ Church scrum, told me that he had not been amused, visiting his old school, to be pelted with bread rolls by its pupils.

For one reason or another, Catholic parents were voting with their feet.

I flattered myself that, as a young (sic) husband and father, bringing with me the experience of working in one of the best and most professional schools in England, I knew better than the clergy what was desired by Catholic parents and needed by their offspring. I was certain that boys were more likely to 'find themselves' and develop their personalities and characters within a secure structure of discipline, where sensible codes for dress and appearance would be steadily and firmly upheld. Prior Park's pupils did indeed seem genuinely pleased to feel and look smarter than they had been and smarter than those in competing schools – although the funny thing was that during the next few years, as I went round the South West circuit of HMC schools, I found that they too had successfully tightened up on the appearance of THEIR pupils!

How much deeper did my programme for improvement go? Imitating Father Bernard in Ealing, I initiated a 'Seventeen Club', composed of the intellectual few, so that they could acquire skills in discussion and have minds broadened and perception sharpened by visiting luminaries like Jonathan Smith. Meanwhile, concerts, plays and exhibitions, along with impressive success in rugby, hockey and cricket, demonstrated that Prior Park was a community bearing fruit. Less tangible were the moral and spiritual dimensions of education, but these were really more important to a Catholic school. From Prior Park boys and girls should emerge deeper in their wisdom, stronger in their character, more assured in their values and beliefs and more generous and enlightened in their concern for others. All this, indeed, was our aim at Prior Park.

Ten years later, when I collaborated with Eric Anderson in the HMC training course for new Heads, he would tell them that there was a very simple way of recruiting pupils. It never failed. *'Run a good school.'* Had I heard this advice in 1983 I might justifiably have seen it as infuriatingly facile. How can you run a good school without good pupils? In that case I would have been wrong. My experience of Prior Park left me convinced that you will succeed if you are single-mindedly committed to the improvement of everything that your school is trying to do. That is the minimum entitlement of pupils and their parents. The 'market', of course, will judge you less by your efforts than by your perceived success – but nobody ever achieved success in education without trying.

I became certain of two priorities. The first was to win the hearts and minds of those boys young enough to change, the group who would sit their Ordinary Level examinations in June 1984, so that Prior Park College could hold its head high as a HMC school worthy of that association's academic standards – so that I could 'sell' it in good faith as a school to which I would send my own son. Matthew would enter Prior Park as an eleven year-old in 1984. Emma would be ready for entry in 1986. I invested my hopes, my ambitions and my affections in the group who would sit their Ordinary Levels in June 1984.

The second priority was to persuade the Governors of the need for coeducation throughout the School. The Governors were very nervous of this further extension of coeducation. They were rightly concerned that, in seeking to make Prior Park coeducational for the teenage years, we would endanger the support of those parents who had so far, through thick and thin, adhered to the single-sex school. They wanted the assurance of 'Market Research'.

I immediately undertook to do this myself.

To the existing parents I sent a lengthy Questionnaire. Its first section sought information about themselves. Parents of 204 pupils at the two schools replied, there being a minimal response from overseas parents. It emerged that the fees of nearly a quarter of pupils were funded wholly or partially out of the Service Grant and that the Armed Services constituted by far the largest category of parental employment. (Of these the proportion of commissioned officers was relatively low.) About 25 parents were in business of some kind and as many were in the professions. Nearly 20 were in some form of engineering and 10 were civil servants.

We knew from our records that roughly 65% of our pupils were Catholic, but that a relatively large number of these had a non-Catholic parent. Altogether the two schools listed 115 non-Catholic parents. Another Catholic school (of 333 pupils) claimed to have only three non-Catholic parents. That school boasted 27 Old Boys among its parents. Prior Park had five. We had 71 non-British parents, they had 19.

Most parents chose Prior Park primarily because it was a Roman Catholic school, with Location, Reputation and Size the next most important reasons. When asked, however, why they had chosen Independent education as such, parents ranked Religious Education an indifferent sixth. Academic standards, Manners and Morals, Small Classes, Discipline and Character training emerged as greater priorities.

From the parents' ticks of approval or crosses of dissatisfaction I extracted crude 'quotients of approval' in respect of various aspects of Prior Park and its performance. On this basis parents were happiest with Prior Park's Size, Music, Pastoral Care and Religious Education. Their estimate of the School's Academic Standards was less complimentary. 64 praised, 26 found fault. Only in Drama did Prior Park achieve a lower quotient – and I was confident that this reflected the past rather than the present.

But the main thrust of the questionnaire was to discover parental attitudes to the issue of Girls. In my introductory letter I emphasized the heavy 'fixed' costs borne by the School and observed that a wider revenue base would increase the scope for improving facilities and restraining the growth of fees. I referred to the fact that the Cricklade girls would be seeking 13+ schooling in 1987. I informed parents that, at 11+ and 12+, the number of pupils at Prior Park was usually between 15 and 25. With such small numbers it was difficult to 'set' pupils into groups appropriate to their previous attainment, '…an argument for taking 11+ day girls into Prior Park College.'

The key responses were encouraging rather than conclusive. 23% favoured the status quo and 76% an extension of co-education. Parental opinion was evenly divided over the admission of girl boarders, but some of those in favour wished to limit girl boarders to the Sixth Form. Of the parents of current boy boarders, a small majority said that they would consider Prior Park for sisters if it admitted girl boarders.

Parents with younger sons were asked whether coeducation would make it less likely that their sons would come to Prior Park. Just under a quarter thought that this would be the case. However, attitudes towards coeducation were much more positive at Cricklade. There, in the first year of coeducational boarding, 89% of parents were happy that girls and boys were being educated together. It did not follow, of course, that such sentiments would necessarily endure into adolescence.

As Service parents constituted the largest single element in the current Prior Park market, and as the Governors had expressed particular concern that the Service attitude to coeducation might be exceptionally conservative, I extracted their views for separate analysis. Almost to a man, or perhaps his wife, the responses favoured coeducation, even if there were no daughters in the family.

What then of the market that had yet to consider Prior Park College? In a few weeks I managed to cover a great deal of ground in one of the most fascinating exercises of my teaching career. I analysed national, local and Catholic demographic trends and perused Michael Murphy's similar survey of the Diocese of Clifton. I visited Michael Hornsby-Smith, the Catholic Church's leading sociologist, and I read *Roman Catholic Opinion*, his study, co-written with R.M. Lee, of English and Welsh Roman Catholics in the 1970s. I issued questionnaires not only to our parents but also to the Common Room, to eleven 'feeder' Preparatory schools and to the three top year groups in the school. I visited and consulted six HMC schools which had become fully or partially coeducational. I also investigated why two Catholic schools had abandoned coeducation.

I concluded that Prior Park could not assume that there was an untapped market for what we were currently offering. The Independent Schools Information Service (ISIS) was registering a record number of parents seeking financial assistance towards school fees, a sign of the economic pressures of the time. A significant proportion of pupils left HMC schools at 16 to attend Sixth Form Colleges. There was a noticeable decline in applications for boarding places.

Of more immediate concern were the patterns in the diocese of Clifton. Until the mid-1960s much of Catholic education in the diocese had been provided through Independent schools, of which many were convent schools run by nuns. Thus in 1965 there had been 8,271 pupils in 35 Independent schools in the Clifton diocese, representing 35% of all pupils. By 1981 there were only 4,624 pupils in the 19 Independent schools that remained.

Nor was there any evidence that Catholic maintained schools had benefited from this cull of their Independent rivals. On the contrary, the average number of pupils in each Catholic Primary School had dropped from 285 in 1961 to 171 in 1981. In the next decade the Clifton diocese anticipated a further fall of about 15% in the numbers of pupils at its schools. The education committee and most of the diocesan clergy remained firmly hostile towards Independent schools. Better, it seemed, no Catholic schooling than Independent Catholic schooling!

Only one parish priest, of a parish on the outskirts of Bristol, was prepared to challenge political correctness in pursuit of what he saw as the true educational and spiritual interests of the children in his parish. He arranged for me to come across to meet interested parents and the impact was immediate. It threw into sharp relief the price that Prior Park paid in most other parishes for the diocesan party line.

Michael Hornsby-Smith's research was particularly interesting in this regard. His evidence revealed a steadily diminishing proportion of Catholics who believed that it was vitally important that their children should go to Catholic schools – with the wealthiest Catholics least committed to specifically Catholic education. Catholics wished to be convinced of the specifically *educational* worth of the Catholic maintained school before entrusting their child to it. Already fewer than half of the Catholics in the South West had had all their schooling in Catholic schools. Hornsby-Smith argued that it was difficult to demonstrate that Catholic schooling actually succeeded in promoting the religious development of their pupils. Home attitudes and practice were far more important determinants. He conceded, however, that Catholic schooling made it more likely that a child from a less religious home background would sustain his or her faith. The increasing proportion of mixed marriages could only accentuate such developments.

The impact of such influences and developments on Catholic Independent schools had been to make them ever less Catholic. Over 30% of boys in these schools were not Catholic and over 50% of girls. Only 5.4% of Catholic school pupils – and only 4.7% of Catholic boys – were at Catholic Independent schools.

There was a further worry. Catholics tended to be over-represented in the Armed Services and the Service Grant was a correspondingly important foundation of Catholic boarding schools. However, the Catholic emphasis on the family made it more likely that the priority for servicemen would be to find a school near to grandparents, or, increasingly, to settle wife and family in an area where the children could enjoy domestic stability – and day education.

Finally, I considered trends in Prior Park itself and, more crucially, at

Cricklade. With the Preparatory School taking fewer boys, it was becoming less effective as the reservoir for a single-sex Prior Park. There too an increasing proportion of parents were non-Catholic and their allegiance to Prior Park after Common Entrance or 13+ Scholarship could not be assumed. Whereas, in June 1983, I had envisaged a school population of 334 by 1988, by September I had had to reduce that projection to a mere 289 pupils by 1987.

My 'Conclusion' was mildly stated but unambiguous. The market for Catholic Independent education was finite and currently diminishing. The boarding market was unlikely to expand and Prior Park was finding it difficult to make inroads into a fierce and relatively cheap day market. One avenue to increased market share, the steep path, lay through the improved reputation of the School, above all academic, but our academic reputation was determined primarily by the quality of the entry. Other avenues to single-sex growth were either unrealistic or undesirable. Coeducation constituted the only other viable route to growth.

I look back with pride and satisfaction on my Market Research Report. It was the coherent rationalization and effective presentation of the case for change. My Report had the effect of convincing even the most sceptical of Governors and the decision was taken that Prior Park should become fully coeducational.

Prior Park College now has over 500 boys and girls. It is larger, as it happens, than virtually all of the illustrious schools against which Margery and I measured ourselves that day in Sherborne. It has been a huge achievement by Prior Park's Governors, splendidly impelled by Fergus Lyons. The key to this transformation was the agreement of the Christian Brothers to vacate the Priory in 1986, thereby enabling us to make it the basis of the Girls' boarding house. John Leay skilfully negotiated with our bankers the funding for our extra accommodation. Rear Admiral John Robertson, first as governor, then as a professional consultant, charted the way ahead and patiently undertook months of tortuous and sensitive discussions with Bath City Council.

Lest the reader should conclude, from all of this, that the author has exaggerated, for the sake of effect, the parlous situation from which Prior Park escaped, I offer this footnote. On holiday in Chideock some time in 1983, I decided one Tuesday to buy *The Guardian*, Tuesday being its Education day. I opened the section and 'Prior Park College' kept popping from the page. The article was a diatribe written by the journalist wife of a St Paul's house tutor against the conditions in which she lived. She claimed that the other staff, overworked and underpaid though they were, knew better than to protest because they understood that the school was on the brink of closure. I was appalled. Then I collected myself. How many of my parents read *The Guardian*? I received no comments whatever on the offending article.

What, meanwhile, of my first priority, the cultivation of attitudes and raising of ambition among the current pupils of Prior Park? I would find out the hard way that changing people is a far more difficult and questionable enterprise than planning for material change. If I gave my brain to the second campaign, I poured my heart into the first. By 1986 I knew that I had lost and that I had been lucky indeed to escape the fate of Bishop Baines.

CHAPTER 14

Painful Lessons

At the root of the profession, if a man is really to succeed in it, is a genuine sensitivity to youth; but there can be deeper instincts too, which may sometimes rest dormant or unsuspected for years until some mysterious chemistry impels them to the surface, so that in the mutually vulnerable relationship between the teacher and the taught, the consciousness of some particular or personal rapport becomes quite literally a sort of heart-hunger…At that point professional detachment is most severely put to the test. What, after all, is true vocation if it is not the yearning to arouse, to enkindle, to elevate, to improve, to open up new horizons, to share excitement with others, above all – to give? These are all functions which lie athwart the tenuous dividing line between the intellect and the affections. This line is the tightrope that many schoolmasters have to walk. But not all who walk it can perceive the abyss at their feet; and even those who do, and who are brave enough to keep on walking, cannot always reach the end.

(David Newsome)

I READ THESE sentences of the Master of Wellington in 1995, six years after I had left Prior Park for my infinitely less emotional job in Edinburgh. They struck me then and they strike me now as self-revelatory to an extraordinary degree. David Newsome, in effect, threw a brilliant light on the three 'middle' years of my first headship, the period when I sought to add a very personal dimension to my management and leadership of Prior Park.

Looking back on my career I recall relatively few close friendships in the Common Rooms in and with which I worked – and none of these was intimate. I was not a colleague who bared his soul or provided a shoulder for others to lean or cry on. Margery and the children formed the loving core of my life. Holidays apart – and often holidays included – the job was its focus.

As a headmaster I found myself distanced from pupils and placed on a pedestal by most colleagues and parents. In Bath and then in Edinburgh I was immensely fortunate in one crucial respect. I knew that I could count on the unqualified support and dedication of my Secretaries. An unspoken affection permeated these relationships and each has metamorphosed into lasting friendship. I have often consoled myself with the thought that those closest to me in my work have seemed to enjoy my company and their jobs.

If I needed such consolation it is because I was too 'driven', idiosyncratic and stubborn to be an easy colleague for others who worked with me. I fear that I took the loyalty of my Deputies far too much for granted and that, at one time or another, I was careless of the feelings of all of them, Sidney Ash perhaps excepted. With most other colleagues, I fear, I was too caught up in the 'persona' of headship to be more than a generally smiling face. I was, as my first appraisal informed me, 'not good at small talk'. In time, I generally gained their respect and trust but our association rarely went deeper than the superficial. If this is the experience of most Heads, the wisest will have given more time to people than I did.

I was the more fortunate that I found it easy and congenial to share confidences with successive Chairmen of Governors – Fergus Lyons in Bath, Michael Walker, James Laurenson and (briefly) Iain Gotts in Edinburgh. Few conversations extended too far into issues and anxieties without laughter and discovery of the absurd. Perhaps it was this that persuaded all of them, in the last resort, that I was not completely insane!

I had proclaimed Prior Park the Catholic 'family' school. Some may have feared that school and family were becoming too conflated. Nicholas and Michael Flanagan, the sons of my cousin Peter, became boarders. Margery increased her teaching and took on pastoral responsibility for the Sixth Form Day Girls. In September 1984 our son Matthew entered the 11+ form of Prior Park College. John Bogie had encouraged us to send him to Cricklade as a boarder but there was little enthusiasm for this idea. As with Emma and Lucy later, Matthew had all his Primary education at the nearest Catholic maintained school, St John's, and like them he was not at all disadvantaged.

In time all four of our children would have me as their headmaster. It is fair to say that Matthew and Lucy generally disliked this complication, while Emma and Sophie rather enjoyed it. I knew that parents in Bath and Edinburgh would note our decision as a 'vote of confidence' in their respective schools. This calculation was of greater importance to Prior Park in the 1980s than to The Mary Erskine School later but I have no doubt that both schools were the beneficiaries of our unorthodoxy. We would like to think that the same applied to our children. The time would come when Matthew would be delighted to see me heading north, but at the outset he was pleasantly removed from any pressure. 'Matthew,' Paddy Cox asked him one day, 'What does your Dad do for a living?' 'He's a headmaster,' Matthew replied, warily. 'Oh! Where?'

The truth of the matter was that I was far too busy with the Lower Sixth to trouble the lives of the Lower Third. I have mentioned earlier how I focused my hopes and ambitions on this year group, the last to derive from 'old' Cricklade, and how to win their hearts and minds. I had coached some of them for rugby. I had even tried to teach them RE. When the new Allen and Roche Houses were formed, I invited myself into them and into St Peter's, on a different day for each house, to say night prayers in the dormitories. I read to the boys Peter Levi's lyrical memories of his old school, along with other passages that might

Taking the children on their first continental holiday.

have fostered their belief that they were fortunate indeed to be pupils under
more enlightened management.

So I fussed when I saw the good habits I had so carefully taught on the rugby
field being dissolved in the Second XV – and I 'flipped' when I saw my men
kneeling down with the others before the match in what seemed to me like a
grotesque parody of religion. I prevailed on Denis Clarke to hive them off into a
separate Under 16 XV and they then won every match. I formed an 'Amnesty'
group which met in Kent House each week. One weekend Margery and I drove
them all down to our house in Chideock and this was the base for a three day
charity walk along the cliffs. I encouraged them to watch the superb Channel 4
rendering of Paul Scott's *The Jewel in the Crown* and then, when they fell away
from observance in their day room, I had a group over to watch in my living
room. I drove them to London to see Leo McKern's one-man performance of
Kipling. I was trying to turn the last young rascals of the Christian Brother era
into my future leaders. I entrusted them increasingly with the crucial task of
conducting potential parents around the school and they proved to be eminently

good salesmen. Pat McMahon remarked sagely that I was trying to put old heads on young shoulders.

It was about this time that the Catholic chaplain at Cambridge University complained that the products of Catholic schools were notable only for their absence from Sunday Mass. What, he asked, was the point of a specifically Catholic education? I duly urged the School to make God the centre of their lives and to be very careful of anything that reduced religion to a meaningless ritual. The place for formal prayer was Chapel. It was a good thing to make a point of kneeling and praying as soon as one arrived. I noted that my group did so. When Father Paul made his annual announcement that he was seeking volunteers as sacristans, they volunteered, without any prompting from me.

And I watched their work habits like a hawk and prowled around their carrels during 'Prep'. I told the year group and their parents that the hurdle for entry into the Lower Sixth would rise from 4 to 5 0/L passes – and that they would also have to obtain Grade 'B' passes in their chosen A/L subjects. The Common Room trembled – would there *be* a Lower Sixth?! I drove to Cornwall to persuade the parents of one young man that he should not attend the local Sixth Form College but stay at Prior Park and succeed where his brother had failed.

The stress and strain of it all was already beginning to get to me. Margery found that I was beyond sense or reason. On one occasion she and I were invited to dinner at Marlborough by our Australian friends, the Prestons. As usual I left it to the last minute before returning home from my study in school. Ian Fox arrived to 'baby sit'. Suddenly I realized that Margery was not in the house. Nor was the car. Margery had obviously 'had enough' and left for Marlborough without me! What was I to do? I trudged slowly across in the direction of the school gate. I decided to confess to Stewart Woodward and ask if he could, perhaps, drive me to Marlborough. At that moment, the familiar blue Peugeot swept in, Margery at the wheel. She had been to collect Lucy from Brownies. Together we returned, to be greeted by an ashen-faced Ian Fox. He had looked everywhere but there was no sign of Lucy!

At the end of this year my group volunteered to do a week of paid employment, painting our historic swimming pool – allegedly the oldest indoor school swimming pool in England? – and Margery and I gave them supper in Kent House.

In short, during my fourth year at Prior Park, I had cast aside the shackles of orthodoxy and restraint and I had done things my way. A month later, the Ordinary Level results seemed to justify everything. 86% of the boys achieved the old minimum of four passes, while the number achieving eight passes corresponded to previous norms for six. The number and percentage of 'A' and 'B' grades also rose sharply to record levels.

If only, I sigh as I look back, if only I had the sense to 'back off' and watch, with confidence, the blossoming of all that I had worked for. Why didn't I? I knew that the job was only half done. I had risked much in the belief that the boys of Prior Park were capable of ever so much more than they had previously achieved, or than had previously been expected of them. The little voice whispered that it would be folly for me to disengage now, at the very point when the real battle had to be fought, for Advanced Level success would be the acid test as to whether Prior Park had made the grade. Far from backing off from the group in whom I had invested so much time, energy and attention, I decided that it was time for me to return to teach Advanced Level History – for which many of my group had signed up.

But I knew then and I know now that the overriding reason was personal. What was it that Sir James Darling had written about the need for a headmaster to be certain of the 'purity of his motives'?

At the first assembly of the new academic year I proclaimed my manifesto for improvement.

> Sixth form preps will be extended and a real drive mounted by house staff and Common Room to ensure that these preps will be of a genuinely high standard. However, we also believe in the importance of creating the right overall tone. The plain fact is that pop music belching out of windows, or football being kicked around in front of the St Paul's doorway, adds up to a Butlins-type atmosphere instead of the relatively quiet, academically-based atmosphere which should be prevailing on boarding houses dominated by the Sixth Form…In similar vein, we are looking to the Sixth Form to find in the boarding house a development of their communal religious identity. It might have been said in recent years that in the Sixth Form the School encouraged you to stop praying and start smoking.

This Sixth Form would be encouraged to continue to pray. I introduced voluntary Sixth Form prayers every weekday evening. The sacristans led the way dutifully and for a time I flattered myself that I was keeping open the doors to spirituality. But the pastoral and the authoritarian were too intimately intermeshed, in my psyche and in that of the boys. When, early in 1985, I finally ended the right of the Sixth Form to smoke in their study bedrooms, this was seen as an attack too far on the pupils' traditional liberties. Today's reader will be incredulous that the decision took so long. Then it was a frontal challenge and it was resisted and resented as such. It would have to be enforced. Under such pressure, the morale that had so promisingly flourished wilted and withered.

Nor did the girls of 1984 exercise the wholly elevating influence that, naively perhaps, I had attributed to their predecessors. Prior Park had come on a long way since the advent of the founding girls of 1982, when, as I liked to quip, the male chauvinism in the lunch queue evoked Noel Coward's remark, that he always preferred to travel by Italian lines because there was none of this nonsense of women and children first. By 1984 the Lower Sixth had become a much more immediately congenial experience for new girls. They, for their part, could not be expected to understand, let alone subscribe to, the expectations that

I had attached to their highly personable friends. The more gregarious of these boys immediately 'paired off' and I worried, with some cause, that we were in danger of realizing the worst fears of those who had cautioned against coeducation.

This was one tension that produced a genuinely positive outcome, in that Wilfred Hammond produced a magnificent 'Personal Development Programme'. This anchored our 'PSE' curriculum firmly in a Christ-centred theology and its ideals bear repetition today.

> We try to touch those aspects of growing up which cannot be covered within the classroom and we base it very firmly on a Christ-centred theology. We see ourselves as partners with parents in the equipping of our young people for responsible choices, both as teenagers and as adults. The central thrust is positive, pointing boys and girls towards those attitudes and beliefs which, we believe, lead to happiness and fulfilment for them. We seek to help girls and boys to become good wives and husbands, mothers and fathers, employers and tax-payers, integrated people.

Meanwhile, I thrashed around, in my own doomed cause, as I tried to impose a Sixth Form culture characterized by ambition and worth. When it suited my friends to conform with my hopes and wishes they did so, but not at the expense of their 'image'. In calling on my front-line troops to go over the top and stand unequivocally for what I wanted of them I was asking for miracles of perspicacity, loyalty and moral courage. In the end, as was to be expected, their loyalties lay elsewhere. I spoke much about 'trust' but my group knew that I did not really trust them and a vicious circle took hold whereby pressure created dishonesty, dishonesty undermined trust and distrust led to further pressure. Familiarity inevitably degenerated into contempt. Good young men paid the price.

I doubt whether matters would have been any happier if my Lower Park family had not descended into crisis. Koo, now over eighty, was in hospital for another hip operation. Michael was in remission from bowel cancer but his mental health was as poor as ever. My father, driven into depression, had taken to his bed for the best part of a year. Only my mother kept going. Finally, she took action. First she put Michael into hospital, then Denis. On 4 October 1984 she arrived unannounced in Prior Park, mistook Nicholas Flanagan for her grandson Matthew and was surprised that I had not expected her – 'It *is* your birthday.' She wouldn't stay. She had to buy some fish. We took her to the supermarket and then to the station. Next day my aunt Mabel rang. Paul had found Una in a very confused state in Lower Park. She had then collapsed. It transpired that she had suffered a brain haemorrhage. I found it extraordinarily mysterious that some instinct or premonition should have impelled my mother, for the first time, to travel alone to Bath to see the son in whom she had invested so much of herself.

Between then and Christmas we paid hurried visits to the members of the Lower Park family in their four separate hospitals. Una lingered on and seemed to be making a very slow recovery. Then, three days after Christmas, the hospital phoned to say that she had died. As Margery and I drove up to London, past cars that had skidded off the icy road, I mourned that I had not had a lucid word with the person who had been the strongest influence on my life – and, above all, that I had not expressed my gratitude for all that she had given me. Visiting my father, in his gloomy Victorian hospital in Tooting, I broke down in tears. 'How has it all come to this?'

But the treatment in hospital seemed to restore my father and they released him to go home. This was a mistake. Being on his own, in a flat which brought back so many memories, was a recipe for renewed depression. I placed Denis in a residential home, the fees paid by letting of the flat, and he spent the remaining decade or so of his life in a boarding environment of his own, reminiscing of India, seemingly content that I should administer his affairs. Thereafter, my Lower Park family life degenerated into a rushed circus of calls at three fairly dismal institutions.

There would be further reminders that term of our common mortality. I attended the funeral of the young man who had found it so impossible to cope with me during my first year. His parents and his younger brother, still at Prior Park, were noble in their anguished fortitude. And then we were saddened afresh by the death of a Lower Sixth Nigerian, Steven Ogunniyi. This gentle boy had suffered for years from sickle cell anaemia but his death shocked his peers. Once again, parents came from a distant country to bury their beloved son. At the Ash Wednesday Mass, two days after Steven's Requiem, God's presence at Prior Park seemed palpable.

There was much to celebrate during the remainder of that year. The Hockey Eleven had yet another magnificent season, so that in four years Alan Hall's teams had lost just two matches – and this included an unbeaten record on a tour of Holland. Gerald Davies took his Seven to Oxford and they returned as winners of their tournament.

And there was my 'Ascension Day Outing' to Paris, wherein I drove Margery, Matthew, Emma and the combined Advanced Level French and History sets for a two-night stay in the Jesuit College of St Louis de Gonzague. It was mostly enjoyable, even though the Headmaster's wallet was snatched. I had been chatting with my group in the Metro when I was approached by a gypsy-clad girl, probably a refugee. Courteously I listened. Then she jumped quickly off the train at the next stop. Clutching for my wallet I found that it had gone. A police van took us to a gendarmerie, where we found a whole bevy of girls lined up for questioning. 'Yugos,' the gendarme curtly explained. But the girls, when challenged, simply lifted their skirts to show that they were not 'in possession'. Margery and I reached Notre Dame in time join our group for the Ascension

Day High Mass. They expressed sympathy. 'People are more important than things,' I replied, with Pecksniffian sanctimoniousness, yet that Mass too yielded a cathartic feeling of solidarity.

In my Prize Day address, I tried to express something of my emotions concerning Prior Park.

> What a vivid community it is. I walk back to my house on a May evening and I am overwhelmed by the sheer beauty of it – the trees and the blossom, wild garlic, the rabbits, that magical valley. Yet at other times, such is the vibration of the place, I feel with that nineteenth century educational prophet, Dr Gentili, that the devil is in the place. It is a testing ground for headmasters as well as for pupils. Sometimes it is good to be brought down to earth with a bump, as I was one day when a seven year old was told by her parents to say 'goodbye' to the headmaster. Brightly she turned to me, extended her hand and said, 'Goodbye Mr Toad.'

I kept my sting for the tail.

> How does one bear fruit? Very much through development of personal maturity…Partly, importantly, through realizing our talents – and this is why parents, teachers and pupils lay such stress on examination results and academic progress…Your questionnaires last year expressed – very rightly – strongest reservations concerning our academic achievement. The next strongest reservations concerned our Sixth Form, a related subject. We have tried very hard this year to cajole, entice, threaten, manipulate, drive our Sixth Form into a different valuation of study and cultural enthusiasm for their own sakes. There are times, I confess, when I feel that I am banging my head against a giant blancmange. The world of pop militates against reflection and intellectual growth, too often drowning thought or conversation. The Walkman must surely be the most inherently anti social invention yet known to schools.

It was hardly surprising that Father Paul gave me two books about the psychology of the adolescent. I never looked at them.

At the end of the year sense demanded that I give up teaching my Sixth Form History set. I wavered, then stood firm. That ensured that the next year would begin as the previous one had ended.

As before, there was the contrast between the agonizing headmaster and a school that was striding forward. In September 1985 the first day girls arrived and I was able to boast a school population of 307 pupils, with 34 day girls accounting for the difference between this number and my gloomy prognostications of two years earlier. We welcomed a new Head of Geography in David Hope, while in Gerard Kilroy, a fellow Old Priorian, I recruited a truly gifted teacher of English and man of culture. He arrived in time to nurture the huge talent of Joanne Riches and I would entrust him progressively with the mission to bring Athens to Sparta.

Meanwhile, I was coming perilously close to self-destruction. I lost weight, as

I prowled around the grounds of Prior Park, achieving a fitness and slimness that I had not known since I was at school. Fergus Lyons offered me a sabbatical and I told him that it was out of the question. Father Paul became ever more concerned about the pressure on myself and about the pressures that I was applying to others. He came across to Kent House and told Margery that he had never seen anyone get as *ANGRY* as I did. She told him that a visit to Lower Park would have explained everything!

Bishop Cormac had Margery and me down to stay with him in Storrington and was marvellously affirmative. As a Rector in Rome, he too knew that a headmaster had to *notice* what was happening in church. In our own house, however, he quietly gave me words of wisdom. 'Patrick, if it is God's will that Prior Park should succeed, it will succeed. If it is not His will, it will not.'

The root of the problem was that I was too *possessive*, to the ultimate detriment of strategic purpose. At Sixth Form prayers one night, Jacob Schwarz, typically, had the honesty to express the prayer that we should all have the grace to 'let go'. Would that I indeed had had the grace and wisdom to do so. Instead I taxed to their limits the good will, patience and tolerance of some pupils, their parents and, indeed, those governors who were aware of the problem and who were trying to help me. As incident succeeded incident in my skirmishing with the Upper Sixth, bemused parents murmured and complained. Governors became worried by the tittle tattle in Bath. Challenged, I dug in. I made endless attempts at reconciliation, but it was always on my terms, that the young men should toe my line, and they knew that in any such relationship it is the pupils who call the tune. I, for my part, was determined not to allow them the satisfaction of victory. Yet when one of the group finally went too far and swore at me after I had caught him late for breakfast, and when Wilfred Hammond pronounced that the young man would have to go, I at least had the honesty to say that it was 'my fault', as it indeed was, and that we must reverse our verdict.

I suppose that it remains an open question as to whether I was right or wrong to force the pace of change. At the end of this fraught year I was able to give parents the good news that Grades 'A' and 'B' constituted a record 34% of Advanced Level results and that two thirds of the Upper Sixth had gained places at university. These included five at Oxbridge, pro rata as good an achievement as could be boasted by schools like Tonbridge. Only one of these, Head Boy Peter O'Donoghue, had derived from Cricklade. Miles Hember, an endangered species as a Day Boy in 1980, had blossomed with the arrival of newcomers like Jacob Schwarz and Patrick Tan. I was delighted when Patrick invited Margery and me to join him above the Mansion to peer through his telescope at Halley's Comet and when he arranged a meeting of the 'Seventeen Club' in Miles Hember's house for a talk by the astronomer, Patrick Moore. Joanne Riches' exceptional progress on all fronts included History. She would sit silently in my classes unless and until I specifically invoked her contribution, whereupon she would so perfectly analyse and correlate that the mouths of her awed peers would literally fall open. That apart, the intelligentsia of the new Prior Park owed nothing to me, except my good fortune in bringing them all together. Nor could I claim credit when John Cooke, who had come to Prior Park four years earlier in the hope that he might become a priest, passed from the Upper Sixth into his seminary. John is now a parish priest and chaplain to the Prior Park Association.

The same could be said of Prior Park's more traditional areas of strength. Gerald Davies and Denis Clarke led a successful rugby tour to the South of France and the First Fifteen spoiled Monkton Combe's Open Day to the tune of 46-3. Our Hockey was as strong as ever. Ian Fox's Cricket Eleven put up a good performance against the side that John Inverarity brought from Pembroke School in Adelaide. Prior Park was becoming more securely established. Martin Pike observed in his strong Ulster tones that the school was changing – 'all those Volvos and BMWs!' Seen in this light my continuing skirmishes with the Old Guard appear the more futile and irrelevant. Some humour and affection remained. The Rosslyn Park Rugby Seven went to see *Clockwise*. John Cleese's demented headmaster reminded them of one person only.

We all put on a good show in April 1986 to say 'Goodbye' to the Christian Brothers. The Provincial, Brother Gillespie, had been a delightfully friendly and supportive presence. He accepted my invitation to preach to the School on the Sunday before the departure of his brethren and gave a rousing address, in which he apologized for any hurts that the Christian Brothers may have committed but urged the boys and girls to go on being Christian brothers and sisters in the years ahead. On the Brothers' final evening in The Priory Bishop Mervyn attended a special supper to celebrate the Brothers' contribution to Prior Park. Among the 90 guests were Doctor Maurice McGinn, who was already an Old Boy of St Brendan's in 1924 when 70 of that school moved across to Bath to refound Prior Park, Brother Carroll, who had come as a Brother to Bath in 1925, and Brother Miller, the last President. A month later, Brother Gillespie was our Guest of Honour at Prize Day. In my speech I expressed to him my heartfelt gratitude that the Christian Brothers had agreed to the transfer of the Priory to the School and thereby made possible the opening of the girls' boarding house at the very time that we needed it.

Once again I looked back to Baines, as this was the eve of the 150th anniversary of the great fire that nearly destroyed Prior Park. He had, characteristically, been planning a great basilica above the school. Instead, ten thousand Bathonians stood on that slope and gazed at him, as he pondered the wreckage of his dreams. That night he sought refuge in the nearby house of one of his most recent converts, the Honourable Mrs Crewe. That house was the Priory.

To an extent that now surprises me, I expressed many of the opinions that I later voiced as a Scottish Principal or as Chairman of HMC, for instance my concern about the future supply of teachers, my belief in the crucial importance of the personal relationships within the school community and the need for an effective partnership between School and Parents. I decried the adolescent cult of 'cool'.

But into this speech I also injected more of myself and of my lifetime's convictions than in any other. It was my last opportunity to explain my 'educational philosophy' to those for whom I had cared so much, fought so much, probably scandalized so much. I wanted them, despite everything, to leave strong in the Faith. As Prior Park became more attractive to the market, I hoped that it was not becoming open also to the old gibe about public school religion, 'just enough religion to be respectable and not enough to be dangerous'.

> I believe that we need to do much more to generate in our senior students the excitement of a spiritual world to find, in prayer, in the knowledge of the Old Testament and the New Testament, an awareness of the length and breadth of Christian witness across the centuries and of the Church's teaching in all its relevance and authority. I see in religious life in School a sort of silting process, with the streams of faith clogged up by the boredom of habit, the confusions of self and the indifferent examples of others. Heaven knows, it is the School's responsibility to provide the dredger rather than the silt (to) prevent the religious aspect of Prior Park from being the aspect least understood, most taken for granted and most vulnerable to the pressures and seductions of the world outside. As Prior Park becomes more attractive to the market I hope that it is not becoming open to that old gibe about Public School religion – 'just enough religion to be respectable and not enough to be dangerous'...
>
> We do not need to look very far, no further indeed than Britain today, to see that society needs Christian teaching and Christian values. When we Catholics were in the ghetto, we were never worried about being the 5% – and ours was a Church that would stand on soap boxes in Hyde Park, found Catholic schools in the inner cities and work for the conversion of England. Now, in a more complicated society, out of the ghetto and into the virtues of mixed marriages and ecumenism, we need to value our convictions, protect them and share them with others. In last week's *Sunday Times*, we read that the Church is agonizing over whether to allow girls to act as altar servers. But read the previous page and there find Irena Ratushinskaya – beaten, force-fed and kept in icy solitary confinement for her Christian faith and her poetic genius. (What was it that Osip Mandelstam said about Russia and its poets? 'Only Russia attaches so much importance to poetry. We kill people for it.')
>
> In Russia issues like conscience and freedom can come through with greater clarity, if only to the few. Ratushinshaya became a Roman Catholic at about the age of our Sixth Form, reverting to the religion of her grandmother.

Appropriately, I ended this, the most heartfelt of my 30 Prize Day speeches, with my personal sentiments.

I am kept sane by two people above all. Wilfred Hammond is the best possible Deputy Head – unflappable, discerning, balanced and untiring. There are no prizes for guessing who the other is. My own better half brings up four children, teaches half a timetable of French, has learned the arts of mass catering, supervises our more boisterous Sixth Formers in the Swimming Pool, works with Maureen McMahon, Eileen McPeake, Lesley Richards, Jane Floyd and Elizabeth Moran to beautify the Chapel with flowers every week: I hope that she is not taken for granted by the Prior Park community. She takes Sixth Formers occasionally down to Squash in Bath, with Sophie in the back. Sophie's idea of Squash is a somewhat distorted one, relating to Sixth Form knees rather than to rubber balls. She said to Margery, the other day, with great enthusiasm, 'I like Squash at Prior Park, Mummy.'

I think that we are all enjoying the squash, although the temperature rises from time to time. We shall all miss this year's Upper Sixth, those émigré nobles from the Ancien Regime who will probably say with Talleyrand that those who have not lived before the Revolution will never appreciate the sweetness of life. We shall continue to work to enable Prior Park to combine the graces and wisdom of earlier generations with the needs and best insights of the twenty-first century.

Sixteen years on, the speech and its sentiments ring true.

So there were happy occasions in the Spring and early Summer of 1986, yet I cannot think of that time without sadness. Koo died on 2 March. She had never got over the loss of Una and the break up of the Lower Park family. Sadder yet were the events of Palm Sunday 1986. Father Paul had arranged that the palms should be blessed on the Mansion steps in front of the whole school, before the congregation processed to the chapel. Stewart Woodward's wife, Terry, was the reader. By the evening she had taken herself and the two children away for good. Stewart asked to be released at the end of term from his housemastership and the school. Next term, Peter O'Donoghue, who had somehow managed to remain above the civil war between his headmaster and his friends, wrote to me from Oxford and mentioned in passing that some were attributing the break-up of the marriage to the pressures that I had imposed on the boys in Allen House. I did not feel that I could respond. I hoped that it was not true, but I could not prove it.

There was a predictably infernal climax to the year. On the previous night I had woken Margery to say that there was a mouse in our bed, was told not to be silly and went back to sleep. The final assembly and Leavers' Ball had passed without incident, but I was tipped off that there would be sixth formers out of the House that night. I went to bed regardless. But in nearby Rainbow Woods 'travellers' chose this night for their own nocturnal concert. I imagine that this awoke us at 3 a.m. This time I was certain that there was a mouse in our bed – it was nibbling at my toe. Margery resignedly pulled back the sheets – and there it was. We carried the undersheet to the open window and eased the mouse (Bishop Mervyn's old friend?) outside.

From Rainbow Woods continued the 'thump, thump' of heavy metal. Furious I sallied forth to sort out the travellers. They were just packing up to go. On my way back into school I decided to pop into the boarding houses to see whether my tip-off was correct. It was – a number of those with whom I had been most closely associated were clearly missing. In the morning I told John Moran. He looked despairingly at me. 'Patrick, what were you *doing* in the House at three in the morning?' 'Well, John,' I started, 'you see, there was a mouse in my bed.'

CHAPTER 15

Exit the Hireling

I came to Prior Park from a superbly run school, in which it would have been inconceivable to appoint a housemaster without very many years of service, not only to the school but as a tutor in a house. By this token we should have sunk without trace...We have had to compromise, improvise, massage and conceal. Yet we have got somewhere and we have got there because we did not see ourselves as treading in the steps of the clergy. We wanted to go our own way, picking and choosing what we wished to emulate and what we wished to ditch.

(Talk to the Boarding Schools' Association
Conference for Housemasters, January 1988)

THE OPENING of the Priory House in September 1986 was a decisive moment in the story of lay Prior Park. Although Prior Park had had Sixth Form day girls since 1982 and 11+ Day Girls since 1985, and although the Preparatory School at Cricklade had been admitting boarding and day girls since 1983, it was by no means axiomatic that Prior Park College would become a fully coeducational boarding school. In theory at least it could have emerged as a day school for boys and girls, with a steadily contracting section for boy boarders.

If the departure of the Christian Brothers to Liverpool in 1986 supplied the key to an 8 to 18 fully coeducational Prior Park, the way ahead had first to be charted, agreed and funded. The very beauty of Prior Park's situation was a potentially fatal obstacle to our plans. With extraordinary skill and patience Admiral Robertson negotiated with the City planners and our architects an acceptable plan for the Prior Park estate as a whole. We could then assume the granting of planning permission for the new boarding house. Meanwhile, we needed to raise a seven figure sum, without any financial reserves and in advance of any revenue from our girls boarders. In seeking a loan from our bankers, we were handicapped by the fact that we did not own the Prior Park freehold, but were merely tenants of the Christian Brothers. It was an enormous relief when John Leay announced that terms had been concluded. These were the necessary preliminaries before the decision by our Trustees and Governors that Prior Park would admit boarding girls.

In one sense, it was an enormous gamble. Prior Park would be encumbered by debt for years to come and its ability to meet interest payments would depend entirely on the success of the enterprise. Yet Prior Park had become used to walking its tightrope. Having got half way across the gorge, it would have been silly to have lost heart and turned back to where we had started. We agreed that we would have to launch another Appeal and, on John Bogie's suggestion, we appointed as our Appeal Director the former Middlesex and England cricketer, Eric Russell.

Just over four months after the departure of the Christian Brothers, the Priory House opened. Most of its first boarders were thirteen or sixteen year olds, but the House also became the base for Prior Park's day girls. Anne Hammond had gallantly accepted my request that she should be the resident Housemistress. She brought to the Priory her own unique brand of gallic perfectionism and, with Wilfred at her elbow, ensured the best possible start. In the following year, to provide room in the main House for the first arrivals from Cricklade, we built a small Sixth Form annexe. I named this 'Allworthy', Henry Fielding's pun on his friend and patron, Ralph Allen. The major extension needed for the planned Priory House complement of sixty girls was completed a year later. I imagine that the months of dust and scaffolding are etched on to the souls of Anne and Wilfred Hammond. My debt to them is enormous.

September 1986 also saw the entry of Emma Tobin into Form Lower Three, along with an encouragingly large number of other girls from Bath. That too portended well for the future.

There was another sense in which the School entered a new era in September 1986. Almost without exception, the boys and girls of the School had known no other Headmaster but myself. Of the pupils who had been at Prior Park under the Christian Brothers, only Andrew Hadley and Peter Smith remained. Andrew had been an exceptionally relaxed member of the 'old guard', but I was certainly not going to allow that to inhibit the return of so talented a sportsman. Peter Smith had come to Prior Park in 1979, when he was barely ten, and in consequence had 'repeated' a year during his passage through the School.

The first day of term dashed any hopes that there had been an end to drama in my dealings with boy boarders. The parents of a fifteen year old boy in Oxford had, for year, been wrestling with his refusal to attend school. For some reason the Oxford social services recommended Prior Park to them. Perhaps the answer to 'J's school phobia was for him to move to a friendly boarding school and thereby be released from the daily anguish of going to school. I happened to be standing outside the Mansion as 'J', flanked by his clearly worried mother and father, arrived on foot and approached along the main drive. I shook hands warmly and welcomed 'J' – whereupon he fled down the drive, through the main gates and down Ralph Allen Drive. In hot pursuit I managed to overhaul him, in front of two men working on a gas main. Calmly, I walked him back to his parents. Even so, I was still panting as I said, not

September 1986, Kent House – Emma joins Matthew at Prior Park.

unkindly, 'J, you won't do that to me again, will you?' 'No,' he said, and promptly bolted. Wearily I set off after him, and again I caught him just as he drew level with the gas men. Once more we returned to his parents, standing transfixed where we had left them. A third time 'J' shot off towards the gate. Kevin Ryder, the smallest of my new prefects, had seen these events unfold and he must have feared for his headmaster's health. Before 'J' had time to move more than a few yards, Kevin hurtled across and rugby-tackled him to the ground. There was now no question of 'J' escaping. On the contrary, his injuries were such that he had to be taken immediately to Eileen McPeake in the Infirmary. I wondered how many other schools had seen a new boy admitted to the Infirmary before he had even set foot in a school building and on account of injury by a prefect.

I persuaded the parents to leave 'J' in Eileen's care. On Monday morning I drove Sophie down to her school in Bath and was returning up Ralph Allen Drive when, just level with the two gas men, I saw a by now familiar figure striding purposefully down the hill. I screeched to a stop, bundled 'J' into the car and returned him to Prior Park society. By now I knew that the experiment was doomed to failure. Margery and I took him out with a number of his peers for an excursion to Exmoor but it was clearly a matter of time before we lost him for good. Yet 'J' made only one further bid for freedom, and then embarked on a career that would bring him into the Catholic Church and take him to

Head of House, Oxford degree, doctorate and marriage – in Prior Park, of course!

On 21 November 1986 Bishop Mervyn Alexander came to Prior Park to say a special Mass of thanksgiving. 150 years to the day since Bishop Baines had launched St Paul's his successor now formally opened the Priory. Next day the Choir excelled itself in their performance of Mozart's Requiem. We had done our best to beautify the old St Paul's building and I decided that it was also time for a fresh look at our boarding arrangements for boys. Such planning coincided with the arrival of new housemasters in St Paul's. Paul Fisher had succeeded Stewart Woodward as Allen Housemaster in September 1986. Next Easter, Gerald Davies moved to Surrey as the first lay headmaster of a girls' school previously run by nuns. His final season in charge of the First Fifteen yielded thirteen wins in 14 matches, including a 'clean sweep' in Bath. Denis Clarke took over from him both the housemastership of Roche and the coaching of the First Fifteen, while continuing to carry on his broad shoulders responsibility for the History department. Of such men are good small schools made.

My tussles with the tyranny of the St Paul's peer group had inclined me towards a 'vertical' house system, whereby boys did not transfer en masse at 14 from St Peter's to the two St Paul's houses, but instead spent five years in one of three 13 to 18 houses. At the end of the year we carried through our plans for a such a system. For the first time ever, thirteen year old boys entered the St Paul's houses, Allen and Roche, while John Moran now led 'Clifford House', a 13 to 18 house based in St Peter's. The 11 to 13 girls and boys now constituted 'Baines House', with Richard Wells as its founding Housemaster.

Father Paul Edward left Prior Park in the summer of 1987. His health was never strong and the strains and stresses of Prior Park and its headmaster by now outweighed the pleasure and satisfaction that he gained from the school and its community. He returned to a small parish in Sussex but sustained his links with Prior Park. At Easter 1989, as priest and patient, he accompanied the Prior Park pupils and staff in the 'jumbulance' memorably organized by Bobby Simmonds. Three months later he was dead. I hope that Father Paul realized how much he meant to us all.

In his place I recruited a young and furiously energetic Benedictine monk from Farnborough Abbey. Dom Stephen Darlington had been serving as Director of Studies at another prominent Catholic Independent school, but he was attracted by a post that more closely expressed his priesthood. Philosopher, sprinter and general activist, Father Stephen eventually found the 'passive' role of chaplaincy less suited to his intellect and personality than the leadership of schools, but that was after my time. For reasons of personal association I was a little sad when he moved the small Oratory out of the Mansion and created its equivalent in a room off the main chapel, and I put my foot down when I learned that he was intending that his GCSE Religious Studies group should focus on Judaism rather than Catholicism, but I was fortunate indeed that my last years at Prior Park were with a chaplain of kindred temperament and that he made such a dynamic impact on the School.

The fact that Stewart Woodward and Gerald Davies had performed so many key roles increased the difficulty of replacing them. The gap in the R.E. department was nobly filled for a term by Sidney and Mary Ash, before Bobby Simmonds arrived in January 1987. Who would compile the school timetable? I solved this conundrum by persuading Brian Bane, the longstanding Head of Mathematics, to accept this thankless task and by enlisting Robert Summerson, who had already established a considerable local reputation, to come to Prior Park to lead its Mathematics department. We agreed that it was unreasonable for Brian to accomplish the timetable for 1987/88 at such short notice so I spent the Easter holiday doing it myself. As it happened Margery was leading our French exchange to the Vosges. I did not make myself popular with her by secreting myself in the loft of our host family while I juggled and manipulated people and arrangements. I commend the exercise to any Head who really wants to know how the School functions and who is doing most of the work.

The School had grown gratifyingly by September 1987, its roll of 366 pupils including 95 girls. Increased numbers necessitated extra teachers and I took care that these should be young women. Angela Webster and Deidre Barrett duly launched their teaching careers at Prior Park. Angela is now Deputy Head of a famous HMC school. Deidre is still a valued teacher at Prior Park. The teaching profession needs both types of professional dedication.

The only problem with these enlightened appointments was that they failed to address the loss of Gerald Davies and Stewart Woodward as rugby coaches. So Patrick Tobin, who had thought that he had hung up his boots for good in 1983, embarked on yet another stint with the Under 15 XV. Matthew Tobin was one young man who was extremely unhappy with this unkind turn of events.

By now it seemed that nothing could check the emergence of Prior Park as a force in boys' sport in the West Country. The Hockey Eleven had yet another outstanding season and Martin Woodhouse became the first Prior Park boy to play for English Schools. In Cricket, all the hard work of Paul Fisher and John Gibney bore fruit in seven victories over other schools. It was a delight too to see some of the longest serving teachers deriving great pleasure from the arrival of girls. I was extremely grateful to Tony O'Sullivan for coaching girls' hockey with huge enthusiasm and success.

It was a great thrill to me when Peter Levi chose to make Prior Park the focal point of a highly idiosyncratic Channel Four programme. He wandered around the St Peter's wash room, that remarkable central area (now no more) where each boy had his own wash basin. In the rococo Academy Hall in the Mansion he asked that a young boy should play *Jerusalem* on our (reproduction) harpsichord and Matthew Tobin duly obliged. Then the scene changed to the main school chapel and the entire school sang Blake's great hymn of yearning. I invited the poet and professor into Kent House to talk with the 'Twenty Club' (as it had now become). The boys and girls acquitted themselves excellently. Peter Levi left amazed that everyone seemed so happy.

Another very welcome and memorable guest was the Duke of Norfolk, who was the guest of honour of the Prior Park Association at their dinner. Walking round St Peter's he met Miles Dyton. 'Hello, what's your name?' 'Miles, Sir.' 'Mine's Miles too! Here's ten pounds.'

For the 1988 prize giving we had another illustrious guest, Archbishop John Ward. For the first time we held the ceremony at the end of term, a change that removed any pressure from exams but also cost us the attendance of many of our leavers. By now the increased size of the School had forced us out of the gymnasium and into a marquee in front of the Mansion. I bade a final farewell to Peter Smith, whose return for a further year in the Sixth Form had enabled him to extend his Prior Park career to a record nine years, as well as to the six boys who had joined the Lower Third in 1981 – Edgardo Robinson, Paolo Chiarotti, Tony Foo, Thomas Grove, Marco Hughes and James Powell.

> I was told two days ago that, on his first night in St Peter's, Paolo went to Andrew Mock to ask him where he should leave his shoes to be polished. Mr Mock, also on his first night, said that he would have to be consult Mr Moran. We have all grown older and wiser since then.

By now I had commissioned our own video film from a Lower Sixth boy, Andrew Downey, as part of our efforts on behalf of the Appeal. Vivaldi accompanied the camera as it panned around the sumptuous valley, the choir sang Bruckner's *Locus Iste a Deo Factus Est* and there were a few excruciatingly stilted words from the Headmaster. Margery and I took the film out to Hong Kong, where we showed it in our hotel at a reception for all our Hong Kong parents. Our visit was funded by a great friend of the school, Dr Deanna Rudyard, and she also arranged for us to stay in her hotel in Canton, a vivid insight into a very different culture. On our flight home we heard that there had been a devastating hurricane throughout England and we arrived somewhat ashamed that we had been enjoying ourselves during such an appalling trauma.

The old tensions between pre-1981 and post-1981 staff had receded into history. The introduction of appraisal seemed to arouse no fuss or apprehension. When Vic Ferguson, that doughty and crusty Careers Master and Head of Science and Biology decided that he would retire in July 1988, it was clear that Prior Park was losing one of the finest teachers it had ever had, yet no-one doubted that Richard Wells would be eminently capable of sustaining his standards. Pat McMahon decided that this was the appropriate time for him to pass on to Gerard Kilroy the leadership of the English department. Pat became

Senior Master, with responsibility for organizing our programme of appraisal, and Gerard Kilroy Prior Park's first Director of Studies.

On the face of things, therefore, all was serene. In reality, my moorings had been loosened. HMC met in Cambridge in September 1987. We were greeted by an announcement that a Mr Crouch, the Chairman of Governors of Sydney Grammar School, was staying in a Cambridge hotel and would welcome contact with anyone who cared to discuss the impending vacancy in his school's headship. I went and had a chat, then returned to Bath and wrote a polite letter saying that the time was not right. We were in the early stages of an Appeal at Prior Park and I wanted to see it through. About nine months later, Mr Crouch wrote to ask if circumstances had changed and I would be interested in meeting him during his next visit to England. I agreed and then took off on our family holiday.

For some years we had stayed in a small caravan on a seaside campsite at S. Bartolomeo di Cervo, half way between Nice and Genoa. In the summer of 1988 we combined this with our second canal boat expedition. A week on the Oxford canal in 1987 had persuaded us that it would be marvellous to hire a long boat and sail westwards on the Canal du Midi as far as Carcassonne. One day, the repose of the canal was disturbed by a man shouting that he had a telegram for us. Mr Crouch wanted to interview me in London, all expenses paid. So I deposited the family in Cervo, drove to Nice and flew back to England. There were two interviews, Mr Crouch having discovered after our first that he had forgotten to switch on his tape recorder. The outcome was a request that Margery and I should fly out to Sydney in September.

I knew that my one-time Tonbridge colleague, Michael Mavor, had earlier shown an interest in the Sydney Grammar post and I telephoned him for advice. I discovered later that he had been offered the headship, but had decided, on his return to Scotland, to decline it. Christopher Everett, as one of my referees, informed me that there was a short list of two. I think that Margery and I flew out to Sydney on the assumption that we would probably accept the post if I was offered it. This thought alone cast a shadow over the marvellous week that we spent in the Australia Club overlooking Sydney Harbour, revisiting The King's School and seeing all our old friends. Perhaps life in Sydney would be possible, but what on earth would we do with the children?

A week or so after our return Mr Crouch phoned. 'I am sorry, Patrick,' he began – and my heart soared. We would be staying in Prior Park after all.

It was not to be. A few weeks later, I had another phone call. It was Michael Mavor. Michael Walker, the Edinburgh Merchant Company and a fellow Old Lorettonian, had asked him whether he knew any headmaster who might be able and willing to become the Principal of Daniel Stewart's and Melville College and The Mary Erskine School, the two schools administered by the Merchant Company on the north side of Edinburgh. Michael had mentioned me. It happened that Michael Walker would soon be visiting his son in Bristol. Would I be interested in meeting him? I agreed.

As one of Matthew's friends remarked, it was odd that I should be wishing to leave just when I had at last achieved my aims for Prior Park. That September there were 389 pupils in the School, of whom 121 were girls. Prior Park was on course to its target of 415 boys and girls. It was deeply satisfying to reflect that coeducation was proving such a success – and that Prior Park would have been facing closure had it remained a single-sex school for boys. We had the largest influx of new staff since 1981 and they were excellent. On 7 October 1988 Fergus Lyons declared open the Priory extension and we called it the 'Alexander Pope Wing' on account of two happy coincidences – that it was 250 years since *One Thousand Seven Hundred and Thirty Eight*, Pope's tribute to Ralph Allen, and 300 years since his birth in 1688. That year had also seen the establishment of the Western District, so on 20 October the five bishops whose sees had been carved out of the former district concelebrated a tercentennial Mass of Thanksgiving in the Prior Park Chapel. I had moved the Common Room into the Mansion, so that they enjoyed the rooms that had previously been the 'Large Parlour' and the Headmaster's Study, while I moved into the 'Small Parlour' overlooking the valley.

Why, then, did I countenance the abandonment of the job I loved? I was undoubtedly tired, perhaps even a little bored. The work of reorganization seemed complete, for the time being at least, and it is revealing that, by September 1988, I had committed myself to teaching History to Advanced and GCSE level and to coaching the Under 15 group in both rugby and cricket. I threw myself into mastering a new Advanced Level syllabus on the French Revolution, and rediscovered in Robin Tjolle the joy of teaching a young historian fired by the subject.

But there was also a feeling that I was banging my head against a wall. I found it difficult to cope with staffing problems for which I alone was responsible, having imported the teachers in question. After one interview in my study, I found that I had 'levitated' on to the playing fields above the mansion. Merely brooding about another colleague was twice sufficient to leave me in a faint. I became thick-skinned towards others and thin-skinned about myself. I was quick to take offence. Having challenged John Bogie's prospectus for Cricklade on grounds of literary style, I was mortified when the Governors, who had previously allowed me a completely free hand, now asked to review my own third prospectus. In fact, they backed off and I was justly pleased with the outcome, but I am amazed now that I could have allowed myself to become so much the 'overmighty subject' in my own imagination. I found it particularly galling when Cricklade parents decided to send their children elsewhere, having had their expectations raised by our Preparatory School's magnificent new swimming pool and classroom block, while my beleaguered galleon wallowed along with no new facilities whatsoever other than the Priory House and a storage hut on our rugby pitch. Above all, I saw the Appeal's failure as a reflection on myself.

I have no recollection of the sum that Eric Russell and I eventually raised. Several parents were very generous but the overall sum seemed pifflingly insignificant and I took the failure to heart. Perhaps we needed an Ian Botham rather than an opening batsman as our Appeal Director, but I felt that the main cause of the need to increase the run rate was the pedestrian performance of the Headmaster. Our failure with the Old Boys was total. I remember, in particular, a long and wearisome journey to Altrincham. Eric had managed to secure the presence of Father Jack Keegan, the very popular former Housemaster of St Paul's who had left the Christian Brothers to become a parish priest, and his presence indeed attracted many former pupils. They listened politely to me and to Eric but did not give a penny. One of them asked Father Keegan whether he had heard from 'x'. 'He broke my heart,' was his startling reply. What was it about Prior Park, I have asked myself many times since, that it should induce such sentiments in those entrusted with its leadership?

Margery and I went by sleeper to Edinburgh. As we inspected the gloomy Gothicism of Stewart's Melville College and met the apparently dour teachers of The Mary Erskine School, Margery was confident that I would see the folly of moving. Instead I was once again attracted by the challenge. It was confirmed that I should travel a second time to Edinburgh to attend a formal interview by the Merchant Company Education Board.

Before then, we had to lunch a former Chairman of HMC and Principal of George Watson's College, Sir Roger Young. To Margery's delight he told me that he 'would not touch the job with a bargepole'. Already, however, I knew enough about the politics of the Merchant Company to realize that this was a move by the 'old guard' to head off a dangerous interloper. Rightly or wrongly, for better or for worse, I was determined to make the move. The interview was enough of a formality for me to get away with mixing the Christian names of Roger Young and my predecessor, Robin Morgan. When asked how I would deal with smoking behind the bike shed, I said that I would 'inconvenience the malefactor', to the great amusement and satisfaction of my audience.

The final two terms in Bath flashed by. Thirty-seven boys and girls were confirmed by Bishop Mervyn. We had a centenary party for our swimming pool. I played my last innings in cricket, taking care to declare before I was dismissed. Damian Ettinger became my last Prior Park recruit to the Common Room. (He has just been appointed to his first headship.) There was a Charity run by the teaching staff around the Prior Park grounds and my eyes filled with tears as the procession of my gallant young teachers, male and female, sped past the Mansion in front of me. Otherwise I kept my emotions in check.

29 June 1989 was sunny and warm. The school packed into the old gym-

nasium for 'my' last assembly. I do not recall what I said, only what followed, for Wilf Hammond took the microphone and told me that, for once, I would not have the last word. Vanity demands that I repeat the penultimate paragraph in his sumptuously generous tribute:

> If you want a basis for judgement look around you. You see a full school, a happy school, an achieving school. No headmaster could achieve more than that. There could be no more eloquent testimony to any headmaster's achievement. Look at each other, look at the school, look at its precarious past and its promising future, and you will see something of the achievement of these last eight years.

29 June is the Feast of Saints Peter and Paul Father. Father Stephen invited me to choose my favourite hymns for the Mass. In his sermon he drew smiles to many faces when he enlarged on the more difficult aspects of St Peter's character. In the gospel, however, with his eye not far from me, he delivered Christ's parable about leadership. The good shepherd stays with his sheep. The hireling deserts them.

Chris Patten was the Guest of Honour. We recalled his early days in the St Benedict's First Eleven. He said that I was a fine example of the Catholic schoolmaster. As we walked away afterwards, he told me that the great thing in life was to go when they were all cheering you.

I spoke at inordinate length to my sweltering audience. I paid my belated but utterly sincere tributes to Susie Holmes and Wilfred Hammond and, above all, to Margery and her secret of eternal youth. I recalled the Lower Third boy who, after a few weeks in the School, had suddenly exclaimed. 'Oh! Mrs Tobin, I had not realized. Is Mr Tobin your father?' …'To the world outside Kent House she has been, as a Governor told me in her presence, "charm and eminent good sense". Within Kent House, she has been to me the indispensable, if all-too-often submerged, rock of sanity, wisdom and total support.' I thanked Fergus Lyons for the privilege of working at Prior Park and for supporting me through thick and thin. I told the boys and girls that I was immensely proud of them.

In seeking a peroration I had initially been at a loss for an anniversary but I had been rescued by Matthew, who had pointed out that it was 225 years to the day since the death of Ralph Allen! Then I remembered the battle of Kosovo in 1389, and I drew inspiration for the last time from Rebecca West and the poem that she had placed at the heart of her wonderful book on Yugoslavia, the poem of the Grey Falcon.

> Six hundred years ago, in June 1389, Tsar Lazar perished in battle on Kosovo and the Kingdom of Serbia perished for nearly five centuries. But it remains as true today as it was then that a civilization can only live and endure, as the Serbian civilization has indeed endured, not through material triumphs but through the community of values and beliefs. Prior Park College was created to educate Catholics for this world, yes, but not so that our boys and girls should choose the earthly kingdom before the heavenly kingdom.

Farewell to Prior Park.

'An earthly kingdom lasts only a little time
But a heavenly kingdom will last for eternity and its centuries.'

At the end, I received the first and last standing ovation of my life. I would not work again in a Catholic school.

CHAPTER 16

Incomer

I feel that I have now got the top brass at both schools solidly behind my schemes, but it has been quite nerve-racking pushing my ideas through the planning stages. I am pleased, because I came to believe at Prior Park that if you didn't pull the school round to your way of thinking in your first (honeymoon) year, it is always more difficult to move people afterwards. And if that is true of one school it is trebly difficult when there are two schools to persuade and neither will move without the other!

(Letter to Emma and Matthew 28 February 1990)

IT WAS A massive shock to our systems. The Dorset heat wave was a fading memory as we infiltrated the grey outskirts of the grey city. At last we stopped outside the sixties house in Ravelston House Loan where we would live until the Merchant Company settled our permanent accommodation. 'It's gross,' said Emma. We spent the night as guests of the Honeymans in Heriot Row. Then we met the removal van from Bath. The driver expressed amazement that we should wish to leave Kent House for this!

Fourteen years later, we are all very much more positive about our great trek to the North than we felt at that moment. Matthew, with me off his back, grew prodigiously in size and gregariousness and moved on to Merton College – specially chosen, I suspect, because it had twice rejected his father – to read History. Emma also stayed at Prior Park, initially to be with Matthew and friends, then because there was no obvious alternative for her Sixth Form education, but she paid the highest price for our move. She became Head Girl, won her place at Oxford and treasured her Prior Park friendships – they would all be there on a magically sunny April Saturday in 2002 when she was married to Rob at Prior Park by Cardinal Cormac Murphy-O'Connor. But she missed home dreadfully, or, perhaps, realized that her home was missing her. Most Saturday mornings, throughout Matthew's and Emma's time as boarders at Prior Park and undergraduates at Oxford, I would type out on my Amstrad a common letter with individual variations, a practice later extended to Lucy. It was for me a form of catharsis and the thick file now takes me back into recesses otherwise hidden from the memory.

Our younger daughters became Scottish pupils. Because year groups in Scotland are calculated from February rather than September, Scottish boys and girls are on average six months younger than their English counterparts. Both Lucy and Sophie would leave school a year earlier than would have been the case in Bath. Lucy was heartbroken that she would not be moving to Prior Park but put a brave face on things until the first day at Mary Erskine. She felt so savaged by that experience that she locked herself in her bedroom and would not emerge for hours. For a year or so she could not bear to be close to me in public and she never fully lost her feelings of vulnerability, yet she thrived at Mary Erskine, won Colours for her Music, became a sergeant in the CCF, followed her sister into a Modern Languages course at Oxford and made friendships that have endured. Sophie moved into the Mary Erskine and Stewart's Melville Junior School at eight. She assimilated immediately and she bounced irrepressibly through the next ten years. To Lucy's achievements she added one that meant much to me as an 'incomer', the status of premiere Highland Dancer at The Mary Erskine School and, indeed, in all the competitions that she entered. She too went to Oxford, as a historian.

Margery also looks kindly on her Edinburgh years. The Edinburgh Royal Choral Union was the finest of the many choirs in which she has sung and she left it as its Secretary. At Mary Erskine she soon became a full time and highly respected teacher of French. In the Staff Room she was seen as the human and humorously subversive face of Tobindom. She enjoyed the 'buzz' of Edinburgh, admired the attack and capability of the Scots and developed an affection for the panoply of Merchant Company connections in whom the schools rejoiced, an affection clearly reciprocated towards her.

The downside? We kept our house in Chideock and took off for Dorset each holiday and half-term, but Margery felt out of reach of her parents as they aged and I was similarly removed from my father and my brother. All of these would die before we left Edinburgh. Only in the case of Denis was either of us present at the end. He gently slipped away on 5 January 1997. Michael had died two years earlier, on 9 January 1995. His bowel cancer had been in remission for many years and it was merciful that he died within days of its re-eruption. I rushed south but was met at the hospital by Matthew with the news that Michael had died a few hours earlier.

And because we headed south for our holidays, we never saw Edinburgh as a place of relaxation or enjoyment and we never made time for sheer gregariousness. I am sure that many of the HMC members of the Scottish Division saw more of one another – over the dinner table or on the golf course. Being Principal of The Mary Erskine School, Daniel Stewart's and Melville College and their Combined Junior School was, first and last, a job.

Perhaps this was just as well. Edinburgh is a consumers' paradise for the patrons of Independent schools. It is said that when two Edinburgh castaways meet each other on a desert island, the first question they ask is, 'Which school did you go to?' You could not attend a cocktail party in Edinburgh without hearing the parents of another school vigorously backstabbing their Head and I have no doubt that the same applied to me. During the next decade others came up from England to lead Edinburgh schools and soon retreated, licking wounds. One of these described the world of Edinburgh Independent School parents as 'the piranha tank'.

Shortly after we arrived, the BBC showed a short television play, *A Week in August*. It was about a state school boy who won a scholarship to Stewart's Melville. In Aitken & Niven's, the school outfitters in Princes Street, the salesman walks past the Watson's and Heriot's blazers before ushering mother and son towards the black and red uniforms of Stewart's Melville. 'Ah yes! Quite the best results in the whole of Edinburgh. The school where all the cabinet ministers send their children.' It wasn't true, of course, but gratifying nonetheless.

'It's a big job,' said Robin Morgan, as he briefed me over a typically generous whisky. That was an understatement. It was, in terms of number of pupils, by far the largest job in British Independent education. The Mary Erskine School was Scotland's oldest girls school. Founded by Mary Erskine and the Edinburgh Merchant Company in 1694 as a 'Hospital' for the daughters of deceased or destitute Merchants, it had become overnight in 1870 a large day school for several hundred girls. Over the centuries it had wandered to many locations, but since 1966 it had rejoiced in purpose-built new buildings in its own parkland in Ravelston.

A mile away, at the other end of Ravelston Dykes and facing Queensferry Road, stood Daniel Stewart's and Melville College. This was a hybrid of two more recently established institutions. Daniel Stewart, who had made his fortune in India, left it in 1814 to the Merchant Company for the foundation of a Hospital similar to those of Mary Erskine, George Heriot and George Watson. The survival of an indigent niece meant that the first boys did not come to Queensferry Road until January 1855. Those thirty waifs must have been awed beyond measure by the size and soaring cupolas of David Rhind's fantastic edifice, originally designed for the House of Commons but evocative, rather, of the Kremlin.

Daniel Stewart's had chugged along for nearly 120 years as the 'poor relation' of George Watson's College – in endowment, in public perception and in the Merchant Company pecking order – until a seismic upheaval transformed the more famous schools of Edinburgh. The four electoral victories of Harold Wilson and the Labour Party threatened the very future of selective education. Faced by the loss of the Direct Grant, some schools, like James Gillespie's (of Muriel Spark and Miss Jean Brodie), accepted their comprehensive destiny. Some, like John Watson's (now the Modern Art Gallery), closed. And some amalgamated. Thus did the hitherto separate George Watson's Colleges for boys and girls come together under Roger Young to become a single school of over two thousand pupils.

On the North side of Edinburgh, the future of Daniel Stewart's College became more secure in 1973 with the absorption of the boys of Melville College. This small school, founded in 1830 by the remarkable Robert Cunningham, was in many ways more distinguished than Daniel Stewart's, notably in rugby where fiery ladies in the Junior School fostered the talents of Calders and Brewsters. The merger of the red blazers of Melville with the black of Stewart's had a catalytic effect on the Queensferry Road establishment. It became a force in the land.

Less happy seemed the prospects of The Mary Erskine School. The Merchant Company saw no future for a fee-paying girls school in competition with the many other girls' schools in Edinburgh. Ten years after Miss Jennings had moved her school from Queen Street to Ravelston (over an October half-term!), the Merchant Company negotiated the sale of its oldest school to Lothian Region. At the eleventh hour an unlikely saviour emerged, the redoubtable Labour Secretary of State, Willie Ross. Not for Willie Ross the modern hypocrisy, whereby middle class parents purchase educational advantage through their postcodes. He was adamant that the denizens of Murrayfield and Barnton would not have free prestige education on the rates and he vetoed the purchase.

By now The Mary Erskine School was haemorrhaging badly. The Merchant Company decided to join its Junior School, up to Primary 5, with that of Stewart's Melville. The senior schools would remain separate, each with its own Head, but the two Heads would be asked to apply for the new post of Principal of the North Side schools. Robin Morgan had been in post for a year. Jean Thow had been Mary Erskine's Headmistress since 1967. The Merchant Company selected Robin Morgan. For an anguished year he shared the leadership of The Mary Erskine School with Jean Thow. From 1979 until his retirement ten years later, he was the Head of Mary Erskine AND of Stewart's Melville.

Both schools had small boarding sections. These stood next door to each other on Queensferry Terrace. The boys lived in Dean Park House, a heavily impressive mansion once owned by the Salvesen family and more recently detested as the place where Army Medicals had been conducted during the War. The girls occupied a much more modest terrace of houses.

This was the job that I inherited. There was a job to inherit because of Robin Morgan's panache in broadcasting the virtues of this extraordinary arrangement. He argued that it was 'the best of both worlds' – coeducational primary schooling, followed by single-sex adolescent education that yet brought boys and girls together for drama, music and (his great passion) the CCF. I have no reason to disbelieve the report that the Merchant Company imagined that, in time, numbers at each end of Ravelston Dykes would fall sufficiently to make a coeducational merger the obvious and necessary outcome. Robin Morgan made such speculation superfluous. Malcolm Rifkind, who had been a pupil of

Robin's at George Watson's, was fond of telling the story that Robin's History set had invented a caption for their teacher – 'First know your facts, then you can do with them what you want.' It was, the future Foreign Secretary remarked, a lesson that had stood him in good stead! They were skills employed to the full by the 'Laird of Ravelston', as Robin's HMC colleagues affectionately dubbed him. Even so, I suspect that he never really felt at home in Ravelston. Although the numbers of those who had worked under Jean Thow dwindled, there lingered in the Staff Room a feeling that Ravelston had fallen to an occupying power from the other end of the Dykes. Robin was at Ravelston for two days each week and he had two studies, one in the main block, the other in Ravelston House. 'Patrick,' he said often to me, 'the girls are *marvellous*. It's the staff that gets you down!'

The other half of the 'dynamic duo' who had fashioned the Erskine Stewart's Melville conglomerate was the Junior School Headmaster, Brian Head. He elected to depart with Robin Morgan in 1989 and I had been invited to participate in the selection of his successor. Bryan Lewis, the Head of Middle School at Stewart's Melville, was the clear winner. A Dublin Protestant with a silver tongue and lightning wit, Bryan had joined the school precisely at the point when Melville came to Stewart's and had, indeed, been the co-historian of Stewart's Melville's first decade. In the previous year he had directed a wonderfully successful Appeal to bring Technology to the schools. Bryan now adapted effortlessly to the Junior School, made it the best as well as the biggest of its kind and was to me an ally beyond price. With incomparable flair, boundless drive, marketing genius and a quiet but steely determination never to be second, he ensured that I would never again have to worry about numbers. Bryan Lewis was a one-man guarantor of growth.

In 1989 some clouds obscured this rosy outlook. Cabinet ministers were more likely to favour Watson's or boarding schools either side of the Border. The upper echelons of the Law inclined towards Edinburgh Academy and St George's, these being smaller and more 'English' than the Merchant Company conglomerates. Bryan Lewis and I were determined to challenge ancient ascendancies and we were backed to the hilt in such ambitions by the new Erskine Stewart's Melville Governing Council and its outstanding Chairman.

Until November 1989 all the Merchant Company schools came under the direction of the Merchant Company Education Board and its Secretariat in Hanover Street. While the two Principals were broadly independent in their recruitment of pupils and staff and in the general running of their Schools, they had to operate within the budgetary and policy parameters prescribed by the Board. In practice, therefore, they shared their sovereignty with the Board's longstanding Secretary, Bill McDonald, and his Deputy, Judith Sischy. I gathered from Sir Roger Young that he had been entirely happy with this arrangement at George Watson's College, presumably because the Education Board's decisions were those requested by Sir Roger. Robin Morgan and Bertie Bellis, however, had chafed against the glass ceilings and not always subtle patronage of Hanover Street. Joan Bellis told me subsequently that she determined that her husband should leave Daniel Stewart's when he was asked to send his Prizegiving speech to Hanover Street for approval by Judith Sischy, recently appointed as Assistant Secretary after a few years of teaching experience.

Michael Walker perceived that the Merchant Company schools would never attain their full potential unless and until they were able to fashion their individual destinies. He was successful in importing like-minded men into the Court of the Merchant Company, without whom it would have been impossible to accomplish the revolution within his two-year period of office. The Merchant Company followed its Master and resolved to delegate responsibility for the running of its schools to newly constituted governing councils, with the role of 'Chief Executive' henceforward pertaining to the two Principals and not to the Secretary of the Merchant Company. Used as I was to being my own boss, I would never have considered the move to Edinburgh without Michael Walker's assurance that the 'Promised Land', as Robin Morgan habitually described it, was indeed within sight. The handover would take place in November 1989.

At Stewart's Melville College and then at Mary Erskine I was formally inducted into my post by the new Master of the Merchant Company, Sir Peter Heatly. I must have looked tense as I waited for the doors of the huge assembly hall at Queensferry Road to be thrown open. 'Feeling nervous?' asked Jack Matthew, resplendent in his janitor's uniform.

Otherwise I remember little of those early weeks. I recall standing in the study in Ravelston House, surveying the scene and wondering what exactly a Principal was supposed to do. It was no coincidence that I should commit the Tobins to two follies at this time, the purchase of a timeshare, against Matthew's emphatic and absolutely correct advice, and the acquisition of a croft in Newtonmore. (The timeshare has been exchanged annually for places that we would never otherwise have visited. The croft became a much loved Highlands headache.)

My first three months were a curious period. On the one hand, I served as an old-style Principal, seeking Bill McDonald's authority for any purchases or appointments – and trying to explain to him why Mary Erskine had purchased its first minibus without his approval. On the other, I was liaising closely with Michael Walker and James Laurenson, shortly to be the first Chairman and Deputy Chairman of the new Erskine Stewart's Melville Governing Council (ESMGC), and making plans for the brave new world into which we would enter. It was, in its way, a throwback to the excitements of 1981, when Fergus Lyons and I had been establishing the ground rules for the lay Prior Park.

It was planned that the Tobins would live in a new house in the grounds of

The Mary Erskine School. Judith Sischy would be our first Bursar, with rooms in 11 Queensferry Terrace. It was a bombshell when we learned that Judith would instead be the Secretary of a reconstituted Scottish Council of Independent Schools (SCIS). Hitherto, Bill McDonald and she had 'run' SCIS from their Merchant Company headquarters – an effective subsidy of Scotland's Independent Schools by the parents of Merchant Company pupils. It was the more questionable that the new arrangements for SCIS should have been negotiated behind the backs of the Merchant Company and its schools.

The Merchant Company expressed its outrage and threatened for a while to pull its schools out of SCIS. I was left without a Bursar. For several weeks, until the arrival of the excellent Fred McLeod, I was the effective Bursar of ESMGC. This at least enabled me to get to grips with the finances and to confront the truth that my three schools were effectively trading at a loss of nearly £140,000 per annum, with The Mary Erskine School accounting for most of this deficit.

If we lost Judith Sischy we otherwise did well out of 'devolution', securing the best of the Hanover Street technocrats. In Sylvia Honeyman we gained a superb Estates Bursar, while Dorothy Scott and Faye Mowat were the Merchant Company experts on Fees and Assisted Places.

Bryan Lewis and I used the weeks before the November revolution to hatch great schemes for the future arrangements of the ESMGC schools. The Technology Appeal had raised the best part of a million pounds in cash, promises and kind. But what was Technology? And where was it to fit into the curriculum? How could you insert Technology worth a million pounds into the curriculum, without pushing something else out? I rapidly found that these questions had not really been put, let alone explored.

One question led to another. The decisions as to where to locate the two new Technology Centres had a bearing on all future planning. I argued that we must not proceed until we were satisfied with the present shape of the Schools. That opened Pandora's Box! By the time we had finished, we had decided to build a new classroom block for Nursery and Primary 1 at Ravelston, move Primary 2 and Primary 3 into the rooms at Ravelston previously occupied by the Primary 6 and Primary 7 girls, and move the latter to Queensferry Road so that Primary 6 and Primary 7 could be genuinely coeducational. This meant a net shift of pupils from the overcrowded Queensferry Road to the spaces of Ravelston. My eye fell on the substantial Victorian house in Queensferry Terrace that had originally been earmarked for the Bursar and a relocated Art department. The Art department should stay put, the Bursariat would be more happily located at Ravelston, 11 Queensferry Terrace would be an ideal home for the Principal and his family. 'It's a bit large,' James Laurenson remarked. 'It's a lot cheaper than building a new house,' I replied. We moved into 11 Queensferry Terrace in February 1990 and would remain there very happily for the next ten years.

Top Highland dancer – Sophie (and trophies) in Queensferry Terrace.

Meanwhile, I made room for Technology in the curriculum by persuading my colleagues to expand the working week. By then I had realized that the famed breadth of Scottish education was something of a myth. Boys and girls at the school studied only seven subjects to Standard Grade. In consequence, very few embarked on a second Modern Language. Introducing Technology on a large scale could only make the curriculum less 'liberal', unless the timetable itself could be expanded. I decided that the North Side schools should strike out on their own. Boys and girls would take eight Standard Grades, most would study German as well as French and I would use this enhancement of educational provision as the justification for increasing fees beyond the level envisaged by George Watson's College. The North Side would no longer be the poor relations! From September 1990 the hapless pupils of Mary Erskine and Stewart's Melville would now have 46 periods of 35 minutes. This was to be the first of three new timetables that I shaped and negotiated during the 1990s. By the time I left, each class lasted an hour.

What of Technology itself? At Prior Park I had asked Wilfred Hammond to plan the introduction of Design Technology. In Edinburgh I rapidly realized that there was no one to whom I could turn. I worked hard at my brief and concluded that each senior school should have its own Technology Centre and that the subject should centre on the design process, rather than on the mere teaching of craft skills. At Mary Erskine, where there had been no Technology as such, the Art and Home Economics departments expressed consternation about this cuckoo in their nest. At Stewart's Melville, with its craft-based team of three long-serving teachers, the Head of Department, Peter Stoddart, told me that I should advertise for a Director of Technology who could guide the schools towards the sort of Technology that I envisaged and plan the new Centres accordingly. I took this excellent advice and was extremely lucky to attract the interest of a lecturer at Trent Polytechnic, John Forth. Single-handed, John designed the layout and equipment of two fine Technology Centres that placed the schools ahead of any local competition. I was closely involved with John in the presentation and explanation of his plans, not least because John stayed with the Tobins in 11 Queensferry Terrace until he was able to buy his own house.

Once again I enjoyed the backing of a Governing Council who were not terrified of going into debt for the sake of a brighter future. We found a good site for the Mary Erskine Technology Centre and realized that the reformed Stewart's Melville department required very little extra space. (The Duke of Edinburgh, when he spoke to the boys after opening the Centre in 1992, referred to it as 'Your little thing'.) Building the new classrooms for the Nursery and Preparatory One threatened to be a more taxing assignment. The tenders all came in several hundreds of thousand pounds higher than we had envisaged or ESMGC could afford. A switch to a design-and-build route produced an affordable and eminently satisfactory solution and the way ahead was clear.

After all the years of scrimping and saving in Bath, it is hardly surprising that the pleasures of mould-breaking went to my head. If Prior Park had taught me anything, it was that nothing is gained by the avoidance of evident weaknesses. I was by now an experienced headmaster. I should act on my first impressions and not allow myself to be deflected from their solution. This, of course, is the occupational hazard of second headships! *You* come with a somewhat arrogant belief in your ability to identify issues and crack problems, forgetting perhaps that the need for reform and renewal in this second and bigger job is neither as urgent nor as self-evident as it was in your first. *Your colleagues* do not see you as the friendly young man in need of encouragement and support, but as a potential threat to their equilibrium, someone who comes 'with a reputation', via the ever fluid grapevine that links one HMC Common Room to another.

I was aware of two reasons why I should tread carefully – I was English and I was Catholic. An Englishman with the hide of a rhinoceros would have sensed in 1989 that many Scots disliked England. It was the heyday of the Corries, whose snide wit and patriotic jingles enlivened many a car journey and whose 'Flower of Scotland' acquired the status of national anthem at the never-to-be-forgotten 'Grand Slam' match at Murrayfield in 1990. It was the first and last rugby international Margery ever attended. She found the xenophobia hard to take. Had *we* ever objected in London to Scots as such?! Yet here the English seemed to be universal pariahs. Our own personal experiences were very different. There were countless expressions of welcome, even if they were invariably accompanied by the enquiry, 'And how are you settling in?' We would be asked the same question for about eight years.

There are two types of Independent School in Scotland, those who adhere to the Scottish curriculum and those who do not. The Edinburgh Merchant Company schools were rooted in the Scottish camp. In the first three centuries of The Mary Erskine School there had been only English Head before me, the formidable Miss Muriel Jennings. When she wrote her tercentennial History of the School five years later, Lydia Skinner remarked of Miss Jennings that she made the mistake common to the English of imagining that silence in Scotland amounts to consent. I wondered whether the remark was aimed also at the new Principal. But Daniel Stewart's had much more benign memories of its only English Headmaster, Bertie Bellis, and the Deputy Heads of both senior schools were English, as had been the outgoing Head of the Junior School. Looking back, I am impressed and grateful that my colleagues never challenged my ethnic capacity to lead them. No-one ever called me an 'English prat', although many must have been tempted.

Nor did they ever speak openly of my religion, but I have little doubt that it instilled far greater mistrust of me in the Schools and in the Edinburgh community at large. Indeed, my Catholicism should, technically, have posed an insuperable obstacle to my appointment, as the statutes of Daniel Stewart's College had specifically prescribed that the Headmaster should be of the reformed religion. Years later, James Laurenson told me that another Governor, soon to be a great supporter, had warned the Education Board that Stewart's Melville would lose half its pupils if I was appointed. He was certainly not reflecting any bias of his own, only his worry that Scottish sectarianism was alive and well. I am glad that I was not informed of this at the time, although it might have alerted me to the need to reconnoitre and 'cover my back' more carefully before some of my staffing appointments. By then, I had developed real friendships with men like the Reverend Hugh Davidson and the Very Reverend William McDonald. Hugh Davidson, the Minister at Inverleith, had been on my interviewing panel – he had asked me where I stood in relation to the Second Vatican Council – and would be a Governor throughout my period of office. Bill McDonald was my first Founders' Day speaker at Stewart's Melville and next year preached memorably on 'Stewartship' during the commemorative service in St Mary's Cathedral 250 years after the birth of Daniel Stewart.

At the first of these ceremonies, Bill was Moderator of the Church of Scotland. For my second Stewart's Melville Founders' Day I invited Finlay Calder, fresh from his triumph in leading the Lions to victory in Australia. Ernie Wilkins happily quipped that it was not every school that could boast the captains of the Christians and the Lions.

Stewart's Melville and Mary Erskine were schools vividly different in atmosphere and character. Stewart's Melville College pulsed with energy and self-confidence. School assemblies throughout my time in Edinburgh were litanies of individual and team achievements, with the table in front of me groaning under the weight of silverware to be presented. The School had a great tradition in rugby, thanks to the selfless dedication of scores of teachers. Every Saturday morning Stewart's Melville put on an extraordinary number of teams to play a variety of schools, there being few that could emulate us in our breadth of participation, and it was rare indeed for the First Fifteen to lose more than a handful of games. But the same competitive edge permeated the whole range of boys' activities, great and small. During my first year three Fifth Form boys became World Debating Champions and strutted around with justifiable self-satisfaction in the 'Melville Red' of the School's Colours blazer.

In the Stewart's Melville Management team I was the only 'Arts man'. There were three Mathematicians. Paul Caton, the Deputy Head, had spent the whole of his career at Melville and Stewart's Melville. He compiled the timetable, coached and refereed rugby and ran the outstanding CCF. Donald McDiarmid was a Watsonian who had been at Daniel Stewart's before the merger with Melville. I came rapidly to depend on his good judgement, administrative capacity and quietly unfailing loyalty. Graeme Wilson, Bryan Lewis' successor as Head of Middle School, had won Robin Morgan's admiration through the extraordinary talents that he had displayed on the hills and mountains of Scotland. Ernie Wilkins, previously Head of Chemistry, was Head of Upper School.

It was a buoyant and generally cheerful place but not one for the faint-hearted. 'It's a rough school,' Ernie murmured to me, as we stood on the steps leading into the School. Ernie was responsible for overseeing the discipline administered to senior boys by the eight Housemasters. Like so many of his colleagues he had seen the amalgamated school march to eminence from its inception, it had educated all four of his sons and he loved it with passion. Ernie has no recollection of his comment but I noted it. For me, roughness was a failing to be redressed.

For there was a long 'tail' at Stewart's Melville College. The HMI Inspection of 1988 had warmly praised the School but its academic results seemed mediocre in comparison with those of most of its competitors and too many boys left, disenchanted and underqualified, after the Fifth or even Fourth Forms. From my Study I peered across the playground at the registration of a

House group in an opposite classroom. Nearly forty boys herded together daily for twenty minutes, hardly an image of good pastoral care.

The Mary Erskine School seemed demure and ladylike in comparison with its younger brother down the Dykes. There were three Assemblies each week, the girls sitting cross-legged on the floor, and noise and overt enthusiasm were curbed. On Saturdays there were Hockey matches against other schools but there seemed little incentive or pressure to participate. Only in Music did the School exceed Stewart's Melville in verve and commitment, thanks to the brilliance and dynamism of Helen Mitchell. I was sure that the girls would respond to a more challenging atmosphere. Scores of them loved the CCF, even though none of the officers came from Mary Erskine, and one of the boarders had even participated twice in the Nijmegen Marches. Janice Rankin was a devoted curler, who in 2002 would be a member of Scotland's world-beating team. Too few of The Mary Erskine Common Room, however, would have wished or felt able to compete with the extra-curricular commitment of the Prussians of Stewart's Melville. The exception to this was Carbisdale, the joint Third Form outdoor education programme in Sutherland, and even here the organizer had always been a Stewart's Melville teacher.

To some extent, appearances of demureness lied. Skirts could be skimpy – May Burns inveighed vainly against the exposure of 'unsightly flesh' – and rumours of out-of-school licence abounded. Many of our girls and boys had to contend with difficult home circumstances and even with acute deprivation. In those days, the two schools together educated more holders of Assisted Places than any other establishment in Scotland. ''T' is a poor, wee thing,' said Nan Howe of one particularly troubled girl, and we made allowances accordingly. But the corridors were broader, the classrooms lighter, the floors more polished and the green acres more inviting than at Stewart's Melville.

Nor did the Mary Erskine Staff Room possess the same phalanx of hardened veterans. Many of the teachers were close to retirement, but only a few had been at Ravelston during the traumas of the 1970s. Among those who had battled through those troubled times were Eileen McCamley and May Burns, the Deputy and Assistant Deputy Heads. It was hardly surprising that their faith in the good intentions of the Merchant Company was tenuous. 'Mr Tobin,' asked Eileen one day, 'Will they leave us our beautiful school?' For my first Founders' Day at Ravelston I broke with tradition and invited an English Headmistress, Olive Peto, to be guest speaker. I was pleased rather than offended when Eileen enthused about her address and added, in her wry fashion, that it had reminded her of how 'nice it would be' to have a headmistress again. Eileen had been devoted to Jean Thow and, while appreciative of Robin Morgan, always feared Stewart's Melville emissaries bearing gifts. Robin Morgan had imported Nan Howe from Stewart's Melville to inject a more robust style and the tensions were often evident. It was a great help to me, then and thereafter, that Judith

Barton should have been such a cheerful, positive and welcoming Head of Middle School.

Mary Erskine was loss-making because it was heavily overstaffed. The numbers of girls studying Standard Grade German, Italian and Spanish could be counted on two hands. I culled Italian and Spanish from the timetable, believing that such small numbers were undesirable educationally as well as financially, and promoted German in their place. I asked the teachers of very small sets to add more periods to their teaching load. I encouraged more elderly teachers to retire and ensured that their replacements were very young and much cheaper. Costs fell and revenue, miraculously, began to soar. I liked to think that word was getting around Edinburgh that new blood was beginning to course through Mary Erskine.

To a degree, Mary Erskine benefited, and Stewart's Melville struggled to sustain past numbers, in consequence of the gradual change in the distribution of boys and girls in the Junior School. What had been in 1978 a predominantly boys' school had by 1989 become genuinely coeducational. It was timely, therefore, that the Junior School should cease to be seen as a physical appendage of Stewart's Melville College. From now onwards it would be divided more or less equally between the two sites. For those who loved Mary Erskine and who had previously feared for its future it must have been heartening to see new building at Ravelston for the first time since 1966. Whatever the reason, numbers of girls at Mary Erskine rose sharply from my arrival and went on rising.

In the early months of 1990 such evidence of success lay hidden in the future. A wiser man might have kept a low profile, practised the politics of consensus and eschewed change. I did the opposite. Why?

I was keen to demonstrate the virtues of devolution from Hanover Street. No longer would the North Side Schools be hamstrung by the diktat of the Secretary or by the argument that we should keep in step with George Watson's. I had not left Prior Park to stop being a schoolmaster or to become a 'roi faineant'. I believed that Michael Walker had been looking for a leader. I knew before I arrived that, in a sense that went deeper than nationality, this would be for me a new culture. All of my previous experience, as teacher and pupil, had been in schools that had been Independent since their inception. The Merchant Company schools had until recently been funded by the State. There was a 'no frills' aspect to them, especially at Stewart's Melville, that I found hard to take. (Bertie Bellis subsequently told me that had to campaign vigorously in the 1960s to persuade the Merchant Company to provide indoor toilets for the boys.)

I wanted to broaden the constituency of the two schools. I never challenged their 'Scottishness', indeed fostered their 'custom and ceremony', but, with Assisted Places under constant threat and with a steady tide of English immigrants into Edinburgh and its 'silicon' environs, I felt that it was my job to make the Schools truly acceptable to incomers like myself.

When I had consulted Christopher Everett about the possibility of exchanging Edinburgh for Bath, he had said that the beauty of a really big job was that you left the minutiae of management to others and could focus simply on the things that you wished to change. My problem in 1990 and 1991 was that I found too many targets. Reforming the senior school curricula, changing their timetables, introducing Technology, recasting the structure of the Junior School and writing new prospectuses for both senior schools was not enough. Bryan Lewis and I devised an enormously long Questionnaire to parents, designed to elicit from them views and preferences that would support the cause of Reform. I undertook the rewriting of the Teachers' Contracts and became involved in tortuous, if ultimately successful, negotiations with the staff room representatives. I decided that we needed entirely new arrangements for School lunches. I argued that the House system at Stewart's Melville could only function adequately if the number of House tutors was increased. At Mary Erskine I added two new Clans to the historic four – and reworded the School Song accordingly.

In that letter to Emma in February 1990, quoted above, I had rejoiced that I had managed to change so much in my first term but referred to the inherent problems of managing change in two or three schools at a time. Not the least of the shocks facing me in Edinburgh was the shortness of the school day. Eighteen years in boarding schools had accustomed me to leisurely discussion, after-school meetings and evening chats. Now, suddenly, there seemed no time for anything. 'Macro-strategy' was relatively easy, because it hinged around a very small number of key individuals. Any intended change in school arrangements, however, was likely to unleash hours of consultation in pursuit of elusive consensus. Such issues dragged into and through my second year. Contracts, to the undisguised exasperation of James Laurenson, were being discussed until April 1992. I certainly did not behave like a bull in a china shop. Stickability was the name of the game.

If there is one responsibility that no Head can safely shelve, it is the disciplinary tone of his school. I found this a much more elusive task than in Bath. It took us six months, off and on, to terminate the careers of four young men who had led us all a merry dance. They were four out of 780. Ernie Wilkins was surely right when he observed that it was important with boys to 'catch them being good'. The occupational hazard for me in Edinburgh was that I tended to see only the bad cases.

In a big city day school the power to shape or amend the attitudes and behaviour of the peer group will necessarily be limited. Even so, I know that I was right to insist that a day school had a legitimate interest in the behaviour of its pupils *out of school* whenever one pupil got another into difficulties or when collective misbehaviour derived from common attendance of Stewart's Melville or Mary Erskine. Hence my notorious letter on Parties.

When he had briefed me Robin Morgan had told me a graphically sad tale of parental delusion. There had been a party of sixteen year olds and the parents had obediently vacated the house. They returned to find their house in a distressing state. The father then wrote to Robin, requesting that the School should meet the cost of replacing a carpet as all the 'guests' were from Stewart's Melville. By my second term, I had heard too many tales of similar excess and I decided that it would be a good idea to write a general letter to parents in order to 'fortify' them in their responsibilities. In it I stated that there should always be an adult present when there were parties in their house. Parents should also make a point of finding out where their children would be and of contacting the hosting parents to assure themselves that arrangements were as they should be.

There was general outrage. The pupils demanded to know what business it was of mine to interfere in what they did outside school. One father observed that there was a difference between backing up parents and putting teenagers' backs up. The Parents' Liaison Committee spent an hour debating the matter – good humouredly.

Drugs were the most serious example of the impossibility of divorcing the welfare of pupils in school from their activities outside it. After my first Carbisdale I had to expel or suspend four boys and two girls for consuming cannabis. I adhered to a rigid line that if a pupil brought drugs into school or supplied them to others, he or she would have to go. I also maintained that any taking of illegal drugs, at any time, would put at risk the pupil's future in the school. In time, my consistency in this area won general support from colleagues and parents and I have no doubt that this relatively robust disciplinary stance, complemented as it was by an increasingly sophisticated programme of personal and social education, enhanced the schools' appeal to the more discerning parents of Edinburgh.

More controversial were my attempts to infuse the public occasions of the schools, especially Stewart's Melville, with my personal views. Every good Head will wish pupils and colleagues to know what he or she stands for. The Stewart's Melville Remembrance Day address was a traditional and entirely acceptable vehicle for the Principal's values and people liked what I had to say. Before I left Edinburgh, indeed, James Laurenson would commission and generously finance the publication of these addresses, under the title *Sweet Wells*. (I thank Christ College, Brecon, for my introduction to Wilfrid Owen.) But in those early days I probably used school assemblies too freely for the airing of my views on whatever issues grabbed my attention – Kuwait, Communism or Corruption.

Perhaps a little voice was whispering to me that I had sold my soul in taking my pagan job in Edinburgh. After votes in the Commons on abortion and embryo experimentation had provoked Cardinal Hume's comment that Britain was no longer a Christian country, I wrote to *The Tablet* to urge committed Christians in the Commons to establish a Christian Democrat Party and to the *Independent* to denounce the 'moral cul-de-sac of the media's liberal consensus'. Neither letter was published.

At the beginning of my first Summer Term, I was invited to two Fifth Form RE classes for 'general discussion'. One red-haired young man asked me what attempt I had made to come to terms with Edinburgh attitudes. I confessed that I had made none, but I asked him why, if he expected me to adjust my attitudes to my new city, I should not expect him to change his beliefs if and when he went to London. He replied that Edinburgh was a deeply conservative society. He told me that he could not bear it at school assembly when I prefaced remarks with the phrase, 'As an Englishman'. I asked him to supply a single instance when I had used the remark in any other sense than to point to Scottish superiority. I was, in any case, an Irishman! After that, we had a pleasant discussion. In January 1991 I received a letter from of an Iraqi Sixth Former accusing me of indoctrinating impressionable youths with American humbug and hypocrisy.

Six weeks later, I accepted an invitation from the Debating Society to oppose the motion, 'This House believes that there is no place for Religious Education in Schools'. Afterwards, I shared my grief with Matthew and Emma.

> In my debate yesterday I was confronted by the blank wall of anti-religious prejudice in Scotland. We lost 43-15, even though there was scarcely one thoughtful argument on the other side, and it suddenly becomes very clear that, in a society which does not acknowledge God, the herd mentality simply takes over, because there is no ultimate reason for attaching *value* to the individual who fails to conform. There is no *reason* for love, forgiveness, compassion, anything.
>
> The big argument of the other side was that religion indoctrinated. I would have thought that the size of the vote was proof in itself of how ridiculous that argument is!…The problem in Scotland was that Scottish Calvinism was a hellfire type of religion, which went well with repression and coercion. The Irish Christian Brothers would be the Catholic counterpart. So generations have grown up resenting the part played by religion in their childhood and passing on their antipathy to the young. All very understandable; all totally NEGATIVE!

The Stewart's Melville staff room found that it was starkly divided as to whether school assemblies should have a religious content. The School had a 'Chaplain' who did not wish to be seen as a chaplain but as the Head of RE. Wally Shaw, a delightful American, had been involved in a protracted struggle with my predecessor on this issue. I happened to agree with Wally that school assemblies should benefit from the active involvement and witness of the Common Room as a whole. As part of my search for a route forward, I put to the two Common Rooms the question, 'Do you think that school assemblies should have a specifically Christian character?' At Mary Erskine the staff were massively in favour of this proposition. At Stewart's Melville, there was an exact split between 'Yeses' and 'Noes' – with no 'Don't Knows' at all! One of the 'Noes' came from a very vocal Young Turk. 'This is an absurd question. Stewart's Melville belongs to the great non-denominational Edinburgh tradition. There is NO place for religion in school assemblies.' He left for a school closer to his tastes a couple of years later.

The Governing Council agreed with me that the secularist position was narrow, prejudiced and illiberal. It made no more sense to exclude religious education and the spiritual dimension from the life of a school than it would to exclude music, art or drama. The Governors ruled that 'non-denominational' should not mean 'non-religious' and they adopted the formula that we were 'non-denominational schools in a Christian tradition'. I compiled special hymn books for the schools, *Singing Together*, containing about eighty hymns selected by staff and pupils, plus my own selection of prayers, scriptural texts and exempla of other faiths. When I left in 2000, my final contribution to the Schools was to endow prizes for Religious Education.

I applied to school lunches the same principle, that the good school must not limit itself to what the pupils already possessed. I disapproved of the way in which the teaching staff ate separately from the pupils and I disliked the cafeteria system. We should at least provide a proper two-course meal for pupils and there should be an emphasis on 'healthy eating'. Teachers would enjoy a free school lunch, which would be tax-free precisely because they would be in the same hall, 'supervising' the pupils. Pupils could 'opt out' and bring sandwiches. Otherwise, parents would fund the school lunch through a fixed addition to termly fees. I steered this concept through the Management Teams, the Governing Council, the Parents' Liaison Body and, finally, two general meetings for parents. Margery and I were dumbstruck by the extent to which parents allowed themselves to be slaves to their children's fads. One mother complained of her problems in feeding a vegetarian daughter who did not like vegetables. Compass Catering were duly awarded the contract and we eagerly awaited parental responses.

I applied the opt-out principle to another innovation based on my Prior Park experience, the pre-paid life subscription to the two Former Pupils Clubs. A decade later, The Mary Erskine Former Pupils Guild and the Daniel Stewart's and Melville Former Pupils' Club bask in revenues and a range of activity that would previously have been inconceivable.

All these changes were broached and developed without reference to the Merchant Company school on the other side of Edinburgh. If we were happy to be cast as the radical Governing Council, there was no reason why the George Watson's Governing Council should not have been equally innovative. The setting of fees, however, was a different matter, as this prerogative had been reserved to the Merchant Company Education Board. My Governors had agreed with me that our parents should have a full term's notice of the annual increase in fees. Accordingly, we submitted our proposals for ratification at the March meeting of the Education Board, before George Watson's had discussed their fees. On the day, so many members of the Board absented themselves that there was no quorum. Ratification would have to be postponed until the Summer term. I persuaded the Master that it would be in order for me to inform our parents of the proposed fee increase, 'subject to ratification by the Merchant Company Education Board', and this formula enabled us to proceed independently of our South Side friends.

We made one change that materially affected George Watson's College. Hitherto all teachers employed by the Merchant Company Education Board had the right to fee discounts for their children at any of the Merchant Company schools. When I was appointed, there was only one child of a George Watson's teacher at a North Side school. On the other hand, there were scores of North Side children at George Watson's. This meant that after 'devolution' a very considerable sum would be transferred each term from the Erskine Stewart's Melville accounts to those of George Watson's. I thought that it was outrageous that North Side parents should be expected to provide this subsidy to the (then) richest of the Merchant Company schools and my Governors agreed that no ESMGC teacher who had not previously sent a child to George Watson's would be entitled to the staff fee discount. I was a happy man when Fred McLeod told me a few years later that this drain on our finances had ended. But my pleasure was more than financial. I did not want any of my teachers to act on the assumption that there was a better school elsewhere. At least I was setting a good example in this regard, as the first modern Principal to send his children to his own school.

I am less happy to recall a linked decision, that we should end the right of support staff to staff fee discounts. By today's standards this cost-cutting initiative was thoroughly unenlightened. I can only plead that my schools were neither well endowed nor into satisfactory surplus and I console myself with the thought that the considerable increase in our support teams during the past decade would have been less affordable if it had carried with it an increased liability to discounted fees.

For these were critical days. I had persuaded my Governors not only to invest heavily in new buildings, in the belief that they would attract extra pupils, but also to support Bryan Lewis and me in reducing class sizes, even though this meant the employment of more teachers – and all this amid acute economic uncertainty and an uneasy political outlook. Numbers of pupils at Mary Erskine and in the Junior School were indeed rising impressively, but the ultimate success of the enterprise would depend on matching achievement to declared aspiration. And behind me were some uneasy colleagues.

Bryan Lewis and I saw eye to eye on everything and he had no problem in carrying with him the Junior School Staff Room. Eileen McCamley and the Mary Erskine Management Team were quietly pleased that I was doing things my way and not the way that Stewart's Melville's movers and shakers would necessarily wish. Paul Caton was, as always, loyalty personified, but the remainder of the Stewart's Melville Management Team were anxious indeed as the new Principal practised a form of leadership with which they were not at all familiar.

Stewart's Melville College colleagues, especially those who had grown middle-aged in its service, very understandably tended to see proposals for change as implied criticism. The Housemasters, for instance, were digging in against my proposal to double the number of Stewart's Melville House Tutors. To a man they had opposed the idea when I first advanced it in 1990. I had pointed out then that, because they had become Housemasters by virtue of their long-established personal reputations within the school, a new Principal brought something that, by definition, no Housemaster could have, his 'first impressions'. They were clearly unimpressed. In my darker moments, I suspected that the only reason they opposed my 'reform' was the premise that, if it was a good idea, they would have thought of it first.

Yet the School was remarkable for its esprit de corps, never more conspicuous than at Carbisdale each May. Hierarchy cut no ice in this, the largest school-based outdoor education project in Britain. The operation was run by a director elected from within the ranks and status attached only to those who had earned it through their competence and zeal. The scores of teachers from the two schools slept in Spartan dormitories in Carbisdale Castle or the youth hostel at Strathpeffer or in bothies sufficiently primitive to satisfy the exultant Puritanism of Jock Richardson.

This phenomenon left me feeling suitably humble. Nevertheless, I pushed ahead with my desired increase in the number of House tutors and I overrode a majority report when I decided that there should be Integrated Science in Form I. It seemed to me that the balance of argument rested with David Girdwood, the excellent Head of Chemistry at Stewart's Melville, and I appointed him Head of Science, along with Joan Houston at Mary Erskine, so that they could provide leadership to their colleagues.

With so much being changed and questioned, nerves became frayed, rumours raced and trivial events mushroomed spectacularly. The Summer Term of 1991 began with a series of hoax bomb calls. Paul Caton, with his usual robust good sense, argued that we should only take note of these if there seemed to be particular reason for doing so. Evacuating the school on every occasion merely encouraged the hoaxers to continue. When I was told that there had been yet another scare, this time at Mary Erskine, I asked Linda Hourston, my excellent Deputy Head Girl, to go around the classrooms and ask the teachers to report if they saw any suspicious package in their classrooms. The Bursar, meanwhile,

The joys of Carbisdale.

took it upon himself to enlist other girls to help him look under cars. The reward for such initiative was a banner headline in the *Daily Record* – 'GO AND FIND A BOMB GIRLS'. In no time, photocopies were pervading Stewart's Melville, the local councillor wrote to express his concern and parents were telephoning the School to ask whether I intended to issue a statement. I duly sent out such a statement to those parents who requested it, making the point that to give hoaxers the oxygen of publicity was simply to invite other hoaxes and was, therefore, undesirable.

A house divided cannot stand. Was it for this reason that disciplinary problems multiplied? My second year ended with a plethora of suspensions against boarders for drinking. On June 15th 1991 I wrote to Matthew and Emma:

> It was a nice surprise to be woken by you this morning. When the phone rang my first thought was that it was probably another abusive call. I had two in five minutes yesterday evening – 'You fat bastard, you fat bastard,' each time. The first time it was a broken male voice. The second time it was a girl squeaking and I am afraid that I simply burst out laughing. The car was not vandalized but tonight is Saturday night.

By now the crows were circling. *The Scotsman* ran a story to the effect that English Heads were being eased out of Scottish schools – there had been two notable casualties that term – and a kind soul ensured that a copy of the article was pushed through our letter box. Paul Caton told me that rumours were rife that I intended to jump ship. I must say something to the Staff Room. I went in and said that I understood that doubts had been expressed about whether I wished to stay. There was no substance to such rumours. Why on earth would I wish to leave?

Michael Walker was superb in his support. He never rushed into endorsement of my ideas but would listen gravely and patiently discuss. When necessary he steered me gently towards reconsideration or compromise or retreat. I cannot remember a major issue on which I lacked his backing in meetings of the Governing Council. As the pressures mounted, he and James Laurenson came in each week for half an hour before school began and that in itself was therapeutic. If they were worried, they never showed it.

The same applied to those other lynchpins, my secretaries. At Ravelston in August 1989, Dorothy Leurs had kindly stayed on for a fortnight to 'see me in'. Judy Mottram proved a worthy successor. When I was cast down by some aspect of Mary Erskine, she would say to me, 'Mr Tobin, there are some funny people at Mary Erskine.' Kay More, my Secretary at Queensferry Road, had been part of the fabric for years. I think that she was secretly annoyed that I made the job so difficult for myself and so lengthy for herself, but she resisted the call of the golf course until the summer of 1991. Dorothy Silver stepped ably and confidently into her shoes.

As at Bath but on a much wider front, I had forced the pace of change and, by so doing, created tensions and aroused opposition. I had at least avoided all personal and emotional entanglement, but it had been a tough couple of years and I had pushed myself and others to the limit. Back in October I had been interviewing a Sixth Form girl about her UCAS applications. After a while, she asked me why I kept on saying, 'Yes'. 'Yes,' I murmured and then came to with a start. I doubt if the girl was impressed that her Principal had fallen asleep on the first occasion she had talked to him.

Looking back, I neither regret the decisions that I made nor the positions that I adopted during those first two years. At the time, however, it was hard to avoid the sense that I was walking along a ridge above the precipice. 25 June 1991 became a critical date in my calendar, the day on which I would know whether or not parents would opt into 'my' new Catering system. It was, in effect, the first plebiscite on the Tobin regime. I shared my feelings with Matthew and Emma.

> Excitement is mounting in the Schools. Returns to the great question, 'Will you or won't you?' are due in by Tuesday. We are saying that parents have to commit themselves for the whole year. It is a great bargain to them but their children fear that they are placing themselves in a fiendish trap set by the Principal. Much hinges on the outcome.

In the event, over 1,800 children were signed on for next term, an outcome that did wonders in appeasing the doubters.

In a sense we had to wait a further year for the first harvest. In August 1992, we returned from our holidays to find that my bullish determination to increase the number of Standard Grade subjects for each boy and girl had been triumphantly vindicated. Not only had the number of passes increased by an average of over one but, contrary to the staff room pessimists, the grades too had notably improved. Nothing succeeds like high expectations!

Buoyed with such pleasure, I was rehearsing Stewart's Melville successes with my new Head Boy and his Deputies when I blacked out. When I came to it was to find an irate Dorothy Silver. 'Mr Tobin,' she said, 'You've given those boys a very nasty scare.' It was a delayed reaction, perhaps, to the stresses of being an incomer to Edinburgh.

CHAPTER 17

Excursions, Aggravations, Celebrations

I see the next year or two as critically important for Stewart's Melville. We have so much that is good, so much for which those who have served here a long time – and there are many of you! – have every reason to be proud. The risk is that this know-ledge, this establishment of traditional attitudes, practices and customs, becomes either complacent or fearful, effectively preventing us from tackling our most real problems and making Stewart's Melville the genuinely excellent school that it can be.

(Address to Stewart's Melville Staff Room, 2 February 1994)

O NE OF THE benefits of being Head of two schools was the charitable assumption of your colleagues, when you were missing, that you were at the 'other end of the Dykes'. It did not take long for me to test such charity to the limits. As I read my letters to Matthew and Emma, from 1990 onwards, I wonder at the hubris that led me to want to be a 'public figure' in Scotland *and* in England. When Tom Wheare of Bryanston found me on his train to Waterloo and asked whether my travels were a compensatory therapy in coping with the enormity of my real job, I suspect that he was close to the mark.

My membership of the SCIS Governing Council had been dictated by the Merchant Company to SCIS as part of the price for their schools continuing to fund Judith Sischy's operation. I was a less than ideal participant in the Committee. I was jealously protective of the independence of Independent school heads and exceedingly wary of the SCIS tendency, encouraged by the more 'corporatist' members of Scottish HMC and GSA, to regard itself as Scotland's 'sixth local education authority'. In consequence, I paraded a Thatcherite distaste for all expenditure that was not directly funded by the provision of services for which the 'customers' were prepared to pay. While there was some merit in this stance, others perceived merely a reluctance to bury the hatchet.

There was – and still is – much of the 'rotten borough' in Scottish politics, educational and otherwise. Membership of the establishment owes little to democracy and much to connection and there is an inveterate tendency towards pluralism. On three consecutive days I encountered one of the most amiable members of the Scottish educational establishment. On each occasion we were both wearing different hats. My own pluralism, of course, was perfectly acceptable. With others I was quick to detect the opaqueness and fudge that stemmed from conflicts of interest.

213

In this culture the unacceptable offence was to 'rock the boat'. Wise men in HMC repeatedly hinted that it did not pay to antagonize the fount of patronage, for instance by complaint about the freezing by the Scottish Executive of the value of Assisted Places. I cannot recall a single instance where such 'appeasement' yielded any ultimate dividend.

At times it felt Kafkaesque. I was invited to the investiture in St Giles' Cathedral of the Headmaster of Loretto, a Governor of the BBC, as Chaplain to the Queen. As we milled around afterwards, I bumped into Lord James Douglas Hamilton, then Minister for Education. With typical courtesy he asked me whether the Independent schools had any problems. I mentioned Assisted Places. 'Oh, do please write to me about your difficulties.' I did. My reward was a reply from his minders, over his signature, explaining that such matters pertained to the normal channels for such discussion. The normal channel was SCIS.

It is only too easy for me now to affect a lofty detachment from the nexus of Scottish corporatism and patronage. Yet I did not hesitate to accept my own nomination to a quango, the Scottish Consultative Council for the Curriculum (SCCC). For all I know I may have been nominated by Judith Sischy! I preferred to believe that it reflected my evident interest in the work of the Howie Committee on the future of Upper Secondary Education in Scotland.

The subject at issue was the future of the Higher examination. For the best part of a century this had provided a steep ladder out of school and into university for Scottish 'lads o' pairts'. If not as young or as enterprising as Thomas Carlyle, who had walked as a thirteen year old from Ecclefechan to Edinburgh University, very many Scottish boys took the fast road out of school, leaving after only a year of Higher study to embark on four-year degree courses at one of Scotland's historic universities.

Able students typically sat five or even six Highers, so that far more Scots continued their study of English and Mathematics than was the case in England. The trouble was that an examination designed for the ambitious few was hopelessly demanding for the masses. Half of those who remained at School after 16 achieved one Higher or none in their Fifth Year. Results for this rump in the Sixth Year tended to be even worse!

By 1990, most Scottish undergraduates had spent a Sixth Year in senior school, but one in five, mainly in the less affluent West, still went directly to university after Fifth Year Highers. For decades, this sociological factor had trumped every educational argument that it was time to remove the 'Gold Standard' status of the Fifth Year Higher. In consequence, able Sixth Year students, their university places assured by their good Higher results, had little incentive to 'stretch' themselves in their final year at School. For many it was a largely wasted year.

The Independent schools that followed the Scottish curriculum felt vulnerable, in terms of intellectual rigour, in comparison with those competitors who followed the Advanced Level courses. With varying degrees of enthusiasm and success, they tried to promote the Certificate of Sixth Year Studies. This claimed parity with the English Advanced Level, and had the additional merit of promoting individual research, but its syllabuses were necessarily limited in scope and light in their demands.

Receiving the customary request for input from schools and being in no doubt that the Scottish Office should wish to read the response of the largest Independent set-up in Scotland, I sent nine pages of detailed argument.

That may have accounted for my selection for SCCC. When I arrived in Dundee for my first meeting, I discovered that my appointment was quite controversial. Michael Forsyth, the hawkish Minister for Education, had reduced the numbers of the Committee and refused to appoint anyone suggested by the teachers' unions. There were jibes that he had only chosen the few who were likeminded with himself. I was the only representative from an Independent school.

Suddenly I acquired a specifically Scottish profile. One broadsheet embarrassingly, if gratifyingly, identified me as one of the top hundred movers and shakers in Scottish education. At the AGM of the Mary Erskine Former Pupil Guild, I was praised as a 'nationally respected educationalist'. Even more erroneously, for it rested on the mistaken supposition that I was a linguist, I was even asked to act as 'Convenor' for a SCCC Curricular Conference on Modern Languages.

In March 1992 the Howie Committee published their Report. It was, by any standards, a formidable effort, as clear an analysis of wrongs and prescription for improvement as has been produced by any modern educational committee, and it remains searingly relevant, not only for Scotland but also for England. It recommended that the Standard Grade Examination should be taken a year earlier, after which young Scots would embark on one of two tracks, an academic track, that led after three years to a 'Scottish Baccalaureate', and a vocational track, that would exit from school after two years via a 'Scottish Certificate'.

Scots were torn for a while between innate conservatism and a desire to identify with this *elegant* diagnosis that was so different from and superior to anything that England had to offer! In October 1992, however, attending an evening seminar on Howie arranged by the Scottish Council for Industry, I heard the experts smother the Report in queries and objections, in front of businessmen who clearly had no understanding of the issues. I lost patience and accused the 'experts' of trying to paper over the Report's massive criticism of the Status Quo. As we dispersed, another Council member of SCCC came up and thanked me. '*Why didn't HE speak out*,' I thought. '*How typically SCOTTISH!*'

In the end, conservatism won hands down, but it took time to clothe obscurantism with some decent arguments. So the Howie Report and its anaemic substitute (entitled, with witty and ironic ambiguity, 'Higher Still') became the main subject for SCCC discussion throughout my remaining time on the board. My term was not renewed, presumably because I was no longer 'persona grata' with the HMI and civil servants from the Scottish Office, and this would free me to speak my mind.

Back in October 1990, at the same time as I was drafting that fateful response to the Howie Committee, I was asked if I would be Scotland's representative on the Professional Development Sub-Committee of HMC. Before our first meeting I attended HMC's Annual Meeting in Aberdeen. On the train south, I found myself opposite the genial Chris Lowe, then the President of the Secondary Heads' Association, and I told him of my interest in Professional Development. 'Have you heard about the Educational Assessment Centre we are running? No? Oh! You must meet Howard Green.' The upshot was that I became a member of the 'pilot' group of Assessors.

The Educational Assessment Centre (EAC) rested on two propositions. The first was that most Heads were only 'moderately competent' in their performance. The other was that the traditional process of selection – references, shortlisting and interview – was no more accurate than shutting eyes and sticking a pin. The EACs put aspiring Heads through a series of exercises designed to assess them in twelve discrete competencies. Only one of these, 'Educational Values' was specifically educational. It was revealing that most participants provided little or no evidence of any competence in this area. Once I had mastered the vocabulary and acquired a proper instinct for terminological 'correctness', I discovered in myself the sort of aptitude with which I had so happily absorbed the grammatical rules of Ordinary Level French in the 1950s.

For this we had to be trained and I returned, twenty years on, to Newport, South Wales. For the first time I rubbed shoulders with maintained school Heads, county education officers and the like. This challenge proved considerably less acute than that of returning by train from Newport to Edinburgh. With the East of England snowbound and Euston closed, I struck up through mid-Wales to Crewe. The toilets were frozen and the train made two unscheduled stops so that passengers could relieve themselves on the platform. At Crewe no trains were scheduled for Scotland, so I got back on to the train, if for no other reason than that Manchester was nearer to home. There was only one train there – to Sheffield. I jumped in. For the next hour and a half our little train climbed through mountainous drifts amid the Pennine hills. The guard, grizzle-haired and lumbering, with strong Yorkshire tones and Wellington boots, took us in charge. He told me to take the train to York. At 10 p.m., refreshed only by two packets of crisps and a piece of stodgy chocolate cake, I arrived at Waverley. Was this a sensible way for the Principal of Mary Erskine and Stewart's Melville to be conducting his life?

Michael Mavor seemed impressed. He had been a colleague at Tonbridge, whence he had departed at the age of 29 to become Headmaster of Gordonstoun. I have mentioned already the key part he played in our move to Scotland. Now, as Chairman of HMC's Professional Development Committee, he was responsible for masterminding the annual training course for newly appointed Headmasters. He asked if I would join the training team.

There were four of us, each bringing his peculiar background, experiences, instincts and very distinct (and often eccentric) opinions to the ardent headmasters-designate and their wondering wives. It could be difficult to strike the balance between encouragement and sage counselling. At Rossall, Richard Rhodes so terrified the 'rookies' that men who had thought themselves strong paled, while their wives clearly regretted the impending earthquake in their previously charmed lives. We trainers each served four years, coming off the team after we had directed the course. For 'my' HMC Training Course, I brought everyone up to Scotland. Glenalmond in the Spring was a gamble rewarded with three days of glorious Perthshire sunshine.

In May 1991, Michael decided that he would be too busy in his new headship at Rugby to continue as Chairman of the Committee. Geoffrey Parker, my predecessor as Head of History at Tonbridge and now Chairman of HMC, asked if I would like to succeed Michael. For some reason I had no qualms about a system of patronage seemingly rooted in previous association with Tonbridge. Indeed, at my introductory dinner in the East India Club, I commented happily on the coincidence to Geoffrey, Michael and the HMC Secretary, Vivian Anthony, himself a former Tonbridge Head of Department. 'Shhh,' they exclaimed, as one. Nor did I stop to ponder the irony that, unlike Michael, I had time for such a commitment. As with everything else at that time, I was determined to take life at the flood.

And so, just as I had at Tonbridge become overnight a 'guru' on universities, I now became HMC's leader into Professional Development. It turned out to be a lovely assignment, because of the people with whom I worked and the people I met. I enjoyed meeting the many Secretaries of State who flitted into and out of the Department for Education and Science. Arriving last at a HMC Dinner, I found myself opposite Ken Clarke. He paid the customary homage to Scottish education. I told him not to believe everything that he was told. Taking a point after dinner from a Scottish member to the effect that he should imitate practice north of the Border, he rumbled with characteristic glee. 'I was talking to one of your colleagues at Dinner and he told me that all is not well in Scotland.' I felt kilted faces glowering at me. I went with a deputation to call on John Patten, newly ensconced in the modern splendour of Sanctuary House. Never have I seen someone so pleased with his promotion. Rarely has the fall been faster or crueller. I interested myself in the Paul Hamlyn 'National Commission' on Schools and in November 1994 I badgered Gillian Shepherd about its warning that a crisis in teacher recruitment was looming. What did she propose to do about this? She dodged the question – just as successive governments dodged the issue until, about seven years later, everyone suddenly tumbled to the fact that there was a largely irreversible crisis in teacher recruitment. Thus is our country governed.

It was not long before I was called upon to justify my new eminence. A rather flat chapter on Professional Development in an HMC miscellany, *Head to Head*, will have done little in this regard. Endeavouring to compensate by industry for what was evidently lacking in inspiration, I drew up, despatched and collated a Questionnaire on Appraisal and I drafted the HMC compendium on Appraisal and Staff Development, *Making Good Teachers Better*. I was very proud of this and I think that it has stood the test of time. I argued that appraisal was professional development by other means, an artificial process which served to improve Affirmation, Communication, Evaluation and Strategic Planning. The good school should be notable for its 'culture of professional renewal'. The Headmaster should be his school's leading professional and appraisal should be a means whereby he knew and understood better his teaching and non-teaching staff. Nowadays, there would be a greater emphasis on classroom observation and, in maintained schools at least, a closer and tighter relationship to 'performance management'. HMC Common Rooms were then very hostile to any linkage between appraisal and remuneration, promotion or disciplining. I pointed out that, in the final resort, it was wrong and absurd to pretend that there was no connection. Nevertheless, I remain happier with the 'holistic' model that I advocated than with the process that today seeks to limit appraisal to the annual measurement of each teacher against the previous year's narrow performance objectives.

In *Making Good Teachers Better* I propounded a triangular model, wherein appraisal, professional development and whole school planning all fed into, and were informed by, one another. It was not enough, therefore, for HMC to confine its attention to appraisal. We should also be promoting best practice in professional development. I wrote to the then Chairman, Dom Dominic Milroy of Ampleforth, with the proposal that HMC should appoint its own Training Co-ordinator. Unlike SCIS personnel, the Training Co-ordinator would be funded entirely out of the proceeds of HMC courses supported by its members. Dominic Milroy commended it to the HMC Committee and, to my astonishment, the proposal went through without debate – so that the only question related to the identity of my proposed Co-ordinator. Put on the spot, I blurted out the name of Geoffrey Goodall, who had just retired as Headmaster of Exeter School.

It turned out to be an inspired reflex. Sociable, interested in people and with the massive experience born of over thirty years as a Head, Geoff displayed untiring flair in launching a series of training courses of which HMC could justly be proud. He extracted his price – my co-directorship of some of the new courses. Is there a plaque in the Belmont Hotel, Leicester, recording HMC's first ever training course, on Appraisal? For our second, in Oxford, Matthew helped Geoff and me prepare the room and overheads. He reported to Margery that he had never seen anything so amateur, and I have no doubt that he was right, but the members seemed to appreciate the relatively informal and jargon-free timbre of these occasions. I would limp back drained to Edinburgh.

The Chairman of HMC Professional Development could hardly allow his school to lag behind such developments. The strongest justification for all my external activity was that I was abreast of the latest ideas and currently best practice in English and Scottish education. Thus it was with Appraisal. I asked Doreen Waugh, Mary Erskine's Head of English, to chair an inter-school Working Party, with me sitting off stage in the wings. The quest for consensus was so tortuous that it lasted over a year but the outcome justified the delay. The teaching staff had a sense of 'ownership' of the schools' appraisal scheme, while the Principal was happy that it was sufficiently rigorous and purposeful.

The new Nursery and Preparatory Department at 'Easter Ravelston' and the two Technology Centres were completed and the Duke of Edinburgh formally opened the Technology Centres, first at Stewart's Melville, then at Mary Erskine. We had been warned in advance that he always added salt to his lunch and our Caterers laid out an impressive array of hired silver salt cellars. Vigorously he shook the one in front of him. Nothing emerged. Michael Walker beckoned urgently for another, with the same result. There were red faces in the kitchens. I had planned the day meticulously but missed one critical point. How was I to see the Duke away from Queensferry Road and be waiting at Ravelston to greet him? I mumbled my dilemma to the Duke. 'You'd better get in,' he said breezily, and I had my first and last ride in a royal car.

By now Compass Catering had become reasonably established as our culinary providers. Their debut, what should have been the triumphant vindication of all my work to provide a better system of lunches, remains for me my most embarrassing memory as teacher or head. At 3.15 lunches were still being served. Somehow we staggered on. The schools continue today to enjoy a civilized lunch and the successors of Compass, by now the largest catering organization in the world, still hold the contract.

In general, my third year in Edinburgh was proving a happier and more settled experience than the second. On 4 October 1991 there was a lovely surprise when all four of our children, including Matthew from Oxford and Emma from Bath, woke me up to wish me a happy 50th birthday. Our cottage in Newtonmore was at last completed in November. I was frequently invited to rugby matches – by the Nat West Bank, in recognition of my debt to them, by the Royal Bank of Scotland, because they were both the schools' and the

Scottish Rugby Football Union's bankers, and through the good offices of our Bursar, Fred McLeod, who was by now moving smoothly along the path that would take him to the Presidency of the Scottish Rugby Football Union.

December found the whole of Stewart's Melville College walking in file to St Mary's Cathedral for a special service commemorating the 250th anniversary of the birth of Daniel Stewart. Afterwards, a group of us drove up to Calton cemetery and there, amid the remains of such great men as David Hume, placed wreaths on our Founder's own mausoleum. The occasion was as successful as it was unprecedented and it helped me to feel more at home in this foreign land.

So too did the FP Dinners, particularly the extraordinary feasts in Aberdeen. In my first year this had been a notably scary occasion. Aberdeen was Robin Morgan's home ground and he had repeatedly told me how to start my speech. 'Patrick, whatever you do, start your speech by saying, "As I passed the road end at Muckles." They will *love it*.' I did so – and they did love it, cheering so tumultuously that I was quite unnerved, knowing that nothing else that I would say could possibly make the same impact. After the next dinner, I was reassured by an Aberdeen doctor that I was 'part of the Aberdeen establishment'. Of the sixty or so at these dinners, only about ten were Stewart's Melville Former Pupils. Most of the rest were doctors. It was never a good night to be seriously ill in Aberdeen! I found every dinner an exhilarating and mildly terrifying experience. From the top table at the head of a long, rectangular room I would run my eye down the two or three longitudinal tables and apprehensively assess my audience. There was no question of their falling asleep, unless they were more than usually inebriated. Rather, there was a constant stream of razor-sharp banter from the body of the kirk. This was an occasion when prepared speech was never enough. Instant repartee and impromptu jokes were the needs of the hour.

A different type of humour and stimulus came to Queensferry Terrace in the shape of the Czech teachers who brought their party of boys and girls from their Music academy in Prague, the first of many such exchanges organized by Roger Askew and Helen Mitchell. Margery and I greatly enjoyed these visits and always looked forward to them.

In March 1992 there was another, more remarkable, contact with the one-time Habsburg Empire. Sally Duncanson, Head of Modern Languages at Mary Erskine, had organized a European Conference, attended by delegates from a number of schools and various luminaries from the new Europe. One of these, Janice Webster, then president of all Europe's lawyers, soon became one of our Governors. For me, the most memorable feature of the day was the address by Otto von Habsburg, the son of the last Habsburg Emperor. I had seen a photograph of him, as a five year old in his parents' resplendent coach as they made their way to their coronation in Budapest in 1917. At 79, he was still fit as

With Stewart's Melville boys in the Library.

a fiddle and immensely alert. I asked him whether he remembered the Emperor Franz Josef. 'Yes, of course, though I was very young.' A handshake linked me to the man who had become Emperor in 1848.

Otto von Habsburg's upbringing came out most strongly in the passion with which he spoke about the unfolding catastrophe in Yugoslavia, in that he adopted a totally pro-Croat position. He emphasized Serb atrocities in recent weeks, Serb crimes after the Second World War and the Serb villainy of King Alexander of Yugoslavia in the early days of his new kingdom after 1918, in other words immediately after his father lost his Croat lands. He had recently been in the front line of a Croat town that was being shelled by the Serbs. I wondered whether he had ever met Rebecca West or read *Black Lamb and Grey Falcon*. (See above, page 81.)

Perhaps it was this occasion that triggered a desire by me to do something for History's victims in Bosnia. I floated a proposal that Mary Erskine and Stewart's Melville should educate a small number of girls and boys for a couple of terms and this idea was embraced with great generosity by parents and others willing to offer their hospitality to our visitors. (Sylvia Honeyman had two.) Mrs Deborah Miller worked tirelessly to make the necessary arrangements but, with only a fortnight to go, we had only four definite guests. In the event, on 21 February 1993, three boys and eight girls, all aged 13 or 14, stepped smilingly from their aircraft to meet their 'foster parents'. Next day they were kitted out in school uniform, much to their amusement, and the enterprise turned out to be a hugely positive experience. It was lovely to see the party really enjoying themselves at a ceilidh at Inverleith and they had a wonderful send-off at a barbecue on an uncharacteristically balmy June evening at the Wyllies' farm in East Lothian. Nor was this the end of the contact. Jana Bosto, who had stayed with Stan and Eileen Elder (a teacher at Stewart's Melville), returned three years later for a whole year in the Sixth Form.

Little by little, as with all new Heads, I was bringing in 'my own' people, promoting others and saluting the achievements of departing faithful servants of the Schools. In the summer of 1991, right at the end of the term, a Stewart's Melville History teacher asked if I could possibly release him so that he could take up a place on a special Secondary-to-Primary conversion course. I decided to take a chance and duly advertised for his replacement. There were two responses. One of these was from a young man with an Oxford First who had gone straight into teaching at his old school without a PGCE. It transpired that he had been appointed Head of History at a nearby school (later to close) and that he had changed his mind and pursued the bird in the bush, at Eton, and been rejected, leaving him without a job. So he came north, on the understanding that he would probably not be with us for long. Until such time as he found a flat, he lived upstairs in 11 Queensferry Terrace, in the room recently vacated by John Forth. The family had their qualms. He was English. He was Catholic. He was 25 and so well spoken that the boys called him 'Little Lord Fauntleroy'. Would he *survive*? In no time, Richard Cairns was a star – 'The best young History teacher in Scotland', said his Head of Department, Andrew Tod.

As I was drawing heart from this undoubtedly successful appointment, Eileen McCamley confirmed her intention of retiring in June 1992. I was gazing at the Firth of Tay in Dundee, doodling through an exceedingly tedious session of SCCC, when an idea hit me. I would ask Paul Caton to become my Deputy Principal, for the whole of ESMGC, and would advertise for Deputy Heads of *both* Senior Schools. I declared an open mind as to whether I would choose an internal or an external applicant, but saw this nevertheless as a great opportunity to infuse the senior management of the schools with fresh vision and expertise.

Thus it was that I appointed a 31 year old at Stewart's Melville, a young Englishman who had, like Richard Cairns and Patrick Tobin once upon a time, only taught in the school where he had been a pupil. At Mary Erskine I appointed the Deputy Head of a Girls' Maintained school in Hertforshire. She was Scottish but had had no experience of working within an Independent school.

In the event David Dunn and Norma Rolls did great things for me and their respective schools. At the time their appointment caused great personal hurt to at least two 'home' candidates with excellent credentials and generated some consternation in the Staff Rooms. At Mary Erskine Nan Howe decided that she would retire altogether from teaching at Easter, a very sad loss to the school. At Stewart's Melville, Donald McDiarmid told me his feelings with great dignity. In the following October, there was a knock on my door and Donald came in and said simply, 'I want you to know that David Dunn is doing a superb job and that I could not have done it as well.' His generosity was as humbling as it was magnificent.

There was a final staffing twist to my third year. Andrew Tod decided that it was time for him to leave – for the post of Head of History at Strathallan. By now Richard Cairns was seeking to put his own career back on its appointed track. I decided that I must at all costs not lose him too and I offered him the succession – without interview, let alone advertisement. Yet again questions were asked in the Staff Room concerning the Principal's judgement. Nobody mentioned the Catholic question but it must surely have lurked in many a mind. Years later, when I was appraised by Michael Walker, I was told that colleagues had seen some of my appointments as 'controversial', but that they conceded that they had also been very good.

David Dunn must have wondered during his first term what sort of school he had come to. He had much the same first impressions of Stewart's Melville as I had had three years earlier, a crazy mixture of highs and lows. On the one hand, the School was awarded the Ernst Enzensperger prize for Outdoor Education, a German recognition of the uniqueness of Carbisdale. On the other hand, when I proposed a new structure of Term Dates and naively imagined that I had the Management Teams behind me, I ran into the usual resistance in the Stewart's Melville Management Team. In exasperation I remarked to Ernie Wilkins that I had never known a School that made such an unprofessional start to its school year. He exploded, with some justification, 'We work bloody hard here,' and slammed the phone down.

But Ernie, David and I collaborated well on disciplinary business. We vigorously investigated rumours of drug taking in the Fifth Year and it transpired that the consequent list of 'known offenders' corresponded more or less exactly with previous supposition, thereby encouraging the surmise that the majority were 'clean'. Then the curiosity of some Fourth Year boarders led to the importation of cannabis into Dean Park House and the expulsion of two of its members. The mother of one of these, a young man who fashioned a good career for himself at his next school, said bitterly, 'If you fly with the crows, you are likely to get shot.' I met the other some years later on Waverley Station. He came across, shook me by the hand and I asked him why he was in Edinburgh. He was just starting at Edinburgh University. I expressed my pleasure. Then, 'I would like to thank you, Sir, for the way you handled things.'

There is often a silver lining to the blackest of clouds and distraught parents too often forget this. In particular, they believe that blind support, amounting often to 'denial', is right for their delinquent child when he – it usually is a 'he' – positively needs to learn his lesson and make a fresh start.

That said, the misery of some situations can seem almost irredeemable. On this occasion I wrote to Emma and Matthew:

> The human reality of getting rid of boys is as horrible as ever. The main culprit lost his father (suicide) and then mother (also suicide). His mother's brother brought him up, before he left home – he is now in jail for drugs. So his mother's brother's wife and her second husband are bringing up the boy and his sister. The latter slashed her wrists a couple of weeks ago. The foster-parents hope that she will be better, now that her brother's problems are out in the open.

The boarding house drugs affair did have one funny side. 'D' was a boarder whose family lived in Thailand. He had puffed a joint but had admitted his offence immediately I questioned him. I suspended him out of necessity but the last thing I wanted was his permanent departure. I telephoned the father and asked where he should serve his suspension. 'You'd better send him home.' I hit on the idea of 'internal suspension'. He would work for a week at Inverleith but board with the Principal and his family. Lucy was horrified. 'D' was in the same year as she. Once more she barricaded herself in her room. Gradually she realized that there were no hard feelings. On the Saturday evening we took 'D' to Mass in the Cathedral – as we knelt, he whispered to Lucy, 'Is it always this hard?' – and on to hear Margery singing in a Chamber Concert, another new experience for him. On Sunday morning we drove up through the mist to the cottage in Newtonmore, where I wanted to fix a bathroom mirror. All went well, until the time to drive home. The battery was flat, because I had left the headlights on. Grimly, I tramped with 'D' through the fields and out into the road, seeking help. Eventually a car emerged. Yes, he had a 'jump lead'. It transpired that he was a Watson's parent. 'D' made the most of his opportunities at Stewart's Melville and afterwards. Weeks before my retirement I found to my delight that one of the co-presenters at the Sixth Year Business Breakfast, the very model of the modern IT entrepreneur, was a very smart and clearly flourishing 'D'.

The worst problem of all in that autumn term of 1992 left David Dunn on the sidelines. The parents of a young man who had left Stewart's Melville in the previous summer reported the school to the Race Relations Board. Despite fine academic results and a place at Cambridge University he had not been awarded a 'Dux' prize. He and his parents claimed that this was the final chapter in a catalogue of racial discrimination, involving such events as the award of a Biology prize to another pupil some years earlier.

We found that it is actually quite difficult to defend yourself against discrimination when it has never entered into your mind in the first place. In those days, before schools and universities 'watched their backs' and ensured that they awarded prizes according to strict numerical data, panels of well-intentioned people would get together and devote their best – and this often meant 'subjective' – thinking to the judicious award of the Dux distinction. It was only after the hubbub subsided that Donald McDiarmid informed us that, had the Dux award been given to the boy, he would have had a bigger Higher score (i.e. worse – 'A's go to candidates who achieve 1 > 5) than any previous Dux winner.

The aggrieved parents, whose elder son had won the Dux prize a few years earlier, seem to have believed genuinely that their equally talented younger son had suffered from the change of regime at Queensferry Road. Told at first by the Commission for Racial Equality that the School did not have a case to answer, they enlisted the interest of the media and the support of a local Labour MP, Gavin Strang, who did not hesitate to express his totally misinformed 'judgement' – and without talking to anyone in the school. I returned from an SCCC meeting to find the case strewn across the front page of the *Evening News* and on the whole of an inside page. The young man, soulful against a Cambridge backdrop, stated that school, 'which should have been the happiest days of my life', had been turned into a misery by the racial discrimination of his teachers, under my leadership. At the foot of the article was my total and indignant denial of all the charges.

Next morning, *The Scotsman* took up the affair on an inside page. Although milder, its article was defamatory in two respects, in that it stated that the 'wrong boys' had been awarded two prizes and it quoted an unnamed solicitor as saying that the evidence showed that the School had been racist.

A week or so later, a journalist from the *Evening News* telephoned with the news that the CRE had finally decided not to proceed against the School. Did I have any comments? I said that I was not surprised, that I was very sorry that the family had such a sense of grievance and that the whole affair had been counter-productive in that Asian children at the School were now being asked by well-intentioned white children whether or not they felt that they were the victims of racial discrimination. Later that day my remarks were published, alongside a barrage of letters critical of the School and a single, long letter arguing for us. After a Council of War I wrote an extended letter to the *Evening News*. This seemed to go down well.

The father was not going to leave matters there. He too wrote to the *Evening News*. His younger son had been a victim of discrimination and not his older because there was a new Principal and because an earlier Deputy Head too had been superior to his successor, Paul Caton. The *Evening News* alleged that I had only appointed an Asian Deputy Head of School for the following year to protect myself from the forthcoming action. I had to write yet another letter, vigorously affirming my distinguished Deputy Head and dismissing the other claim. After that there were threats of court action but the matter gradually subsided, not without the odd outburst that revealed the breadth of what was effectively a conspiracy against the good name of Stewart's Melville.

The affair had its positive aspects. The Parents' Liaison Committee declared their total support and the Stewart's Melville Staff Room organized a special staff revue, in which I starred as Morse and David Dunn as Lewis, that culminated with Jock Richardson leading the singing of *For he's a jolly good fellow.*

By now I was almost too tired to care. I had been leading a crazy life. When my mother's cousin, Winnie Coombes, went into hospital after a fall and it became obvious that she would not able to go back to living on her own, I had to organize her move into a nursing home and the letting of her flat to provide the necessary income. In the fortnight before the eruption of the Race Relations case, I drove Sophie (for her History project) to every Thomas Telford bridge in the Highlands, addressed the Former Pupil dinner in Cambridge, with Matthew's help moved all Winnie's furniture from her third floor flat in Kensington to the family garage at Lower Park, dashed to the Caledonian Club for the London FP Dinner, went with Matthew to the Calcutta Cup match at Twickenham and flew back to Edinburgh in time to enjoy the dessert and make my speech at the Mary Erskine Former Pupil Dinner.

Was it about now that, in my impatience to set Sophie down at Mary Erskine, I drove off while she was still clambering out, so that the rear wheel grazed her leg? If so, she was not the only member of the family to suffer from the collapse of my sense of proportion. I was wrong to believe that my attendance of the Junior School Prizegiving enjoyed priority over Emma's last Prize Day at Prior Park. Margery went south alone to see Emma bow out as Head Girl with a gracious and witty speech of thanks to Cardinal Hume. Perhaps I felt that another outing would, quite simply, be one too many.

We returned from holiday to one of those numbing tragedies that stand out later as landmarks. Iain Hoyle, a fine and justly popular young man who had left Stewart's Melville that summer with a bright future stretching before him, was killed in a farming accident in the USA. His parents were wonderfully brave. His peers were devastated.

This was the moment when David Dunn injected fresh heart. Whereas I had simply felt that the School presented a rather drab and unwelcoming aspect to visitors, he did something about it, designing and achieving a completely revised entrance lobby, replete with the College's Coat of Arms.

The old tensions lingered, nevertheless. By February 1994 David had 'ear-bashed' me enough and I decided that I must address the Staff Room on the need to embrace change. I typed a long speech for comment by the Management Team, half hoping that they would say that it was 'over the top'. They didn't, so I delivered it to the teaching staff, who listened in silence. I gave each a copy to read at leisure.

In essence, it was a 'We're all in this together' rallying call. Numbers of applicants were down, perhaps because of recent knocks, perhaps because the pool had already been drained, and the School had to confront the likelihood that, sooner or later, it would lose its Assisted Places. The only antidote to decline was excellence – in our academic aspirations and atmosphere, in our social and disciplinary tone and in our relations with the outside world. We needed to re-examine and refine our strategies for teaching and learning with a view to effective differentiation. Our 'boisterous' reputation was not helpful nor could Stewart's Melville continue to be seen as a school 'where you had to learn to take knocks'. Our guidance systems should eradicate any vestiges of bullying and 'slagging' through the genuinely open channels of communication and it was time for a wholesale review of our disciplinary codes and sanctions. Finally, it was not enough that the School should be strong in sport, the CCF and outdoor education. The School could be a 'very cold climate' for aesthetes and it needed to enrich its provision in Music and Drama. In short, we needed to change and the management of change was not something that pertained simply to 'management'. Unless everyone felt involved we would not promote real accountability and consensus would leave us always with the lowest common denominator.' Like alcohol, the 'old soldier' act provided momentary solace, but after that it served only to deepen depression.' We must lift up our eyes to the hills.

Apparently, the atmosphere on Thursday was not happy, but it was, for me, a Mary Erskine day. By Friday smiles were back on faces.

I wrote to Matthew and Emma: 'I wish that I felt more comfortable about my role in trying to make the School change. I just feel tired and stressed, but I hope and suppose that good will emerge at the end of it.' It did – and this is the last that I will say about my tussles with the soul of Stewart's Melville. Stewart's Melville's inner strengths saw it through, not without the occasional sleepless night for me, and I can record that my colleagues did indeed respond generously and very effectively to the call that I made of them. As always, it was they who made the School what it is – a great school, with an extraordinary habit of producing the extraordinary achievement.

That summer, Sylvia Honeyman decided that the Principal would benefit from a change in his surroundings. Out of my oppressively gloomy study went the bottle-green wallpaper, the mustard-and-black carpet, the deep red ceiling panels. In came light and gold redolent of a world far to the south of Presbyterian Edinburgh. Henceforward, in my advice to new Heads, I always urged them to look first to their surroundings. Making the study my own in August 1994 did wonders for my morale! So too did my new Head Boy, the remarkable Mark Tweedie.

His year group had arrived in the Senior School at the same time as I did and it happened to contain many very talented individuals. A relatively new member of the English department, John Allan, decided to enter the leading Debaters into the competition to represent the UK at the forthcoming European Youth Parliament in Berlin and his team beat off the best of Britain. David Dunn and I flew out for a weekend to see the Stewart's Melville boys in action in the Reichstag debates. They were in their element. John Allan ensured also that they were at the centre of the social whirl and that his Scottish ceilidh would be one of the favourite memories taken back by the delegates to their countries.

To me there was a further dimension. I found my first visit to Berlin a haunting experience, never more than when we went to a concert in a suburban school and passed some wreaths set against a recessed wall. I looked closer and saw a plaque, saying that it was the site of a synagogue destroyed on 2 November 1938 and that it was from this spot that the first Jews had been taken to concentration camps. As we turned back to the pavement, we saw that it was inset with rails, on which stood a single cattle wagon. In the adjacent children's park stood a tall obelisk in black stone, on which were listed all the train journeys which departed from this place to Auschwitz. What an extraordinary and terrible thing to live a suburban life amid such memories. At least, unlike so many millions today, the Berliners *do* remember the horrors that man has done to man, the perils of living without a God-given conscience.

It was predictably ironic that, in the week after I spoke to the Stewart's Melville Staff Room, I should be plunged into a major disciplinary investigation at the other end of the Dykes. In the end, after hours of interviews, we dealt satisfactorily with five girls involved in offences in Edinburgh. I spoke to the School, as I would always do in such circumstances, so that all would be in possession of the facts. Once again there was a telephone call from the *Evening News*. The young female journalist asked for information, then said that she was the niece of the chaplain at Tonbridge School. Fatally, I thought that I detected a nicer and better side to a journalist and I blurted out, 'There's something else. I hope that you remember that these are only teenage girls and that they are bitterly ashamed of what they have done.' Next day, 'GIRLS' SHAME' was the front page headline of *The Scotsman*.

Yet again there was a positive aspect hidden in the business. A police friend of the School indicated to me that the source of the 'leak' came from within the bowels of the School and he hinted that the police would do their best to inhibit such exposure in the future. That was, as I recall, the last time that a purely internal disciplinary affair was ever broadcast in the columns of the press, 'reputable' or otherwise. The media switched their attentions to other Independent schools, and they are still at it today.

1994 was, in any case, destined to be an 'annus mirabilis' for The Mary Erskine School. Founded in 1694, Scotland's oldest girls' school was 300 years old and we were determined to make the most of this unique occasion. As with many another school, this included an Appeal – for a new building overlooking the playing fields that would have the double function of Sixth Form Centre and Pavilion. It was the sort of facility that is difficult to justify in terms of necessity but gives all the right messages about the School's vision and ambition. For Mary Erskine, after all its recent travails, it was the token of success and security. No Appeal is really enjoyable but we raised enough from parents and friends to achieve our goal.

But the main business of 1994 to 1995 was celebration. For months, a Tercentenary Committee had dreamed and planned. The outcome was a spectacular succession of concerts, lectures, tournaments and works of art. We commissioned a musical from Peter Skellern and in *Poles Apart* he produced a lively parody of Carbisdale. I invited Lydia Skinner to write the history of the school and she obliged nobly with *A Family Unbroken*, stipulating only that I write the last chapter. Doreen Waugh collaborated with the Secretary of the Merchant Company, Robin Wilson, in mounting a fine historical exhibition in Merchants' Hall. And there were many great feasts.

The first of these followed a sunny Founders' Day that brought Jean Thow and Robin Morgan together in a photograph of three Heads. That evening the Former Pupils held their Tercentennial Dinner in the Balmoral Hotel. 359 women and 7 men rocked to the sparkle and sentiment of one fine speech after another, with a notably brilliant contribution from the Head Girl, Lynsey Milne. In January, Merchants' Hall witnessed two dinners on successive nights, the first for 140 of the great and good of Edinburgh, the second for all the teaching staff of the School.

The Former Pupil Guild gave the School a sumptuous legacy of the Tercentary. Audrey Lawrence, the excellent Guild President and a recently retired teacher of the Junior School, had enlisted Marjorie Clinton to design a ceramic mural. This was a beautiful representation of the herbs known to have been grown in the Edinburgh Physic Garden at the end of the Seventeenth Century – the 'stock in trade' of Mary Erskine's apothecary's business and the source, therefore, of her school's foundation. No school can have received a more apposite adornment of a centenary and we made it the focal point of the most important of all our celebrations, the visit of the Queen and Duke of Edinburgh in June 1994.

I defy any Head to say that he or she is nerveless on such occasions. Margery and I woke at four and tested each other on our 'lines'. We identified the Highland Dancing as a potential problem and we memorized the order of dances.

The sun shone brilliantly as the royal car arrived, the Queen and Duke stepped out and I introduced Her Majesty to the welcoming party. We then walked towards the Highland Dancers, Sophie Tobin included, and as we drew nearer I realized that I did not have a clue as to which dance they had reached. The Queen duly asked her question. I mumbled that I thought that it was a

Mary Erskine School Tercentenary – Her Majesty on the balcony of Ravelston House.

Speyside. Meanwhile, Prince Philip was experiencing a similar ignorance in Margery. He shouted ahead, 'What is the dance?' and received the reply, in a familiar drawl, 'He doesn't know.'

The Queen found in Marjorie Clinton an infinitely more authoritative guide to the Mural and she was suitably impressed. I then escorted her into the school hall to meet the assembled school. As our steps echoed along the corridor, the trill of over 600 girls subsided instantly and all were quiet, even tense, as the Queen and Duke mounted the steps of the stage. The orchestra struck up the National Anthem and the Queen winced visibly at a horribly discordant note. However, she began to tap her foot in time with the Purcell – not the happiest choice perhaps, despite its composition in 1694, in that Queen Mary, for whose birthday it had been written, did not live to see another birthday. I then stood up and assured Her Majesty that, though there had been many Queens since 1694, none would have been as popular or welcome as she was today.

I invited Her Majesty to cut the special cake. She took the knife, then looked at me as if to seek my guidance. At the back of the hall, Matthew and Emma froze. Nobody in the world knew less about how to cut a cake than their father. (I suspect that the Queen knew the same.) Gingerly I motioned towards a promising spot. She inserted the knife and the pre-cut slice fell away. 'Oh, it's quite easy,' she remarked, with the trace of a smile.

After that the royal visit was plain sailing. The Queen and Prince Philip stood on the Ravelston balcony to listen to the Pipe Band, then mingled with girls, staff and governors in my Study. I felt numb as I escorted the Queen to her car and as she and the Duke drove off. I hope that they realized how much pleasure and joy they brought to the School that June day.

And I thought of my mother and of the pride and pleasure that she would have had. It was a far cry from Lower Park and Paddy the Putney Pud.

CHAPTER 18

Higher Still?

The Blakes headed north. Helen Mitchell, head of music at Mary Erskine's, met the plane. (Howard) got to the school, made his apologies and rambled on about how Stevenson's verse was out of date for today's children, and how such direct and great text couldn't be set. 'Ah,' said Patrick Tobin, the headmaster, 'so you're saying that you can't respond to that?' Blake rumbled on about song cycles and their problems with language. Silence. 'Well,' continued Tobin, 'I don't think Mahler was troubled with such things,' and he laid out, concisely, his views on Mahler's 'Kindertotenleider'. Then Blake gave his, and conversation hummed, and suddenly an hour had passed, and Blake had the whole of 'The Land of Counterpane' singing and soaring in his mind. He knew that he had to write it.'

(*The Scotsman,* January 24th 1995)

Vanity demanded that I print this extract from Scotland's premier newspaper. Tobin's views on *Kindertotenleider* were necessarily concise – and I can no more imagine that he conversed with a composer for an hour about music than that the Queen talked three hours with a standing butler. Even so, I can justly claim that a lovely piece of music would not have been written but for my felicitous remark.

For a school as musical as Mary Erskine, it was only right and proper that the tercentenary should culminate in the performance of a classical score composed specially for the school's birthday. Helen Mitchell approached Howard Blake, famous for *The Snowman*, with the idea that he should compose a choral work based on R.L. Stevenson's *A Child's Garden of Verses*. On a Saturday morning I drove across to Ravelston to meet our composer, to be confronted with a statement that he wouldn't do it. Classical music and children's verses did not go together. As it happened Margery and I had enjoyed a performance of *Kindertotenleider* and I blurted out, 'Mahler didn't have a problem.' Howard went away and thought again. The premiere in the Usher Hall of *The Land of Counterpane* is for us a glowing memory, the more so as Lucy was the lead cello and Sophie was in the choir that sang so magically under Helen Mitchell's inspired direction. The hairs on the back of my neck still twitch whenever we replay the video-recording of that very special evening.

A feature of that evening was the spectacle of that choir, for all were clad in the new, tercentennial, Mary Erskine kilt. I had long winced at the ever-shortening and skimpy skirts of the girls. Norma Rolls agreed and we came up with the idea that a kilt might be the solution to our problems. Thereupon she took the idea from conception to manufacture, greatly aided by the partnership of Deirdre Kinloch Anderson, whose family were kilt makers to the Queen. She and I went to obtain the approval of the Countess of Mar and Kellie for this variant on her clan's tartan. The Countess spoke fascinatingly of the time from 1932 to 1935 when her father had been Military Attache in Berlin. He had got on well with Hitler, as the two men had fought on the same sector on the Western Front, and he had substituted for the British ambassador when the latter refused to act as host to Ernst Rohm and other leading Nazis. It was the only occasion when the bells rang and the guests told the waiters that they wanted to come down and help with the washing up. Rohm was killed the following week. 'When we said, "How shocking", the Nazis said, "Oh no, he had it coming to him."'

The Mary Erskine girls were far less happy about the kilt. They saw it for what it was, the imposition of the School's tastes on their own, and the pressure was such that I agreed to a general meeting with their parents. Roger Griffiths, the Membership Secretary of HMC, was staying with us that night and I took him along with me. He came out ashen-faced. 'Patrick, I have never seen anything like it.' We toughed it out and before long the kilt was proudly worn by all the girls, Senior and Junior, of The Mary Erskine School.

Perhaps I was too fond of 'toughing'. I detect in my letters to my children a note of 'machismo'. Too many of the weekly epistles began with a 'I can't recall a week like…' and went on to describe an extraordinary confusion of routines, meetings, emergencies, social engagements, fleeting appearances in support of rugby and hockey and, increasingly, excursions to London.

'Delegate,' my successive Chairmen urged me, 'You must delegate.' But how could I remain, in any meaningful sense, the Head of each of the two senior schools if I became further removed from their lives? And, of course, I was also the Chief Executive of ESMGC, the man who kept the top spinning.

The underlying reason is the difficulty of imposing shape on such a diffuse operation. The last fortnight has thrown up massive imprecision in the calculation of our repairs and maintenance programme for next session. It amounts to nearly £300K and yet no-one has a proper fix on what needs to be done – so I have insisted on that before any decisions are taken. Exactly the same applies to MES heating – another memo painfully composed by me to remind everyone else of what we do not know and what they must do! I suppose that it is what I am paid to do and that I would be out of a job otherwise, but the current level of inundation is very high, with the Pavilion already started, with artificial lawns and a new gymnasium at SMC awaiting final approval (the Gymnasium was never built, thank goodness!) and with various firms tendering to MES for the revamping of our Science labs, subject to resolution of the MES Heating strategy! The Chairman of the Building Committee has complained to James Laurenson that he has been asked to run five meetings in two or three weeks and that they are lasting an inordinate amount of time because the senior management at the schools has not got its act together. 'Too right', as they say, but life is simply not long enough for the individuals concerned to come together in sufficient calm and knowledge to crack all the problems. When it is all over, I hope that I shall be able to look back on some concrete achievements. At present, my life feels as attractive and coherent as a building site on a muddy day.

My key file was a small, very tatty one, containing a maximum of three sheets of paper – my 'Balls in the Air' file.

From time to time Michael Walker and James Laurenson expressed concerns about the threat to my health, but I never missed a day through illness. The only outward sign that all might not be well was my proclivity for passing out. In 1991, I fainted at breakfast, inflicting serious damage on my head and my bowl of bran flakes. As I came to, my immediate thought was, 'What is going to happen to my *lovely* job?' It was, in its macabre way, a defining moment for me. Amid any subsequent moaning or self-pity, I knew thereafter the truth, that my job might at times be impossible but I loved it!

I had been particularly keen to be at Mary Erskine that morning, as a seemingly excellent young Modern Languages teacher was coming from London for interview, so I went into work after the doctor had patched me up. Jane Bremner did not allow the gruesome sight to put her off her return to Edinburgh, but Nan Howe proved less tolerant of infirmity. As I pressed a bloodied pad to my wound during the Management meeting that followed, she exploded, 'Oh for God's sake, go home!' I meekly did as I was told.

That was my first faint since Prior Park. Not long afterwards, as previously described, I passed out in my study at Stewart's Melville, but I then enjoyed a lengthy period without similar scares. My only serious intimation of mortality came in the form of a letter from United Artists Communications (Scotland) Limited in March 1995. I replied, tersely and in some confusion: 'You now tell me that the bank has stopped direct debits because I am dead…If you believe that I am dead, why are you still invoicing me?'

My next faint was so public, dramatic and pregnant with notoriety as to arouse serious concerns about my health and staying power. David Dunn had arranged a Fire Practice for Stewart's Melville. The alarms sounded and I took up my place in front of the assembled School. Eileen Elder came up to tell me that Jana Bosto, one of the Bosnian girls of 1993, had just arrived from Split for her second stay in Edinburgh, but that her luggage had gone missing at Heathrow. The next thing I knew was that Margery was with me in an ambulance.

Apparently I had keeled over and smashed the back of my head against a stone that jutted out from the foot of the wall behind me. I lost a consider-able amount of blood. The School dispersed from the scene, the ambulance was called and Norma Rolls went to find Margery to tell her that there had been an accident. In the event, the injury demanded nothing more than a few stitches and I was back at home that evening and in School the next day. Very impressively, no whisper of the incident seems to have reached the Press.

I assured James Laurenson that I was OK, but he had had enough and commissioned a thorough overhaul in Glasgow. They found nothing wrong – and my periodic fainting remains a mystery. Perhaps the brusque Ulster doctor from the surgery was right. Called in after a fourth faint, she asked how long it had been since the previous occasion. When I replied, 'Eighteen months,' she said, 'A faint every eighteen months is nothing to worry about,' and left without more ado.

James Laurenson had replaced Michael Walker as Chairman when the latter took charge of the Trust of the Western General Hospital. The two were extraordinarily different, in temperament as in appearance, but each brought to his weekly meeting with me his acute intelligence, unfailing interest and amused sympathy. While neither could be fobbed off with half-truths, both were tolerant of their Principal's foibles and solid in their support whenever things became difficult. I was remarkably fortunate in my Chairmen.

And in my Secretaries! Dorothy Silver had been in the Stewart's Melville office when Kay More retired and I sensed then that she had the wit and spirit to handle me. When Judy Mottram decided that her time too had come, I asked Dorothy if she would be prepared to be my P.A. at both ends of the Dykes. We became a travelling team and she would each day lug from car into office her laptop and huge bundles of papers. I would bring with me a 'dictaphone' tape or two so that she could get on with my typing while I looked at my correspondence. Between us we cleared a great deal of business. We both enjoyed the speed, buzz and variety of the job and we established our own ways of coping with the constant disruption caused by outings from the Schools. At times we worked *too* fast. A Mr Alasdair Salmond observed in a postscript to a reference, that I had misspelled his first name. Irritated by the apparent pedantry, I dug out the copy of the offending letter – to 'Mr Alligator Salmond'. Spell checks can be dangerous.

Dorothy could be quite fiercely protective of me and this sometimes caused offence, and I could never persuade her to feel part of Mary Erskine in the same way that she loved Stewart's Melville, but her warmth and verve were supremely helpful to me in charming all the Masters, Governors, Headmasters, Former Pupils and others who made up our extended community. To all applicants for teaching posts, arriving for interview, she was their first impression of the School. I learned early to guard against her preference for those who haled from Aberdeen! She was also very good with the boys and girls who came to my Study – as Prefects, or for UCAS 'mock' interviews, or because they were in trouble. She told me that most of the last came back to her office feeling better than when they went in. I think that she played a major part in 'softening' the ordeal for them.

She saw it as part of her job to 'humanize' my existence. She found willing accomplices in my Head and Deputy Head Boys and Girls, notably Lucy Porteous at Mary Erskine and Mark Tweedie at Stewart's Melville. Lucy was friendly charm personified. Mark Tweedie – the first Stewart's Melville boy ever to gatecrash a Mary Erskine Management meeting – was irrepressible. Dorothy seems to have sensed that there was a Teacher in the Principal that was screaming to get out and cross the ever-widening generation gap. So she organized regular lunches for me with my 'leadership teams' in the two schools, in addition to the less personal lunches that I would have in turn with each of the Sixth Year House and Clan groups of boys and girls.

I flatter myself that I generally got on well with my leadership teams. In their very different ways they were all fine young people and it was a privilege to get to know them better. As a rule I selected them, with the help of the Deputy Heads, following interviews of a 'long list', but in two instances I was debarred from the process – when Lucy and Sophie Tobin became Deputy Head Girls. Both handled this potentially tricky relationship with adroit tact and, even though it was impossible to avoid the occasional awkwardness, it helped me to develop a sounder insight into the realities of Sixth Form life.

The most vivid example of 'collusion' between Dorothy Silver and a senior pupil concerned another Deputy Head Girl, Sarah Furness. Sarah was a young lady with a mission – to be a fighter pilot in the RAF. At the time she flew only gliders and she had casually asked if I was interested in going up with her. Finally she cornered me in Dorothy's office. 'Mr Tobin, you haven't answered my question, would you like to come up in my glider?' 'Sarah,' I responded, 'Wouldn't that be a terrible responsibility?' 'Mrs Silver,' Sarah declared, 'I am getting very bad vibes.' 'OK,' I said hurriedly, 'I tell you what. Give me a ring on Saturday morning.'

On Saturday morning the phone rang. 'Hullo, it's Sarah.' 'Sarah who?' I asked, and there was a sigh at the other end of the line. I looked desperately out of the window. There was not a cloud to be seen. 'It's a lovely day,' I said limply, and we arranged to meet that afternoon at her airfield.

Margery came with me as chaperone. We arrived before Sarah and were looking around the huts when a jeep swept in with Sarah at the wheel. 'Jump in,' she said, and we were gone before Margery could register her presence.

We swept up to a line of gliders. 'The commandant has said that we should have his. Would you prefer to go front or back – it makes no difference.' I chose the front and Sarah handed me my parachute. 'Do you mind if I ask a personal question?' I shook my head. 'How much do you weigh?' She thereupon instructed the ground crew to offload all the ballast. We climbed aboard and

Sarah explained how I was to eject myself in the event of an emergency. I decided that it would be simpler to die.

'Do you see that cable?' she asked. 'It pulls us up.' That in no way prepared me for the shock that followed – of being yanked up vertically at such speed that I had no breath to scream even if I had let myself do so. The nose then dipped. 'Don't worry,' she said, 'We're just dropping the cable.'

We flew upwind, circled (roughly above James Laurenson's house, I thought) and came downwind at some speed, before turning again and crash landing into a bank. 'Would you like to go up again?' Sarah asked, and I heard myself saying, 'Yes.' 'I hoped you'd say that.' So I had a second flight and the views were lovely and I resolved that I would dine out on the tale, which I have been doing ever since.

Margery, meanwhile, was standing where we had left her, looking up anxiously into the sky. A number of gliders came across and out of them jumped men in parachutes. 'My God!' Margery thought, and I am flattered that the idea ever came into her mind. She was right, of course. Sarah Furness was a very determined young lady and had she ordered me to jump I would have done it, if only for fear of seeming cowardly if I didn't. Sarah, incidentally, went to Cambridge to study Astrophysics, switched to Theology and is now a Flight Lieutenant in the RAF.

Not every girl was as dynamic as Sarah – or as Kate McGrath and her fellow debaters who matched the earlier feat of the Stewart's Melville team in being chosen as Britain's representatives in the European Youth Parliament. Traditional Girls' Schools had tended, rather, to foster diligence and conformity, virtues that now ensured that girls were excelling boys by ever-increasing margins, rather than risk-taking and flair. When Otto von Habsburg addressed his mixed audience, there were no questions from the girls, although their academic record was generally superior, but several from the Stewart's Melville boys. An irritated Judith Barton sought an explanation and was told, 'The boys' questions were so *clever*!' Caring and conscientious, teachers at girls' schools were perhaps over-fearful of failure and overprotective of their charges. Norma Rolls was ill rewarded one January when she prevailed on us to delay the Prelims by a few days, so that they did not start on the first day of term. A host of girls, Head Girl included, duly absented themselves to grab extra time for revision. Down the Dykes, where the need was surely greater, the attendance of the boys was almost universal. David Dunn found it hard to disguise his satisfaction.

Today's most fashionable heresy is the reduction of the whole of education to the successful preparation of pupils for examinations. For the past decade and more, the trend towards coursework, modular structures and simplified questions has tended to favour girls, whereas the old terminal examinations had penalized them. Each year I would compile my own 'league tables' for Scottish

Independent schools and each year Mary Erskine would be at or near the top of the Higher and Standard Grade lists, while Stewart's Melville would be in the middle. If, on the other hand, I measured Stewart's Melville against the *boys* in coeducational schools, the outcome was much more gratifying. And in the Certificate of Sixth Year Studies, the examination taken mainly by students who wished to stretch themselves, Stewart's Melville tended to excel all its rivals.

Boys posed far more disciplinary problems than girls, partly because they were caught, partly because the Mary Erskine staff did not go looking for trouble. The code on hair, for instance, rigorous at Stewart's Melville, merely prescribed to the girls of Mary Erskine that hair should be of a 'natural colour'. I rebelled finally when I bumped into a girl who was manifestly flouting any conceivable interpretation of 'natural'. From the stage, I observed at Assembly that there *were* rules on hair and that I did not expect to see a 'purple monster' in the corridors. There was an explosion of delightedly shocked whoops and squeals. Afterwards I chatted for a minute or so in the 'Crush Hall', then made my way over to Ravelston House and found my telephone ringing. It was the mother. 'Mr Tobin,' she exclaimed, 'You called my daughter a purple monster. How *could* you?' Wearily I pointed out that I had mentioned no names. She chipped in. 'You are quite right, Mr Tobin, and I am sorry that you had to waste your time. I keep telling her about her hair.' 'Yes,' I thought to myself, 'and why haven't the *teachers*?'

When the girls went to Stewart's Melville for their lessons, they were always struck by the firmness, almost fierceness, with which the boys were treated. The boys, of course, were equally struck by the differences they found at Ravelston. Yet this was as much a 'generational' as a 'gender' issue. Younger staff were much more likely to have been at co-educational schools. The best staff in either school sought to foster excellence through their own high standards and through easy relationships with their pupils. And more and more of these came from a Junior School that was fully coeducational and markedly softer in tone than it once had been.

I saw it as my part gently to nudge each of the Senior Schools towards the strengths of the other, so that 'Twinning' could indeed promote the best of both worlds. Thus I was pleased when Mary Erskine became as competitive in its hockey as Stewart's Melville was in rugby, when Jacqueline Dormand and Linda Thomas stepped forward as Mary Erskine's first Carbisdale Directors and when Stewart's Melville's Nick Fraser proved such a success as the three schools' first 10-to-14 Modern Languages Co-ordinator. The girls' choir under Helen Mitchell was second to none, but Roger Askew and Zlatan Fazlic fought tirelessly against the sexism that tells boys not to be choristers. The friendship and collaboration between the two Schools' Music departments were conspicuously generous, as was their annual alliance with Dr Iain Scott of Mary Erskine in the production of a series of stunning Musicals. Nor did Stewart's Melville

Rugby in any way retreat. Having for long eschewed the semi-professional undertones of the Scottish Cup, Phil Waine and Chris Spence coached their Fifteen to victory at the first attempt.

Richard Cairns, meanwhile, was achieving astonishing success in terms of the Oxbridge places won by Stewart's Melville Historians. He attracted a series of fascinating speakers to the school and did his best also to rekindle his Principal's involvement with History. Thus it was that I drove up to Strathallan to hear Alan Bullock tell Scottish Sixth Formers about Hitler and Stalin, with the happy consequence that I was asked if I would drive the great man and his wife back to Edinburgh. I would have loved to have had a tape recorder running as he talked about his meetings with Khruschev and Speer. He told me that the 'Alan' handed down in his family had once been 'Allen' – after Ralph Allen, from whose illegitimate child the Bullocks were allegedly descended.

Richard Cairns' final coup in my regard was to inveigle an SCCC Conference into inviting me to talk to them about the teaching of Scottish History. This was, for me, surely a bridge too far, although I held very strong feelings on this subject. With every year that passed, it seemed to me, boys and girls knew less about the past and were increasingly devoid of anything resembling a cognitive framework. Instead they were taught 'historical skills', but, without any maturing grasp of cause and effect and the sequence of events, such skills were intrinsically disembodied and therefore of diminished value. When a St Petersburg Headmistress and her Head of English lunched with me at Stewart's Melville, I bemoaned the fact that Scottish girls and boys were debarred from learning about the Sixteenth Century, presumably because it was potentially so divisive, and that in consequence they knew nothing about John Knox or Mary Queen of Scots. The Headmistress replied, 'Our children, when they study the Reformation, know all about John Knox.'

I suppose that my more 'progressive' colleagues saw me as an old codger. I pressed for the re-establishment of mental arithmetic in Junior School teaching. I urged the necessity for a grammatical basis to the teaching of French. The funny thing was that the wheel of educational opinion was turning. Nick Fraser was totally at one with me (and Margery) in the need for a balanced approach in Modern Languages. Lorna Greer, Bryan Lewis' inspired and greatly mourned appointment as Junior School Director of Studies, ensured that the teaching and learning of the 1150 pupils would be held together by an intelligible and coherent spine of assessment, recording and reporting. I worked to ensure that the Senior Schools eschewed the 'fresh start' mentality towards pupils entering their First Form and looked instead to foster their progression on the basis of their prior attainment. In all of this I was, in part, parroting the language that I had learned at SCCC, in part, marrying it to my own opinions and prejudices. Little by little, or so it seemed to me, we were doing things our way and not waiting for the Scottish Office to tell us what to do.

Meanwhile my Deputy Heads were embellishing their respective schools. Norma Rolls, having led a team of staff and girls in designing the interior of the new Sixth Form Centre in the Pavilion, went on to orchestrate the physical revamping of the Art and Science departments. David Dunn had to be more patient. For years the Stewart's Melville PE department had pressed for a new gymnasium to supplement the Sports Hall. For years we delayed. David instead created artificial grass pitches on the lawns in front of the school, an initiative as effective as it was controversial.

It would be wrong to pretend that the job had suddenly become placid, predictable and trouble-free. There were racking staffing difficulties, savage in their pain, for which there were no easy answers. The sudden death of a brilliant Head Girl, Sarah Napuk, while she was in her final year at Oxford brought profound grief to all who knew her. So too did the car accident that took the life of Janie Beeston, the beloved mother of Amy, Matthew and Jessica. Before school the next morning, I found Jessica waiting to see me, one of the rare occasions that found me completely lost for words. Her gentle courage is for me an indelible memory.

Amid such griefs and vicissitudes I no longer speculated, as I had frequently done during my early years, how long the crazy arrangement could last nor did I now ask myself whether I could do the job. Even so, with the excitements of the tercentenary over and political storm clouds overhead, I wondered how congenial my final years would be. Now that I was no longer active in SCIS or SCCC or the EACs, and with my time as Chairman of HMC Professional Development nearing its end, life might perhaps become a little boring.

By 1995, I was left simply with membership of the Girls' School Association (GSA) and HMC. It was hardly surprising that the members of GSA, scarred by years of predatory aggression from neighbouring boys' schools, treated one of the few men in their midst as if he were a Trojan Horse. Most of the headmistresses were unmarried, although several were divorced, and the tone of their annual Conference tended to be at once defensive and indignant. If I developed few friendships I certainly respected the guts, tenacity, humanity and wisdom of most of them. As for HMC, I was reluctant to depart from the organizational hub. After one of my last Professional Development meetings, Chris Evans, the Headmaster of Dauntseys, asked me whether I had thought of standing for Chairman. I consulted friends. They seemed far from sure, wondering how well I was 'known' in England, but I reflected that there was little to lose and that there were, at least, four groups of younger Heads whom I had helped to 'train'. In October 1995 I stood in a triangular contest and came very close. James Lawrenson urged me to stand again next year, and this time I was elected – by the margin of one. I would be the HMC Chairman in 1998, only the second to come from Scotland.

One of the initiation rites for a new Chairman is to receive media training. As it happened, I received training enough during the months before I took office. I had never been far from the headlines of the local press and saw it, indeed, as part of my job to fight the Independent Schools' corner in Scotland and keep my schools in the public gaze. I intervened strongly on behalf of the Headmaster of Fettes, when 'The Scotsman' chose to slander him and his school on its Founder's Day on account of the grudge of a parent whose child he had expelled for alleged drugs offences.

It was 'Higher Still', the Scottish Office's shoddy substitute for Howie, that embroiled me in continuous correspondence and controversy through 1996 and 1997. In January 1996 I attacked 'Higher Still' in an article written for the *Times Educational Supplement*, lamenting its failure to address every academic weakness encountered by the more 'academic' schools in the Scottish system – three exams in three years, the two-term dash to Highers, the aimless Sixth Year and the increasing pressure on Modern Languages. I argued that it was absurd to botch the 16 to 18 curriculum, before the 5 to 14 programme had worked through and without making any changes to the 14 to 16 Standard Grade curriculum. I expressed opposition to the proposed modular structure of 'Higher Still', observed that internal assessment was a licence to plagiarism and criticized the intention to certificate 'core skills'.

I reaffirmed my hostility to 'Higher Still' in my Prize Day address in June 1996 and sent a press statement to the media. For this I was rewarded with the following message from the East Staffroom of Shawlands Academy in Glasgow.

Today our members read your considered analysis of the proposals for the new Higher Still examinations. A hearty Hurrah! to you, Sir, and may God bless you.

There followed a wearisome exchange of correspondence with the Minister, Raymond Robertson, and a much more aggravating running feud with my 'colleagues' in SCIS. The 'Establishment' camp in Scottish HMC disliked my sniping, as did the dogmatically consensual members of Scottish GSA. Frank Gerstenberg of George Watson's, although instinctively emollient, agreed from time to time to join with me in public statements of our position. Behind the appearances of consultation and representation, it became clear that SCIS was not prepared to mount any real pressure on the Tory administration in Scotland, fearing perhaps for the future of Assisted Places after the next Election. It was only too easy for Raymond Robertson and his civil servants, with unfailing courtesy, to shrug off my arguments as 'unrepresentative'.

I fell silent and was not intending to resume my campaign when, out of the blue, I was invited to a special SCCC forum in Dundee – 'The Sixth Year: An Analysis of the problem and of the probable effect of Higher Still'. Under the chairmanship of the excellent Cameron Harrison, nine 'participants' from all over Scotland met with four other officers of SCCC for a thorough discussion. I was the only representative of an Independent School.

It was devastating stuff. A coloured graph exposed the full horror of the Scottish Sixth Year – the relative poverty of Scottish Sixth Year attainment in comparison with England and, in particular, the extent to which the many students who failed to cope with their Highers generally went on to repeat their failures in their final year. I wrote to ask permission to circulate the graph among Scottish HMC and GSA and was assured that there was no problem.

Then Andrew Neil wrote a typically astringent article in *The Scotsman*, denouncing the relative under-performance of Scottish pupils. That was my cue. I wrote a letter about the Sixth Year and telephoned Matt Wells, the Education Correspondent, to alert him to the letter and to the basis of my arguments. He contacted SCCC, who were less than happy about this exposure, but he decided that he had to name SCCC as my source, as his paper intended to run my letter as its main 'story' for the day. Next day, its front page carried my photograph alongside an article with the headline, 'ENGLISH SIXTH FORMERS OUTPERFORM SCOTS', with my letter opposite a leading article entitled, 'LEARNING FROM SCOTTISH FAILURE'. Before the end of the day, I had appeared on television, recorded a radio interview and written an article for the *Scottish Daily Mail*.

It took weeks for the balloon to come to earth. In retrospect, I should have backed away earlier, my points made. As it was I laid myself open to two charges. Elizabeth Maginnis, Lothian Region's Convenor for Education, accused me of an 'elitist agenda' intent on denigrating the maintained sector. I dismissed her 'smears and innuendo' and told her to 'go away for six months and do some reading on the subject'. She replied, revealingly, by commenting that in the maintained sector an individual school would not be allowed to express such views and she wondered whether the Merchant Company might have 'something to say'. Others hinted that I was merely hungry for publicity. The Rector of Edinburgh Academy bluntly stated that I seemed less interested in 3Rs than in PR. Alerted to this by Matt Wells I telephoned back and told him to write that I pleaded 'guilty on all counts'.

A GSA member of one of the sub-committees beavering away to make 'Higher Still' work wrote me a long and exasperated letter about the divisiveness of my utterances. She had a valid point, in that I was indeed being purely obstructive. I wanted to *stop* a measure that would, if implemented, consign Scottish education to decades of further frustration. I replied that she seemed to be arguing that, when the Emperor had no clothes, it was wrong to point this out, but my real argument went deeper.

> I stand by my general contention, that it is unhealthy that individuals should find themselves representing divergent interests…I have the greatest personal respect for Ron Tuck, for Bart McGettrick, for yourself and for most of those I know in the Scottish 'educational establishment'. Nevertheless, I admit to a profound distaste for its current working. I see it as fundamentally unhealthy when systems

of government or of education are seen to breed jobs for those previously entrusted with their care. I also believe that the processes of accountability are blurred when important individuals experience significant conflicts of interest.

Bart McGettrick, a man of intellectual stature, spiritual integrity and a delightful sense of humour, was Chairman both of the Committee of Scottish Higher Education Principals, and therefore committed to the retention of the four year degree course in Scottish Universities, and of SCIS, whose interests lay in the shortening of the normal Scottish degree course. Disarmingly, he observed to me, 'Patrick, turkeys don't vote for Christmas'. Poor Ron Tuck, a thoroughly likable HMI who had been in charge of the 'Higher Still' Development Unit, had recently been appointed Chief Executive of the new Scottish Qualifications Authority (SQA), the single examination board responsible for 'Higher Still'.

Associated with my mounting distaste for the Scottish educational 'establishment' ran my abiding distrust of SCIS. On a matter like the Scottish Upper Secondary Curriculum the views and voices of the members of Scottish HMC and Scottish GSA should have been crucially significant. Instead they were swallowed up and neutralized in SCIS. It was remarkable that, in a SCIS deputation meeting the Scottish Office in June 1996, there were only two HMC Heads and no GSA Heads in a deputation of ten. Truly SCIS was behaving like a local authority! I shared with Frank Gerstenberg my belief that SCIS was exhibiting some of the 'least attractive features of the old Merchant Company'. Members did not receive Minutes of Council meetings and SCIS was thereby unaccountable. No-one knew what it was fighting for, no-one knew when it had failed.

In October 1997, the Labour Party swept to power. In Scotland, not a single Tory MP held his seat. Although neither of us had voted Labour, Margery and I found ourselves moved by the sight of Tony Blair walking hand-in-hand with Cherie into Number Ten. 'I do hope,' I added, 'that it will not be a bonanza for political correctness.'

Such fears were exacerbated by the new Prime Minister's histrionic reaction to the death of Princess Diana. Margery and I rebelled against all the hype and hypocrisy. I lamented to Matthew, Emma and Lucy that no-one appeared to have the courage to say 'how ridiculous the whole thing is'. I was unconsciously echoing the distrust of fierce Thomas Carlyle, a century and a half ago. 'Is not Sentimentalism twin-sister to Cant, if not one and the same with it?' New Labour has answered that question.

Yet my own hypocrisy at this time was pretty rich. On the Sunday evening before the funeral, I was telephoned by the BBC, asking if I could rustle up some boarders for interview outside Holyrood Palace on Monday's Breakfast Programme. None of the English schools was back from the summer holidays, nor were the Scottish boarding schools. Could we help? I had no problem in enlisting three personable boys and two charming girls, to whom I added Sophie and a friend of hers who happened to telephone.

We duly set off at 8.15. As I drove past a florist's in Stockbridge, one of the girls asked if we could stop and buy some flowers. Fifteen minutes later the party emerged with a truly impressive display. John Pienaar, up to cover Scottish Devolution, seemed more nervous and out of place than my young people. I heard two days later that their performance had persuaded one in-coming English family to switch their girls from St George's to Mary Erskine.

While I was watching this charade, I was grabbed by a young cable journalist, who had previously interviewed me about drugs. A doll-like figure, impeccably dressed, she would puff herself up delightfully when introducing her interviews. The camera began to run and she went through her routine. Then she asked me why the girls and boys had come to Holyrood. 'Because the BBC asked them,' I replied. 'You can't say that,' she gasped, frantically beckoning her cameraman to stop. 'You'd better ask me a question I can truthfully answer,' I said. 'Why not ask why they have brought flowers?' She did.

It was not long before we returned to the politics of Devolution and the impending Referendum. Invited to participate in a public debate, I asked Alistair Darling why Devolution would mean better educational government on such issues as 'Higher Still', given that Scotland had been continuously independent of Westminster in all educational matters. He congratulated me on asking the key question. In all his time at Westminster, he could scarcely remember any discussion of Scottish education. In a Scottish Assembly, all would be different.

After further months of dithering, the Scottish Executive proceeded with 'Higher Still'. Two years later, just as I was leaving Scotland, a number of chickens came home to roost. For weeks, Donald McDiarmid and Doreen Waugh had, like Directors of Studies throughout Scotland, warned of impend-ing fiasco. In the event, the great examination debacle, wherein many students got the wrong results and many had to wait weeks and even months for the right ones, exceeded the expectations of the most avid Jeremiah. With Scottish education an international laughing stock, Ron Tuck resigned, taking with him his entire board. The HMI, those largely silent guardians whose overlordship had previously seemed removed from scrutiny, questioning or debate, were confined henceforth to the inspection of schools. In my last column for a Scottish newspaper I quoted Alistair Darling's vision of Post-Devolution accountability and urged that the Minister, Dr Sam Galbraith, should go. He was singularly reluctant to do so, for the New Labour rule seems to be that no minister is ever fully accountable and, in truth, he was probably no more inept than his predecessors, but in the end he paid the price for his failings and theirs.

The title, 'Higher Still', proved only too prophetic. We won marginal and ultimately worthless concessions from the Scottish Universities, after the Garrick Committee recommended that they should make allowance for students with Advanced Highers and Advanced Levels, but the ills diagnosed by Howie endure, a decade after his Report. The 'Higher' continues to be Scotland's 'Gold Standard' and good Scottish schools will go on making the best of this Scottish failure of government.

It is no longer a specifically Scottish failure. The English, ignoring completely the lessons that should have been learned through a telescope on Hadrian's Wall, have now adopted a formula involving three examinations in three years, the damage compounded by their modular structure.

Back in 1997, I was once involved in a radio discussion with Professor Howie and others. John Howie hazarded the guess that his Commission's proposals might well be resurrected some time in the future. They should be. Only a Baccalaureate can prevent the *imbalance and absence of coherence* that characterize the present state of affairs, north and south of the border.

The trouble is that today's politicians place political expediency above strategic vision and are capable only of thinking as far as the next election. Radical reform takes longer than that. It would have taken eight years to implement the Howie proposals. They were too fundamental and too costly for the Tory Government. It was yet another irony that 'Higher Still', cobbled together so rapidly as the opportunistic alternative to Howie, should take equally long to gestate, while leaving all the problems unsolved.

As in Scotland, so has it been in England. 'Curriculum 2000', the botched legacy of Blunkett and Blackstone, was amended with knee-jerk rapidity by Estelle Morris – who then talked about 'some sort of Baccalaureate'. There is every risk that the next generation will be saddled with 'some sort' of half-baked fudge. Is there nobody in Government with the wisdom and humility and capability to plant seeds for long-term change?

CHAPTER 19

Chairman – and Out

There is, of course, a more pernicious and insidious threat than drugs to the happiness and well-being of our boys and girls. I refer to the damage done to children and adolescents by marital break-up or, indeed, by the initial lack of that basic entitlement, two loving parents. Top of the agenda for any government concerned to affirm the values of citizenship would be the rehabilitation of the family in British life.

(Extract from my Chairman's speech to HMC, October 1998)

It might come as a surprise to the reader that the technical status of the Chairman of HMC is that of trade union leader. He is not a Chief Executive nor does he shape policy, which tends to emanate from the more important Sub-Committees. The day to day business is sustained by the Secretary and Membership Secretary and their offices. In my time, Vivian Anthony and David Prince were superb in their respective roles.

The Chairman's main roles are to chair HMC's Committee for six meetings during his term of office, to respond to issues and act as spokesman as and when this is necessary, to take up the cudgels on behalf of members who appear to be the victims of undue pressure or unfair treatment from their Governors, to represent HMC in dealings with other educational associations and to travel the country as an embodiment of HMC's unity. He is also charged with the running of the Annual General Meeting, which occasionally will look inwardly into the nature and running of the organization.

My year would, to a degree, be engaged in such self-appraisal. Michael Mavor, my predecessor, had worked to produce a Development Plan. My job was to see that it came to fruition. In particular, I set myself the task of increasing the number of HMC's Divisions, to improve links between the centre and the respective regions. Over decades the numbers of members of HMC had grown, but the six English divisions had remained unchanged. In the largest divisions, London and Eastern, relatively few headmasters could expect to represent their colleagues on HMC's central Committee. The sheer geographical size of some divisions militated against participation. The South West stretched from Truro to Marlborough and Llandovery, the Eastern from Sussex to East Anglia. The all-important divisional meeting, doubtless an agreeable outing in more leisured times, was weakened by increased absenteeism. There was occasional grumbling, but never the concerted will to carry through reform.

246

With Vivian Anthony and David Prince I set out to parcel the larger divisions into smaller and closer units. Edinburgh had taught me the importance of sustaining patient momentum. After one Committee meeting, when I had eased progress through a series of carefully drafted resolutions, Bill Sillery, Northern Ireland's representative and an old friend and fellow veteran of 1981, remarked with a smile, 'Patrick, you were like a cat. And I tell you, you did not learn how to do that in England!' It was a huge relief and satisfaction when the Annual Meeting adopted our proposals.

Another issue concerned the relationship of HMC with ISC, the 'umbrella body' for Independent schools. While much of my Scottish experience was of no direct relevance to English affairs, I carried from my dealings with SCIS a belief in the importance of 'subsidiarity' – the principle that decisions should be made at the appropriate and preferably lowest possible level. I warned my colleagues in Committee of the dangers of being subsumed in an ultimately unaccountable Independent Schools Council. Four years later, when I congratulated the then Chairman of HMC, Edward Gould, on his splendid leadership in exposing the Advanced Level grading scandal and in forcing ministerial intervention, he simply murmured, 'Subsidiarity.' The interests of Independent schools will always be best stated, defended and promoted by those closest to the action.

I loved my year as Chairman – every minute of it. I visited schools all over the country, stayed with Heads and gained insights into the wonderful work that they were doing. I presented prizes at schools and for friends who meant much to me. I fought battles for people and for schools without any of the angst associated with my own job and my own past mistakes. I received wonderful support – from HMC in Leicester and from my long-suffering colleagues in Edinburgh. I learned how to use laptop and mobile as I zoomed around the country. I ate too many good meals and consumed too much alcohol. Representing the Independent Schools at a Tri-Service conference at Cranwell, I recalled my father and his world-changing moment in 1941.

And Sophie, the last of our children to be at home, tried to instil some self discipline in her father. Shortly before Easter, as I was about to set off for the Secondary Heads Association Conference, she said grimly, 'I suppose you'll be drinking.' (It was Lent.) 'Sophie,' I replied with as much dignity as I could muster, 'It is impossible to survive a conference without some alcohol at dinner.' On the second day, we were informed that there would be a wine tasting before lunch. I thought of Sophie and decided against it. In the afternoon we assembled to hear Professor Michael Barber expound on the subject of Global Citizenship. The Government's Educational Advisor drew heavily on the secularist arguments of the Australian pundit, Peter Singer, that it was time to construct a post Christian ethic based on secular premises. I smelled the further marginalization of Religious Education and of History. I did not like what I was hearing.

There are more scintillating speakers than Michael Barber. When he sat down the Chairman called for questions. I looked around. Everyone was fast asleep. I raised my hand. 'All this talk of citizenship,' I blustered, 'It reminds me of Hitler and Napoleon.' There was perhaps another question, then, as others moved off to take their tea, I dashed upstairs to watch Ireland v Wales. I lingered too long, to see the outcome to an Irish penalty kick, entered the hall just after Charles Handy had begun speaking and was accosted by the SHA Secretary, John Sutton. 'Oh, there you are, Patrick. The press are all looking for you.' Thoughts and fears flashed through my head. What had happened at Stewart's Melville? No, don't be silly, it's probably some bad publicity about another HMC school. It never occurred to me that the press would want my views on Citizenship. But they did. Michael Barber had been told not to accept questions, the journalists did not like this and they wanted to hear my 'knocking' views.

Next day I was on the front page of the *Sunday Times*. On the Monday Roy Hattersley dismissed my 'fatuous' opinions in *The Guardian*. I took the train up to Leicester. My mobile rang. It was Dorothy. The BBC wanted to speak to me. It turned out that they had decided to run the issue of Citizenship in that week's *Moral Maze*. I was deeply gratified and told Matthew. 'Oh my God,' he said, 'David Starkey! He'll murder you.' That dampened my enthusiasm and I went nervously into Broadcasting House. I was told that Professor Bernard Crick would, at his own insistence, go first and last – Crick had been resurrected by his former Birkbeck pupil, David Blunkett, and Citizenship was his quaintly paternalistic hobbyhorse. I sat next door, listening to his interview and to his mauling by David Starkey. I began to cheer up. I remember little of what I was asked and what wisdom I expressed. At the end David Starkey opined, 'I think Tobin is right. The duty of all good schools is to teach a profound distrust of government.'

Thus encouraged I put flesh on the bones of my argument and my essay was attached by HMC's Academic Policy Committee as a 'philosophical' appendix to their pragmatic objections. It was a waste of effort. Citizenship duly lumbered into the National Curriculum, a burdensome and amorphous intrusion into the proper business of schools. I am angered still by the underlying assumption – that ignorance of and disenchantment with the political process can be attributed to specifically curricular shortcomings and can be cured through the good offices of teachers. One can only hope that the consequences will not be as abysmal – and arguably malign – as the equivalent programmes for sex education.

I reacted with similar vehemence to the Government's imposition of tuition fees on university students. I fired off a fax to *The Times*, to the effect that it had been customary for each generation to pass advantage to the next. It was outrageous that we, the generation who had 'had it so good', should now be imposing debt on the next generation, doomed as they were to inherit our many other sins of omission. After telephoned amendments in a train clattering into Waterloo, *The Times* gave my letter pride of place. I took up the charge when Alistair Darling became the latest luminary to respond to Richard Cairns' invitation to Stewart's Melville College. Surely, I argued, a graduate tax imposed on all graduates whose income exceeded a designated threshold would be fairer than a tax on students, most of whom would already be facing unprecedented levels at debt. And in my Conference speech in October, I remarked that the 'capricious imposition of university tuition fees (or tuition debt) on young people foolish enough to be born after 1980' was a poor lesson in citizenship. Since then, the debate has moved on. For the sake of the politically correct and educationally absurd proposition that 50% of any generation is entitled to 'university education', whatever that means and regardless of whether or not the three further years of study will be beneficial to the individual or society, the next generation will go through their twenties encumbered by financial burdens that would previously have been unimaginable. They will then find themselves saddled with all the various PFI burdens devised by government to spare its electors the actual costs of social renewal. Better to mortgage the futures of the young rather than risk loss of office through taxation of today's rich!

In his conference speech, as in the arrangements that he makes for the whole of HMC's Annual Meeting, the Chairman has his one opportunity to be his own man and to make his specifically personal offering. Struck by Cardinal Hume's maxim that schools should educate their children into goodness, and reflecting that educational conferences had become increasingly utilitarian, I decided that 'Educating into Goodness' should be the theme for HMC's 1998 Annual Meeting.

The family became testy during the preceding months as I drafted and redrafted my speech, then the traditional opening event of the conference, but fortune smiled on my choice of speakers – all accepted my invitation. Only two clouds loomed. The first was that the Minister for Schools, Steven Byers, had agreed to address the conference – the first Labour Minister to do so in memory – but had been switched to grander office. It was uncertain as to whether his successor, Estelle Morris, would take up the invitation. The second was more literally metereological. The 1998 Annual Meeting was to take place in Jersey. During the equivalent October week in 1997 not a single aircraft had landed.

In the event every plane landed and every speaker materialized – although I sweated when the first of these, Sir Stewart Sutherland, had not arrived long after the final arrival was scheduled. (The Principal of Edinburgh University explained that a baggage truck had run into his stationary aircraft at Heathrow!) Next morning he brought a philosopher's wisdom to 'The Questions We Should Be Asking'. My old friend, Chris Patten, was scholar, idealist and statesman in his vision of 'Education, Values and Tomorrow's World'. Trevor

Roger Askew and Helen Mitchell with their choir in Jersey – Mary Erskine girls resplendent in their kilts, Sophie in lighter blazer, front row.

Grice, a New Zealand expert on the effects of cannabis, supplied a multi-media presentation based on his 'The Great Brain Robbery'. Another friend from the past, John Inverarity, also flew in from the Antipodes – to lead with Roger Uttley a discussion on ethical questions in Sport. Jonathan Smith, already a satirist of headmasters in his series of radio plays, *The Head Man*, and shortly to achieve greater fame through *The Learning Game*, was my After-Dinner speaker.

In terms of educational significance, Estelle Morris was arguably the most important of my speakers. Had the Labour government actually implemented the policies threatened before its election, these would have been dark times for Independent schools. And if it was an honour that she should be the first Labour minister to address HMC, her typically unaffected interest and engagement made as great an impact. She left to a standing ovation, utterly sincere and spontaneous, but tinged also with relief that she had expressed no hint of menace or hidden agenda.

At our annual Service, Bishop Cormac Murphy O'Connor, to whom I already owed so much, preached the sermon – 'Dear Headmasters...' he began, with inimitable warmth, and from then on he had his congregation in his hand. As is customary, the Chairman's choir sang the anthem, except that on this occasion there were girls from Mary Erskine as well as boys from Stewart's Melville and the Chairman's daughter Sophie was one of its members. They sang beautifully and to general acclaim. I treasure the photograph of the choir from Scotland, flanked proudly by Roger Askew and Helen Mitchell, all flights paid by a remarkably generous Merchant Company benefactor.

It was frustrating that I could attend so few of the Discussion Groups that I had organized. While most of their leaders were headmasters, I was determined that a place should be found for consideration of the place of *girls* in HMC schools. Alison Wilcox and Cynthia Hall effectively banished any vestiges of male chauvinism! I had other very talented ladies to keep me from stumbling. It was the last conference to be organized by Diana Griffiths and would have been special on those grounds alone. I broke with precedent by asking Dorothy Silver to come to Jersey. It seemed ludicrous that a PA should miss an event into which *she* had had to devote so much time. (Needless to say she was a great help to Diana.) Above all, Margery was there, doing her best, as always, to disguise the truth that behind every apparently successful man there is an astonished wife.

My own speech seemed to go down well. It was probably too long. I had too much to say – and much of this was said far better by the speakers whom I had invited – and it was as heavily derivative as always. Even so, I like some of my sentences.

> Our business, quite literally, is to sharpen the intellect, to feed the imagination, to awaken the senses, to instil a sense of poetry, to open paths for the spirit and to practise love.

> As St Paul put it, we are all nomads and strangers in our country. True education is concerned more with *dispositions* and *orientations* than with mere *attainment*. Therein lies a paradox. To use the present only as a means of preparing for the future is self-defeating…The *personal* experience is all, it is so central to good education that it has justly been said that the excellence of a school is determined primarily by the quality of its relationships.

I can claim to have been one of the first to have criticized the Millennium Dome at Greenwich.

> I fear a 21st century Titanic, repeating the tired old vanity that progress eliminated God, or a Tower of Babel expressing the delusion that in a plural society all truths are relative.

I sounded the alarm concerning the recruitment of good teachers, without which the best schools could achieve nothing –

> It is a question of status. It is a question of self-respect. Many who might otherwise have made good teachers are put off by what I call the 'humiliation factor', the dread of having to explain to upwardly mobile friends why they are doing something as unglamorous, as 'unsexy' as teaching –

and about the relative decline in the attainment of boys, left vulnerable by laissez-faire liberalism and feminine emancipation.

I deplored the fact that most boys and girls ceased any study of History at 14 and grew up, therefore, without any sense of cultural inheritance. Instead, the Government was giving us Citizenship.

> Rightly or wrongly I sensed the thread that has led from the Enlightenment through the French revolution to all the secular monstrosities of our century. But I also distrust talk about education into an abstraction called 'Citizenship' when it derives so obviously from the political establishment of the day.

And I lamented the educational politics of fudge that threatened, even then, to leave both England and Scotland without an Upper Secondary curriculum that would promote principles of breadth, balance and rigour.

I hung much of my speech on quotations from Robert Musil's vast and wonderful, *The Man Without Qualities*. Thus –

> Historic periods of permissiveness have never failed, so far, in keeping all who live in them miserable.' Our legislators, lacking Robert Musil's historical perspective, press ahead enthusiastically with the privatisation of personal morality.

It was 'no-one's fault' that the British were notorious for their loutish drunkenness. Drugs, legal and illegal, were now woven into our adult social fabric. Health education in schools tended too often to separate sex from values. All of this might have passed unnoticed, but the next comment did not.

> There is, of course, a more pernicious and insidious threat than drugs to the happiness and well-being of our boys and girls. I refer to the damage done to children and adolescents by marital break-up or, indeed, by the initial lack of that basic entitlement, two loving parents. Top of the agenda for any government concerned to affirm the values of citizenship would be the rehabilitation of the family in British life.

Next day, I was deluged with calls from radio stations that would not normally have been interested in the affairs of HMC. The irony was that this too was not an original Tobin insight. Throughout my year as Chairman, HMC had been conducting its own survey into Drugs and Alcohol, led by the Headmaster of the Leys School, John Barrett. While most of the statistical evidence was based on questionnaires sent to 15 and 17 year olds in 25 schools, a part reflected the views of Heads. We were asked to list in order of perceived seriousness a number of threats to adolescents, including alcohol and drugs. The Heads placed marital break up top of their collective list, and by a considerable margin.

The Chairman's speech behind me, I faced the challenge of chairing HMC's annual AGM. This was usually a perfunctory affair. 1998 was different. My proposals for dividing the larger divisions of HMC into new, smaller units, were not universally popular. So I decided that this issue would be discussed separately from the rest of the Development Plan, ensured that members could not complain of inadequate paperwork and extended the normal length of the AGM.

I asked the 240 members to allow me to provide a brief summary of the steps by which we had reached our proposals and of their underlying rationale. In doing this, I was careful to bring in all the objections which Heads had voiced, in such a way as to make it clear that they had been seriously considered. I then invited open discussion. Most seemed to think that there was not much else to say. One member, saying that he was not really persuaded, challenged me to state the real reason for change. I reminded him that 15 out of 16 elected representatives had voted for radical change, that I could not speak for what was in their individual minds but that I could indeed give my own reasons. At the beginning of my year as Chairman, I had been conscious of a groundswell of feeling that HMC's initial report had been too bland. It was now up to members – Yes or No. HMC had been here before, twenty years earlier, when change had appeared probable, only for caution and conservatism to prevail at the end. If we voted, 'No', the issue would doubtless be addressed by a later HMC – in about twenty years' time. I was told afterwards that this was a decisive moment. The vote was taken – a forest in favour, seven against, with one member putting her hand down sharply on seeing how few were on the conservative side.

On my return to Edinburgh my postbag was massively complimentary. In two quarters alone was there a distinct chill. The President of GSA, a month later, went out of her way to challenge the linkage between stable, married families and the welfare of children. More immediately, I was warned of a concern that we might lose our Founders' Day speaker, Alistair Darling, our local MP, by then a cabinet minister. He had requested sight of my Jersey speech. In the event, he came, but was notably cool and left before lunch. In the very week when relations with Estelle Morris had seemed so cordial, the Scottish Labour Establishment was running true to form.

HMC's Drugs and Alcohol Report emerged early in 1999, just after I had ceased to be Chairman, but my successor, James Sabben-Clare, courteously invited me to 'front' for HMC. I thereby enjoyed my only appearance on the *Today* programme. Retribution was swift. No sooner had I explained that we were advising our members not to resort instantly to expulsion for *all* drugs offences than I was confronted in Edinburgh by the sort of offence that left no room for such manoeuvre. A number of boys had been vigorously involved in supplying drugs to others and would have to go. Others, who had merely purchased drugs, were suspended. All had drifted around Edinburgh for months and years – the focal point being Bristo Square, where they had watched young adults openly smoking dope and where a seller of *The Big Issue* was the main provider. Another provider was a young man who had been expelled from another Independent school for selling at the school gate. The syndrome was always the same. Because the drug was supplied in sizes too big for the individual purchaser, there was immediate pressure on the buyer to find other custom so that he could fund his own purchases. The vendors were often themselves under threat of physical violence from their own suppliers if they did not find fresh customers. No-one spilled the beans and the net gradually widened. Of our eleven, all but one came from broken home backgrounds. I refrained from writing to the President of GSA.

There was no avoiding the human grief in the situation. One of the mothers, when I telephoned her to say that her son would have to leave, wailed that it was 'very harsh' and broke down in tears. She then came back to me and said, 'It was all my fault.' I told her how sorry I was. She responded, 'You shouldn't be having to deal with such things. You should be able to get on with all the good you are doing for the schools.' I was very moved. I went to sleep thinking about it – and woke up thinking about it.

The press had a field day, nor were the Edinburgh Police amused when I indicated that I thought that the police generally had let the drugs situation get out of hand. Elizabeth Maginnis accused me of wishing to criminalize teenagers. I fought my way out of the corner through a lengthy letter to parents, entitled *Partnership with Parents*, outweighing the negative through my vision of the essentially positive interaction of home and school in the upbringing of young children. A number of parents and colleagues expressed appreciation – although one of my secularist colleagues at Stewart's Melville expressed his dismay that I had included religious practice as one of the ways in which parents enriched their children's lives. I referred to the number of Muslims in the School – and saw one of my Catholic colleagues visibly heaving a sigh of content with this unquestionably 'correct' piety.

Before I bowed out, I had some final jousts with the forces of political correctness. One concerned the proposal that the age of consent for homosexual intercourse should be reduced from 18 to 16. As far as I could see, this law served only to protect the adolescents from predatory adults. As a headmaster, I would not have dreamed of invoking it in the case of two consenting youths – on the one occasion when the situation actually confronted me, I treated it as a pastoral and not as a disciplinary matter. So I contacted Ian Beer, the Chairman of the Independent Schools Council, the umbrella body for Independent schools, and asked whether ISC intended to comment on a measure which directly affected schools. He responded, with the wisdom born of three headships, by inviting me to draft a paper.

I did so. As Chairman and then as Vice Chairman of HMC I was a member of the Independent Schools Council. At our next meeting the Prep School representatives of IAPS were warmly supportive – but the Girls' Schools Association was adamantly opposed. Following a President who openly affirmed to her pupils her particular orientation, the leading headmistresses of GSA confirmed that, in terms of priorities, feminism came before the interests of their pupils – and they had done this without any attempt to consult their members. It was a shameful performance. Ian told me that Janet (Baroness) Young, who led the Governing Bodies of Girls' Schools Association, was 'incandescent' in her fury but that there was nothing he could do, beyond obtaining GSA's grudging agreement to a statement that 'many' Independent schools were greatly concerned. He then lodged our objection with the House of Commons Library.

A year or so later, there was a parallel issue concerning the proposal that Section 28 – Section 2A in Scotland – should be repealed. This was the notorious clause inserted by Mrs Thatcher into her Local Government Act, debarring maintained school teachers from promoting homosexuality or from teaching the equivalence of homosexual to married relationships. When the Catholic Church expressed concern about its repeal, Bishop Richard Holloway of Edinburgh, the very liberal and vaguely Christian Primus of the Scottish Episcopalian Church, charged it with a 'fundamentalist' attitude to human rights. I wrote to *The Scotsman*, from my home address, observing that the Catholic Church seemed to be damned if it did and damned if it didn't. Criticized for their failure to denounce Nazi crimes against the Jews, the German Catholic bishops had at least provided perhaps the only case of successful resistance to Hitler in their denunciation of his euthanasia policies. Now the same church was being told that it had no right to teach absolutes as to what was right and wrong.

A week later I sent another letter, this time from the schools. An editorial had opined that heads should simply trust their teachers. This was by no means as easy or as straightforward as he implied. I quoted an eminently liberal and civilized friend in HMC who had been branded as homophobic, because he had refused to allow *Stonewall* literature to be peddled in his school. Another friend, equally enlightened, discovered that his young drama teacher had written a series of millennial sketches, all of which were homosexual in their drift. When he intervened, he too was branded as homophobic. One of the great ironies of the age of political correctness was that discrimination had become a dirty word. Time was when the good parent and good school taught their children how to discriminate. I could not see why it was right now to teach children the importance of discriminating in their eating habits and not in their sexual. If the government was intent on removing Section 2A, then it must 'fill the vacuum', through its carefully stated and enforceable professional ethic. Otherwise, heads would be vulnerable indeed if and when they followed their professional judgement in deciding what was and was not acceptable in their schools. As for ourselves, we tried hard to associate good sex with lifelong, loving relationships. We took care not to offend either the children of broken marriages or those who felt that their inclinations were homosexual, but would be content if our teaching translated into an ideal of lifelong, loving marriage.

In the event, Janet Young mobilized the House of Lords and Section 28 remained unrepealed in England until her death. In Scotland, however, the Assembly pressed ahead.

Ian Beer generously allowed me a final excursion into politics. He invited me to address a politico-educational gathering in Windsor on the place of Independent schools in national provision. I emphasized that we prided ourselves indeed on being 'Independent', and certainly not 'private', and that the reverse side of autonomy was accountability. The maintained sector would improve when it too became professionally independent. I saw more hope for this in England than in Scotland. In this I was wrong. English maintained schools have since been subjected to a regime of centralizing and ultimately stultifying accountability. Only now do we hear from Whitehall the first whispers that professional independence might, after all, be the only sure route to reform.

And that was that, in terms of my public profile. I think that the Scottish media regretted the passing of this turbulent pedagogue – and that others will have heaved a sigh of relief. I cannot pretend to myself that I have seen a successful outcome to *any* of the causes for which I fought! Neither, on the other hand, has the failure been absolute. All the issues remain relevant and topical as I write. Better and subtler men and women may yet turn tides and enter promised lands.

In all my campaigns, I had in mind another audience – the pupils, parents and colleagues in my schools. They knew what I stood for and that seemed to make the schools stronger – and more popular. For instance, they saw my attitude towards drugs for what it was – a detestation of mind-altering and damaging substances which brought profit only to their peddlers – and they supported by more than two to one our proposed policy of administering occasional drugs tests to boys and girls who were evidently at risk of involvement. If I was at odds with the 'liberal' media and the chattering classes, that did not worry the vast majority of my parents. They knew that I was concerned only for the health and welfare of their children. I think that most also enjoyed the feeling that their Scottish schools were in the national and British limelight.

It was at this point, when the progressive loss of Assisted Places revenue should have been causing us to shiver, that the sun broke through and all the building dilemmas that had taxed us for so many years were suddenly and miraculously resolved. Stewart's Melville had inherited from the old Melville College a parcel of land at Ferryfield. Its value rocketed during the 1990s and its sale brought us unexpected riches, with a single qualification – the money had to be spent on another project involving physical education. David Dunn had spent the first tranche on his artificial lawns.

By the late 1990s, the Mary Erskine Swimming Pool, built in 1966, was on its last legs. Meanwhile, the Scottish Cricket Union was looking for headquarters in Edinburgh and guaranteed access to a Sports Hall. Fred McLeod now had his finest hour as Bursar. He negotiated Lottery funding of a new Sports Hall at Ravelston, to be built on the site of the dilapidated swimming pool, on the understanding that on weekday evenings and at weekends it would be reserved for Scotland's cricketers. James Laurenson pronounced that he would 'eat his hat' if the deal came off. I was less forthright, but equally sceptical. Fred proved right and the future fell into place. The Ferryfield moneys gave Stewart's Melville not a Swimming Pool, not a Gymnasium and this was linked to a state-of-the-art Sixth Form Centre. David Dunn at last had a project worthy of his talents. He has his monument on the Queensferry Road.

The Mary Erskine School, in addition to acquiring a second (Astroturf) artificial hockey pitch, became the headquarters of the Scottish Cricket Union and had unlimited access during working hours to the SCU's new Sports Hall. To the construction of this Sports Hall the Lottery Fund contributed over £1 million, an unprecedented award to a Scottish Independent school. Elizabeth Maginnis spluttered her fury.

Behind all this construction lay a windfall as prodigious as it was wholly unexpected. A Melville College Former Pupil, James Wight Rutherford, had practised quietly as a solicitor and lived modestly in Leith. He was known to be a canny man. On the eve of the war, he had bought up several pairs of brown, leather brogues in the expectation that he would never again be able to purchase shoes of such quality and at such a price. Nothing, however, suggested that he was rich. His hobby was to watch Melville College play at rugby and, indeed, he endowed the School the Goal-Kicking Cups that are presented on Stewart's Melville Prize Days. He left his estate to his widow and it was only when she died that it transpired that his estate would pass to the Melville Trust, to be used by them to promote the interests of Stewart's Melville College, and that the value of this inheritance was an estimated £4.25 million.

The Melville Trust, having consulted the School, decided that the bulk of the estate should be used to fund scholarships and bursaries to the School. It was a windfall whose timing was the more serendipitous in that the Labour Government was in the process of abolishing Assisted Places. I reflected on the irony whereby Prior Park, its future hanging in the balance, had sought in vain the generosity of millionaires, whereas Mary Erskine and Stewart's Melville, surfing on waves of good fortune, were now receiving millions from a Former Pupil of whose fortune they had been completely unaware. David Dunn at last had a project worthy of his talents. The fine new building that composes the Sixth Form Centre and Swimming Pool is his monument in Edinburgh.

Before he left in 1999 to take up his well-deserved Headship of Yarm School, David Dunn initiated another profoundly gratifying development, affecting both of the Senior Schools. Each year, we would hold a 'Brainstorming' Weekend, away from School, for Governors and the Management Teams. I asked David to lead a session in which we discussed the closer integration of the two Sixth Forms and his scheme can be recognized in the eventual outcome. While the two Schools remained separate, in that senior boys and girls would continue to hold office and represent teams in Stewart's Melville and Mary Erskine respectively, all Sixth Year teaching would be coeducational and all students would be members of coeducational tutor groups, meeting at one or other end of the Dykes. There would be a Director and Deputy Director of Sixth Form, leading teams of Tutors drawn from each school. We did not know it at the time, but we had invented a future flavour of the month, the 'Diamond' structure.

All of this had the enthusiastic support of the Chairman of Governors. James Laurenson now urged us to grab the moment and restructure the two schools' pastoral arrangements. Instead of the eight Houses of Stewart's Melville and six Clans of Mary Erskine, there would be the same six Houses at each school, with names totally different from those of the earlier groups. Among my last bequests to the Schools were the very Scottish names of the new joint Houses. I wonder how long they will endure!

There was a time, not long before, when any such changes would have involved months and even years of consultation, laced with a fair measure of resistance. Now I encountered only generosity – abandonment of old names, volunteers to serve as Sixth Form Tutors. Many colleagues were equally forthcoming in their membership of various ad hoc working parties, from which emanated Whole School Policies on a range of important issues. Perhaps the boldest of these was the adoption of an Erskine Stewart's Melville policy for Teachers' Remuneration, in that it involved the creation of a number of Salary Scales that were entirely on the Schools' devising and not linked to national scales.

I like to think this transformation in attitudes reflected a confidence that all was well, that it was a good thing that the Schools were once again in the vanguard of change and that the judgement of the Principal was generally to be trusted. I suspect, however, that the most potent cause of the magnanimity towards me was my decision to retire in June 2000. My contract would have allowed me to work until 2002. When I ceased to be Chairman of HMC, I felt that the Putney Pud had been so incredibly privileged and lucky in his career that it would be a shame to blight it through failure to leave when people were clapping. There was a less positive motive. Right to the end, there were acute interpersonal tensions that left me feeling bemused and aggrieved, asking myself why it was that some found it so difficult to get on with me – had power finally and totally corrupted me? One such collision finally pushed me over any hesitation and I found James Laurenson and Iain Gotts generously willing to help me go early.

If I remember my final terms as an orgy of policy writing, a last-minute attempt to give my successor the impression that he was taking over a well run organization, Roger Askew and Helen Mitchell conspired to ensure that they were not entirely prosaic. I had been delighted with their recommendation that the schools' collective celebration of the Millennium should take the form of a community performance of Britten's *Noye's Fludde* in the King's Theatre. Literally hundreds of Junior School pupils would be the animals, their masks lovingly created by Marjorie Douglas and her team at Stewart's Melville, Primary 3 would be the waves, many staff would represent the sun, moon and stars and the combined senior schools would attend the matinee performance and serve as the chorus. We would never have contemplated such a project had we not obtained the full-time services of an inspired choreographer, Jane Duffy. The sting was in the tail. Would I be God?! Thus is was that a middle-aged man, whose only previous stage performance had been as the Two of Hearts, was reduced to quivering terror by the need to deliver five thunderous interventions, at the exact time required by the score. All was well. The two performances were wonderful expressions of teamwork, talent and hope. It was, enthused the *Scotsman* review, 'a wonderful visual spectacle'. Roger Askew 'deserved a medal' for juggling three orchestras on the floor, trumpets and handbells on opposite balconies, soloists and choruses on the stage and, of course, his chorus of hundreds in their seats. At the next school assembly, I called Roger to the stage, where he received a standing ovation, and presented him with an ornamental ark.

Roger's achievement was the more remarkable and moving because his wife Frances was even then locked in her battle against her cancer. Frances had taught History part-time at Mary Erskine, she was the loving mother of Lucy and Greg in our schools and she was dear to all for her kindness, fun and warmth. She died in April 2000, on the eve of the Fauré Requiem for which Roger had been preparing our school and community choirs. Helen Mitchell suggested that I say a few words in tribute to Frances before the concert began.

What followed was incredibly moving – the sight and sound of boys and girls singing out of their skins – and strong men were in tears. Earlier, and this too seemed poignantly apposite, Jessica Beeston had played the violin solo magically in the Beethoven Romance, Opus 50.

Next week, buses took the choir to the Catholic convent church in Lauriston Place where Frances and her family worshipped. Our music teachers formed a string quartet, Norman Mitchell was at the keyboard, Tim Paxton played a cello sarabande during Communion and the Mary Erskine girls sang *In Paradisum* as Frances' coffin left the church. It was, as I wrote to my own children, 'a lovely occasion, the world as it was meant to be.'

Would that everything in my last term was as serene. There were disciplinary matters of a type that had escaped my previous 56 terms of headship. In my final week I had a furious row with a Channel 4 journalist who wished to interview a

14 year old girl who had 'come out'. I told her that an adolescent girl was entitled to privacy with regard to her sexual orientation, whether or not she or her parents desired exposure, that it was nobody's business – neither Channel 4 nor the great British public – and that it was 'sick' and the journalist ought to be ashamed of herself. I telephoned later to apologize and I was told that the programme was proceeding, but in the event the parents withdrew their permission and subsequently complained about the pressure put on their daughter.

It had been a wonderful challenge and a lovely job – of leadership, rather than management, although the devil was always in the detail. I had seen it as my role to be the man on the bridge, setting the course and not down in the engine room. For my three schools I took on the issues that only the Principal could resolve – like the curriculum or the timetable or the shape of the school year. (I steered the schools towards what was effectively a four term year, with a fortnight and three weekends of mid-term each October, another instance where parents generally backed me against the conservatives.) On all such issues we did things our way.

I always put a premium on good communication with parents. Each April, for instance, I composed a detailed explanation of the extent and causes of the annual fee increase. I remain baffled by those schools, governing bodies and other educational institutions who run scared of such 'transparency'.

I left Edinburgh in the comfort of knowing that the Erskine Stewart's Melville Schools were 'in the black'. We had survived the loss of Assisted Places and effectively replaced all our lost pupils. We had also created many fine buildings and facilities.

The 'North Side' Merchant Company schools were still decidedly Scottish, but I believe that they were much more open to other influences than in 1989. Just before I left, I asked the boys at a Stewart's Melville assembly to raise their hands if they had at least one non-Scottish grandparent. Hundreds did. I hope that Scottish Devolution will not encourage native Scots to ignore the cosmopolitan realities of their society.

The schools remained non-denominational, but in an avowedly Christian tradition. I do not believe that I was wholly successful in beating back secularist intolerance but at least I did not allow it a free ride. The bicentenary of the Reverend Robert Cunningham, Melville College's remarkable founder, gave us the opportunity to repeat the walk to St Mary's Cathedral for a special service of thanksgiving. The return of Gavin Park, one of my first sixth formers, to be Head of Religious Education at Stewart's Melville was another cause of great satisfaction.

They were schools of whose staff – those I had inherited and those I had appointed – I was very proud. I am conscious that I have mentioned but a tiny fraction of the hundreds who supplied the motive force to the three schools.

Almost without exception they were capable and professional. The vast majority were also extraordinarily industrious, generous and forgiving. Once they had overcome their initial and entirely proper caution, they amply proved that they were not afraid of change. Like all lucky headmasters, I owe my colleagues, teachers and support staff, a huge debt.

In my final Prize Day speeches I emphasized also how proud I was of our boys and girls. At Jersey I had spoken of the twenty-four schools that I had visited during the previous nine months. I also had Mary Erskine and Stewart's Melville in mind when I expressed this appreciation of my good fortune in being a Head at this time.

> Our young men and young women are, to a degree unknown in the 1970s and 1980s, positive, reliable and pleasant. Never before have our corridors been so tellingly enriched by the art and artefact of pupils or has musical knowledge been more widespread in our schools. Knowledge in abundance lies at the tips of their fingers. Happy, smiling faces attest to a confidence in future possibilities.
>
> The media rarely give our young people – and ourselves – the credit that is due. To read the papers you would imagine that we live in uniquely loose and licentious times and that our schools do no more than mirror the failings of society. This is a travesty of the truth. Our schools, at ease as never before by virtue of so much that has been enlightened this century, express, as they have always done, our best hope for society's future.

I only hope that the politicians, civil servants and special advisers respect and imitate what is good in Independent schools, notably their independence, and do not succumb to the treacherous allure of the politics of envy. There are worrying signs, with regard especially to university entry, of ministerial despair with improvement of the maintained sector and recourse instead to the cold-blooded devaluation of the schools that have demonstrated their academic prowess.

I made a point in my Prize Day addresses of telling the boys and to the girls, more specifically than before, of my belief in the specifically spiritual dimension.

> It is up to you...to ensure that you live in a civilization and not in an intellectual, cultural and spiritual cul-de-sac. My wish for you all...is that you care passionately about the truth – and that you will come to realize that truth is to be found in mystery rather than in the media. To me religion is central, because it alone affirms that life has a God-given purpose. My school taught me the simple question, 'What does it profit a man to gain the whole world and lose his own soul?' In the end, what we achieve materially on this earth is of no importance. Even the best buildings will moulder and decay. It is the love transmitted to our children and to our pupils which can and will go on for ever, during their lives, and on from them to and through future generations, just as Christianity and the great world religions have done and will do so.

The Mary Erskine Former Pupil Guild bids us farewell.

The Putney Pud was taking his last chance to pay tribute to Father George and St Benedict's School.

The Governors threw a dinner for Margery and me and told me to invite those to whom, in all sorts of different ways, we were particularly indebted for friendship and support. They chose the 'Caledonian' Hotel, because that was where I was placed before my interview by the Merchant Company Education Board in 1989, and the gathering included Matthew and Emma Tobin, left to fend for themselves in Bath when their father decamped to Edinburgh, and Matthew's wife Sarah. At the end there was a 'magic moment', the sudden appearance of Roger Askew and Helen Mitchell with members of the two choirs to sing a miscellany of the music we had enjoyed so much from them. Michael Walker held two sumptuous dinner parties to celebrate the appointment he had organized in 1988. There was also a dinner for the Senior Management Team and their spouses, friends to whom I owed more than I could express. And in the Dining Hall decorated by their tercentennial frieze, The Mary Erskine Former Pupil Guild laid on a special lunch, attended by most of those who had led the Guild during my time but also by younger Merchant Maidens – Lucy Porteous, Sarah Furness and Lucy Tobin.

The last two days arrived. Margery and I were told not to come across to the School for the Stewart's Melville Staff Party until we were summoned. David

Orem duly collected us – and there was the Pipe Band, ready to pipe us over to the School, our colleagues standing on the steps of the dining hall. That was a 'last walk' to savour!

Mary Erskine's party had no such overture, but the farewell was as characteristically affectionate. I was solemnly presented with dressing gown and slippers, embroidered by Eleanor Cameron in Mary Erskine's very own tartan, and thus clad I made my final speech to my colleagues.

The final Prizegivings were, as ever, well attended by the Old Masters of the Merchant Company and by others who had befriended us during eleven years in Edinburgh. Thus Cathy Ryden. Thus Tommy and Noreen Weston. To the boys of Stewart's Melville and, then, the girls of Mary Erskine I spoke at even greater length than usual. Nobody seemed to mind. I sensed that many had placed bets on just such an eventuality. 'Summer Suns' at Stewart's Melville had never seemed so lovely nor Mary Erskine more serene. The Head Boy, Ian Cameron, paid an accomplished and humorous tribute. At Mary Erskine, the Head Girl, Frances Pratt, presented me with a book containing the signature of every girl and illustrated most attractively. Afterwards, amid the clink of teacups, various parents and teachers came up to say 'Goodbye', the last being Laura Marshall, one of the many young colleagues who had been especially kind to the old man in his final days.

That evening I paid a final visit to the filing cabinets in my Study at Stewart's Melville, locked the door and stepped into the deserted corridor. A track suited figure emerged from the gloom – Laura. 'Oh, it's you,' I said fatuously, lost for words. Hers was the future – and I was sorry not to be part of it.

Index

265